"The Marv Tolman science activity books were always a hit with teachers and were valuable for use with my science method course students."

—Dr. Donald R. Daugs, professor emeritus, Utah State University

"I love the Hands-On Science books by Marv Tolman. They sit right next to my desk within easy reach. The lesson plans are teacher friendly and student friendly. The books are put together in such a way that it is easy to find any subject. From Kindergarten to 6th grade the lessons are set up for all students to use. I know, I have used them in all grades and my students love to be involved in science. I highly recommend these books for any teacher whether you struggle with science or are an expert in the field."

—Marilyn Bulkley, fifth grade teacher, Garfield School District, Panguitch, Utah

"Our sixth-, seventh-, and eighth-grade students have literally worn out our copies of Dr. Tolman's Hands-On Activities. We have two copies of each activity book and students select them for their concise instructions, excellent diagrams, and easy-to-find materials. Even though the title indicates grades K-6, students and teachers in seventh and eighth grades found the activities very helpful in classroom demonstrations and as a beginning point for science fair problems. I loved the way that the activities are divided into the three different disciplines: physical, earth, and life. It was fast and easy to locate just what you needed using the table of contents organization. There was always an activity for whatever concept my students were learning. Our school will need to purchase the newly revised activity books."

—Rosalee Riddle, science teacher, Red Hills Middle School, Richfield, Utah and science curriculum coordinator, Sevier School District, Richfield, Utah

"Before my current position as science teacher educator, I used these activity books extensively in teaching science to my sixth graders. I found them very valuable and helpful in creating lessons that engaged the students in hands-on activities that effectively taught science concepts. Now, as an assistant professor of science education, I continue to use them as I discuss and model hands-on and inquiry-based science. Additionally, I highly recommend them to the pre-service students in my elementary science methods courses, many of whom use them in lesson planning and unit planning for my class as well as during their practicum and student teaching experiences."

—Leigh K. Smith, Ph.D., assistant professor, Department of Science Education, Brigham Young University

"I have taught many science classes for our district over the last ten years, and I always rely on your Hands-On books for background information. I have them pulled off of the shelf now because I am using them to come up with a science/math activity for my National Board Certification Program. I know I can trust these books. The information is clearly presented, easy to understand, and the activities always work."

—Mary Selin, second grade teacher, Davis District and first grade science trainer for the district, Davis School District, Farmington, Utah

"I have used Marv's science books for several years. I love the experiments. The kids love to try them on their own. They have easy-to-follow directions and all the materials are readily available. I especially like the explanations of how and why. The best thing about these experiments is that they work! I haven't had one fail yet."

—Keetette Turner, kindergarten teacher, Granite District, Salt Lake City, Utah

"I began working with Marv Tolman ten years ago. I was new to the world of elementary teaching. I had heard of a workshop that helped teachers simplify, and pinpoint science concepts that could be taught repeatedly through hands-on, basic application. That workshop was the first of many and I still—ten years later—use the concepts to teach my students. The basic and simple mechanics of science that are incorporated into these lessons reach the gifted and struggling learner and can be adapted and adjusted to time and to the needs of students' individual levels and learning styles."

—Marcie H. Judd, fourth grade teacher, Valley Elementary School, Kanab School District., Kanab, Utah.

"Many elementary teachers lack science background knowledge. The Hands-On Science Activities series provides teachers with both background knowledge and engaging methods to help all students learn science concepts. Marv explains them using simple, clear, and concise language that equips teachers to teach with confidence. These books have increased both the accuracy and the quality of science education."

—Julie Cook, Title I Literacy Coordinator and former kindergarten teacher, Logan City School District, Logan, Utah.

Jossey-Bass Teacher

Jossey-Bass Teacher provides K–12 teachers with essential knowledge and tools to create a positive and lifelong impact on student learning. Trusted and experienced educational mentors offer practical classroom-tested and theory-based teaching resources for improving teaching practice in a broad range of grade levels and subject areas. From one educator to another, we want to be your first source to make every day your best day in teaching. *Jossey-Bass Teacher* resources serve two types of informational needs—essential knowledge and essential tools.

Essential knowledge resources provide the foundation, strategies, and methods from which teachers may design curriculum and instruction to challenge and excite their students. Connecting theory to practice, essential knowledge books rely on a solid research base and time-tested methods, offering the best ideas and guidance from many of the most experienced and well-respected experts in the field.

Essential tools save teachers time and effort by offering proven, ready-to-use materials for in-class use. Our publications include activities, assessments, exercises, instruments, games, ready reference, and more. They enhance an entire course of study, a weekly lesson, or a daily plan. These essential tools provide insightful, practical, and comprehensive materials on topics that matter most to K–12 teachers.

Hands-On Life Science Activities for Grades K–6

Second Edition

Marvin N. Tolman, Ed.D.

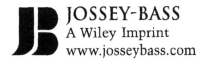

JOSSEY-BASS
A Wiley Imprint
www.josseybass.com

Published by Jossey-Bass
A Wiley Imprint
989 Market Street, San Francisco, CA 94103-1741   www.josseybass.com

Jossey-Bass books and products are available through most bookstores. To contact Jossey-Bass directly call our Customer Care Department within the U.S. at 800-956-7739, outside the U.S. at 317-572-3986, or fax 317-572-4002.

Jossey-Bass also publishes its books in a variety of electronic formats. Some content that appears in print may not be available in electronic books.

ISBN-13: 978-0-7879-7865-5
ISBN-10: 0-7879-7865-5

SECOND EDITION
10 9 8 7 6 5 4 3 2 1

I dedicate this book to
the late Dr. James O. Morton, my mentor, dear friend, and
coauthor of **The Science Curriculum Activities Library,**
from which the current series evolved.

Acknowledgments

Mentioning the names of all individuals who contributed to *The Science Problem-Solving Curriculum Library* would require an additional volume. The author is greatly indebted to the following:

- Teachers and students of all levels.
- School districts throughout the United States who cooperated by supporting and evaluating ideas and methods used in this book.
- The late Dr. James O. Morton, my mentor, dear friend, and co-author of *The Science Curriculum Activities Library*, from which the current series evolved.
- Dr. Garry R. Hardy, my teaching partner for many years, for his constant encouragement and creative ideas.
- Finally, my angel Judy, for without her love, support, encouragement, patience, and acceptance, these books could never have been completed.

Contents

Section One: Living Through Adaptation

Section Two: Animals

Section Three: Growing and Changing: Animal Life Cycles

Section Four: Plants and Seeds

Section Five: Body Systems

Section Six: The Five Senses

Section Seven: Health and Nutrition

About the Author

Dr. Marvin N. Tolman trained as an educator at Utah State University and began his career as a teaching principal in rural southeastern Utah. The next eleven years were spent teaching grades one through six in schools of San Juan and Utah Counties and earning graduate degrees.

Currently professor of elementary education, Dr. Tolman has been teaching graduate and undergraduate science methods courses at Brigham Young University since 1975. He has served as a consultant to school districts, taught workshops in many parts of the United States, and published numerous articles in professional journals. With Dr. James O. Morton, Dr. Tolman wrote the three-book series of elementary science activities called *The Science Curriculum Activities Library*, published in 1986.

Dr. Tolman now lives with his wife, Judy, in Spanish Fork, Utah, where they have raised five children.

About the Library

The Science Problem-Solving Curriculum Library evolved from an earlier series by the same author, with Dr. James O. Morton as coauthor: *The Science Curriculum Activities Library*. The majority of the activities herein were also in the earlier publication, and the successful activity format has been retained. Many activities have been revised, and several new ones have been added. A significant feature of this series, which was not in the original, is a section called "For Problem Solvers" included in most of the activities. This section provides ideas for further investigation and related activities for students who are motivated to extend their study beyond the procedural steps of a given activity. I hope most students will pursue at least some of these extensions and benefit from them.

The Science Problem-Solving Curriculum Library provides teachers with hundreds of science activities that give students hands-on experience related to many science topics. To be used in conjunction with whatever texts and references you have, the Library includes three books, each providing activities that explore a different field. The books are individually titled as follows:

- *Hands-On Life Science Activities for Grades K–6*
- *Hands-On Physical Science Activities for Grades K–6*
- *Hands-On Earth Science Activities for Grades K–6*

More than ever before, children today grow up in a world impacted by science and technology. A basic understanding of nature and an appreciation for the world around them are gifts too valuable to deny these precious young people, who will be the problem solvers of tomorrow. In addition, a strong science program with a discovery/inquiry approach can enrich the development of mathematics, reading, social studies, and other areas of the curriculum. The activities in the Library develop these skills. Most activities call for thoughtful responses, with questions that encourage analyzing, synthesizing, and inferring instead of simply answering yes or no.

Development of thinking and reasoning skills, in addition to learning basic content information, are the main goals of the activities outlined herein. Learning how to learn, and how to apply the various tools of learning, are more useful in a person's life than is the acquisition of large numbers of scientific facts. Students are encouraged to explore, invent, and create as they develop skills with the processes of science. The learning of scientific facts is a by-product of this effort, and increased insight and retention associated with facts learned are virtually assured.

How to Use This Book

This book consists of more than 150 easy-to-use, hands-on activities in the following areas of life sciences:

- Living Through Adaptation
- Animals
- Growing and Changing: Animal Life Cycles
- Plants and Seeds
- Body Systems
- The Five Senses
- Health and Nutrition

Use in the Classroom

The activities in this book are designed as discovery activities that students can usually perform quite independently. The teacher is encouraged to provide students (usually in small groups) with the materials listed and a copy of the activity from the beginning through the "Procedure." The section titled "Teacher Information" is not intended for student use, but rather to assist the teacher with discussion following the hands-on activity, as students share their observations. (Be sure to cover this section before copying.) Discussion of conceptual information prior to completing the hands-on activity can interfere with the discovery process.

Correlation with National Standards

The National Research Council produced the *National Science Education Standards*. Published in 1996 by the National Academy of Sciences, this document has become the standard by which many sets of state and local science standards have been developed since that time. The document is available from the National Academy Press, 2101 Constitution Avenue NW, Box 285, Washington, DC 10055. It is also available online by searching for National Science Education Standards.

For grades K–12 there are seven Standards, identified as Standards A–G. Within each grade-level cluster (K–4, 5–8, 9–12) general sub-parts are identified.

Content Standard A: Science as Inquiry

Content Standard B: Physical Science

Content Standard C: Life Science

Content Standard D: Earth and Space Science

Content Standard E: Science and Technology

Content Standard F: Science in Personal and Social Perspectives

Content Standard G: History and Nature of Science

This is one of a series of three books that focus separately on the Life, Earth, and Physical Sciences. Following is a list of the Content Standards to which the set of three books relate for Levels K–4 and 5–8 of the National Science Education Standards. Collectively, the Standards identified for correlation purposes are Standards A, B, C, D, and F. These Standards and their sub-parts are listed below. In the Standards document, the sub-parts are in a bulleted list. They are numbered here to facilitate referencing them individually within this book. The appropriate Standards and sub-parts are repeated in each section of all three books to provide a section-by-section correlation with the National Standards. This information is found on the page immediately preceding the first activity of each section in each book. Since the activities are designed for inquiry, you will note that Content Standard A is included in all sections of each book.

K–4 Content Standard A: Science as Inquiry

As a result of activities in grades K–4, all students should develop:

1. Abilities necessary to do scientific inquiry
2. Understanding about scientific inquiry

K–4 Content Standard B: Physical Science

As a result of activities in grades K–4, all students should develop understanding of

1. Properties of objects and materials
2. Position and motion of objects
3. Light, heat, electricity, and magnetism

K–4 Content Standard C: Life Science

As a result of activities in grades K–4, all students should develop understanding of

1. The characteristics of organisms
2. Life cycles of organisms
3. Organisms and environments

K–4 Content Standard D: Earth and Space Science

As a result of activities in grades K–4, all students should develop understanding of

1. Properties of earth materials
2. Objects in the sky
3. Changes in earth and sky

K–4 Content Standard F: Science in Personal and Social Perspectives

As a result of activities in grades K–4, all students should develop understanding of

1. Personal health
2. Characteristics and changes in populations
3. Types of resources
4. Changes in environments
5. Science and technology in local challenges

5–8 Content Standard A: Science as Inquiry

As a result of activities in grades 5–8, all students should develop:

1. Abilities necessary to do scientific inquiry
2. Understanding about scientific inquiry

5–8 Content Standard B: Physical Science

As a result of activities in grades 5–8, all students should develop understanding of

1. Properties and changes of properties in matter
2. Motions and forces
3. Transfer of energy

5-8 Content Standard C: Life Science

As a result of activities in grades 5–8, all students should develop understanding of

1. Structures and function in living systems
2. Reproduction and heredity
3. Regulation and behavior
4. Populations and ecosystems
5. Diversity and adaptations of organisms

5-8 Content Standard D: Earth and Space Science

As a result of activities in grades 5–8, all students should develop understanding of

1. Structure of the earth system
2. The earth's history
3. Earth in the solar system

5-8 Content Standard F: Science in Personal and Social Perspectives

As a result of activities in grades 5–8, all students should develop understanding of

1. Personal health
2. Populations, resources, and environments
3. Natural hazards
4. Risks and benefits
5. Science and technology in society

Teacher Qualifications

Two important qualities of the elementary teacher as a scientist are (1) commitment to helping students acquire learning skills and (2) recognition of the value of science and its implications in the life and learning of the child.

You do not need to be a scientist to conduct an effective and exciting science program at the elementary level. Interest, creativity, enthusiasm, and willingness to get involved and try something new are the qualifications the teacher of elementary science needs most. Your expertise will grow and your "comfort zone" will expand as you teach, and as you find opportunities to expand your knowledge in the topics you teach. If you haven't yet really tried teaching hands-on science, you will find it to be a lot like eating peanuts—you can't eat just one. Try it. The excitement and enthusiasm you see in your students will bring you back to it again and again.

Early Grades

Many of these concrete activities are easily adaptable for children in the early grades. Although the activity instructions ("Procedures") are written for the student who can read and follow the steps, that does not preclude teachers of the lower grades from using the activities with their students. With verbal instructions and slight modifications, many of these activities can be used with kindergarten, first-grade, and second-grade students. In some activities, steps that involve procedures that go beyond the level of the child can simply be omitted and yet offer the child an experience that plants the seed for a concept that will germinate and grow later on.

Teachers of the early grades will probably choose to bypass many of the "For Problem Solvers" sections. That's okay. The "For Problem Solvers" sections are provided for those who are especially motivated and want to go further. Use the basic activities for which procedural steps are written and enjoy worthwhile learning experiences together with your young students.

Capitalize on Interest

These materials are both nongraded and nonsequential. Areas of greatest interest and need can be emphasized. As you gain experience with using the activities, your skill in guiding students toward appropriate discoveries and insights will increase.

Organizing for an Activity-Centered Approach

Current trends encourage teachers to use an activity-based program, supplemented by the use of textbooks and many other reference materials, including Internet resources. The activities herein encourage hands-on discovery, which enhances the development of valuable learning skills through direct experience. Opportunities abound for students to work together, and such collaboration is encouraged throughout.

One of the advantages of this approach is the elimination of the need for all students to have the same book at the same time, freeing a substantial portion of the textbook money for purchasing a variety of materials and references, including other textbooks, trade books, audio- and videotapes, video discs, models, and other visuals. References should be acquired that lend themselves developmentally to a variety of approaches, subject-matter emphases, and levels of reading difficulty.

Grabbers

The sequence of activities within the sections of this book is flexible and may be adjusted according to interest, availability of materials, time of year, or other factors. Many of the activities in each section can be used independently as *grabbers* to capture student interest. Used this way, they can help to achieve several specific objectives:

- To assist in identifying student interests and selecting topics for study.
- To provide a wide variety of interesting and exciting hands-on activities from many areas of science. As students investigate activities that are of particular interest, they will likely be motivated to try additional related activities in the same section of the book.
- To introduce teachers and students to the discovery/inquiry approach.
- To be used for those occasions when only a short period of time is available and a high-interest independent activity is needed.

Unique Features

The following points should be kept in mind while using this book:

1. Most of these activities can be used with several grade levels, with little adaptation.
2. The student is the central figure when using the discovery/inquiry approach to hands-on learning.
3. The main goals are problem solving and the development of critical-thinking skills. The learning of content is a spin-off, but it is possibly learned with greater insight and meaning than if it were the main objective.
4. It attempts to prepare teachers for inquiry-based instruction and sharpen their guidance and questioning techniques.
5. Most materials needed for the activities are readily available in the school or at home.
6. Activities are intended to be open and flexible and to encourage the extension of skills through the use of as many outside resources as possible: (a) The use of parents, aides, and resource people of all kinds is recommended throughout; (b) the library, media center, and other school resources, as well as classroom reading centers

related to the areas of study, are essential in the effective teaching and learning of science; and (c) educational television, videos, and resources available on the Internet can greatly enrich the science program.

7. With the exception of the activities labeled "teacher demonstration" or "whole-class activity," students are encouraged to work individually, in pairs, or in small groups. In most cases the teacher gathers and organizes the materials, arranges the learning setting, and serves as a resource person. In many instances, the materials listed and the procedural steps are all students will need in order to perform the activities.

8. Information is given in "To the Teacher" at the beginning of each section and in "Teacher Information" at the end of each activity to help you develop your content background and your questioning and guidance skills, in cases for which such help is needed.

Integrating

Students do more than just science as they become involved in science inquiry activities. Such experiences are loaded with applications of math, reading, and language arts. They often involve social studies, art, music, and physical education as well. This is true of activities throughout this book. Meaningful application and reinforcement of skills learned throughout the curriculum are embedded in the child's science experiences. These connections are noted within the individual activities, as described under "Format of Activities."

Format of Activities

Each activity in this book includes the following information:

- *Activity Number:* Activities are numbered sequentially within each section for easy reference. Each activity has a two-part number to identify the section and the sequence of the activity within the section.
- *Activity Title:* The title of each activity is in the form of a question that can be answered by completing the activity. Each question requires more than a simple yes or no answer.
- *Special Instructions:* Some activities are intended to be used as teacher demonstrations or whole-group activities, or they may require close supervision for safety reasons, so these special instructions are noted.

- *Take Home and Do with Family and Friends:* Many activities could be used by the student at home, providing enjoyment and learning for others in the family. Such experiences can work wonders in the life of the child, as he or she teaches others what has been learned at school. The result is often a greater depth of learning on the part of the child, as well as a boost to his or her self-esteem and self-confidence. An activity is marked as "Take home and do with family and friends" if it meets all the following criteria:

  (1) It uses only materials that are common around the home.
  (2) It has a high chance of arousing interest on the part of the child.
  (3) It is safe for a child to do independently, that is, it uses no flame, hot plate, or very hot water.

  Of course, other activities could be used at the discretion of parents.
- *Materials:* Each activity lists the materials needed. The materials are easily acquired. In some cases, special instructions or sources are suggested.
- *Procedure:* The procedural steps are written to the student, in easy-to-understand language. To avoid interfering with the discovery process, no conceptual information is given in this section.
- *For Problem Solvers:* Most activities include this section, which suggests additional investigations or activities for students who are motivated to extend their study beyond the activity specified in the procedural steps.
- *Teacher Information:* Suggested teaching tips and background information are given. This information supplements that provided in "To the Teacher" at the beginning of each section. This section is not intended for student use, but rather to assist the teacher with discussion following the hands-on activity, as students share their observations. Discussion of conceptual information prior to completing the hands-on activity can interfere with the discovery process.
- *Integrating:* Other curricular areas from which students will likely use skills as they complete the activity are recognized here.
- *Science Process Skills:* This is a list of the science process skills likely involved in doing the activity.

Use of Metric Measures

Most measures used are given in metric units, followed by units in the English system in parentheses. This is done to encourage use of the metric system.

Word Search Puzzles

The final activity of each section is a "Word Search," intended for fun and for encouraging vocabulary development. Each Word Search includes an answer key and a challenge for students to create word search puzzles of their own, with a form provided for ease of use.

Assessment and Evaluation

The activities in this book should effectively supplement and enrich your science curriculum. While a comprehensive testing system is not provided, a small collection of questions, titled "Do You Recall?," is included at the end of most sections. Activities in the "Animals" section are mostly student projects that deal with local animals; the content does not lend itself to questions with specific answers. Similarly, most of the activities in the "Food and Nutrition" section involve students in a study of their own eating habits. Again, the content does not lend itself to questions with specific answers. The "Do You Recall" questions from the other sections could be used as short quizzes or added to other assessments such as pretests or post-tests. They include true/false, multiple-choice, and short-answer questions. No performance assessment items are included. Each list of questions is followed by an answer key, which identifies the related learning activities and provides answers to the questions.

Grade Level

These activities are nongraded. Many activities in each section can be easily adapted for use with young children, while other activities provide challenge for the more talented in the intermediate grades.

Scientific Investigation

Scientists sometimes seem to flip-flop with theories that support a particular health remedy or behavior, then refute it, or alter their position on an established scientific theory. If we understand why that happens, we are less likely to be annoyed with it. It isn't because they are an indecisive lot, but because they are doing what scientists do. If we know of a certain drug that shows promise of helping us with a serious health problem, but is undergoing extended testing prior to approval for public use, we become impatient with the system. If it is marketed without sufficient proof of safety and we suffer ill side effects, we bring a class-action lawsuit against those who marketed it with insufficient testing.

The Tentative Nature of Scientific Knowledge

Scientific knowledge is, by its very nature, tentative and subject to scrutiny and change. It results from empirical evidence, but the interpretation of that evidence is often unavoidably influenced by human observation, inference, and judgment. To be respected by the scientific community, evidence must usually be verified by multiple scientists.

Occasionally, a long-held theory is shown to be flawed and, in light of new information, must be altered or abandoned. In 1633 Galileo was punished and imprisoned for defying the commonly held "truth" that the earth is the center of the universe and that all celestial bodies revolve around it.

If we criticize change that is based on the best current information, we make light of a process that deserves, instead, to be applauded, and we show our ignorance regarding the scientific way of learning. If we understand and encourage the continuous cyclical process of acquiring new information, we will not be frustrated when later on the "new" theory is also adjusted in light of newer data and revised perspectives.

We are bombarded with so-called "scientifically proven" health remedies that are at odds with each other. Two conflicting theories can both be wrong, but they cannot both be right. In such cases, we must wonder why more data were not collected before certain claims were made, and we question the motive that inspired the marketing of the product.

Taking a Less Formal Approach

In our efforts to spawn lifelong learners, we need to capture the general concept that science is an ongoing search for observable and reproducible evidence. Current thinking is leading us away from the once-held rigid sequence of memorized steps of the scientific method. We are, instead, encouraged to think of scientific investigation as a logical process of acquiring information and solving problems, applicable and useful in virtually every area of study and every walk of life.

In the face of a dilemma brought about by a question or problem, we need to first examine the information currently available. If this is insufficient, we pursue possible ways to acquire additional information (data) and to determine the accuracy of the new data. Having done that, we are better informed and thus better prepared to provide an answer to the question or a solution to the problem.

When Mother comes home from shopping and finds milk spilled on the kitchen floor, the problem is immediately apparent. Her mind quickly surveys current information by considering who has probably been in the house and, based on past behavior, age of children, and other information that would indicate who is most likely responsible for the mess. It may be that the child she first suspected is at scout camp and was nowhere around on that day. Mom quickly adjusts her thinking, considers other ideas, and forms a tentative conclusion (hypothesis). As she seeks out the young suspect for clean-up patrol, she might consider alibis, the stories of witnesses, and other new information, all of which contribute to a final conclusion. Her systematic approach might result in evidence that it was Dad, in a hurry to get to work on time!

Although this example does not involve clear-cut scientific experimentation, it does use a systematic procedure for acquiring information and/or arriving at a solution to an everyday problem, which is the very point being made. The procedure is very simple:

1. Examine information currently available regarding the question or problem at hand.
2. Determine the most logical conclusion (hypothesis) from the information already known.
3. Devise a way to test the accuracy of the hypothesis.

The scientific method, in some form, applies to many situations in everyday life, even if it is not commonly recognized as a scientific approach. If students are trained in the use of a logical, simple, systematic way to gather information and solve problems, they will be better equipped to meet life's inevitable dilemmas.

Now let's go back to the drug company that challenges our patience with extended testing delays. The whole process began with a question raised about the possible effectiveness of a particular formula in dealing with a specific health problem or class of problems. Interested scientists likely examined all of the information they could find about the possible effects of the separate ingredients and of this particular mixture of ingredients. They posed their best tentative conclusion (hypothesis), based on the available information. They then devised ways to test the substance for its effectiveness in the intended application, and perhaps other related applications, and the potential side effects. From their new data, they either concluded that their earlier tentative conclusion (hypothesis) was right, or they adjusted it and did more testing and examination of information (data) acquired. They likely will not allow the substance to be marketed as a solution to the targeted health problem until they are quite certain the substance has been adequately proven to be effective and safe—that their hypothesis was right. Even if you and I are impatient with the lengthy process and the substance shows promise of reducing suffering and saving lives, we won't see it on the market until it has been conclusively proven. Even then, the new formula could later be shown to be inadequate or to have unforeseen harmful side effects, and now it backfires. Those who tested, approved, and marketed the new drug are facing the wrath of those who used it—perhaps many of the same people who criticized them earlier for taking so long in the approval process.

Broad Application

Your students may use this approach in a variety of subject areas. For example, in the science classroom they might apply it as they experiment with the effect of light on plant growth or the effect of vinegar on baking soda and other powders. Perhaps they will find ways to check their hypothesis regarding the direction of the earth's rotation and do numerous other scientific explorations.

In another setting, they might study diacritical markings and their uses in unlocking word pronunciations, making logical conclusions or predictions based on information at hand. Testing such predictions becomes a learning experience as students read and study further, compare known words, ask an expert (perhaps the teacher), and so forth.

Your students might also enjoy the challenge of identifying elements of scientific investigation in a mystery story. When introduced to a variety of experiences in applying a basic approach to problem solving, they will recognize its universal application and down-to-earth logic, and chances are they will use it with confidence throughout their lives.

Application in This Book

Good habits of scientific investigation are encouraged in this book in the following ways:

1. Students are encouraged to work together in completing the activities, collaborating and learning from each other as they go along.

2. The form "Science Investigation Journaling Notes" is provided to help students record what they do and what they observe, as they practice scientific behavior in their study of science. It will serve as a template that can be applied in numerous problem-solving situations.

3. To help students make the transition into the use of journaling notes to record what they do and observe, the "Science Investigation Journaling Notes" form is reproduced within a few activities of the book. In each of these cases, the activity number is referenced in the heading, and part 1, the "Question," is provided on the form. In addition, the procedural steps guide the student in making appropriate connections and filling out the form as they complete the activity. This help is provided with the following activities:

    Section 4 (Plants and Seeds): Activities 3, 11, 12, 13, and 16

    Section 5 (Body Systems): Activities 7, 8, and 21

4. Help is also provided for making the next step in the transition—designing an investigation and completing the form independently. The following activities suggest, in "For Problem Solvers" and/or at the beginning of the "Procedural Steps," that students get copies of the "Science Investigation Journaling Notes" from the teacher and use them as they design and complete their own science investigation from the ideas provided.

    Section 5 (Body Systems): Activity 21

    Section 6 (Five Senses): Activities 12, 14, 21, 33, and 35

    Section 7 (Health and Nutrition): Activities 2 and 7. Use of the Journaling Notes is also suggested at the end of the procedural steps of Activity 8.

5. We hope that copies of the following "Science Investigation Journaling Notes" form will be made available for students to use as needed, and that students will prepare journaling notes as they complete these and many other science investigations from this book and from other sources, including those devised by the students themselves.

Science Investigation

Journaling Notes

1. Question:

_____

_____

2. What we already know: _____

_____

_____

3. Hypothesis: _____

_____

_____

4. Materials needed: _____

_____

_____

5. Procedure: _____

_____

_____

6. Observations/New information: _____

_____

_____

7. Conclusion: _____

_____

_____

Final Note: Let's Collaborate, and Learn Together

Discovering the excitement of science and developing new techniques for critical thinking and problem solving are major goals of elementary science. The activities in this book are written with the intent that students work together in a collaborative way in the learning process. The discovery/ inquiry approach, for which these activities are written, also must emphasize verbal responses and discussion. *It is important that students experience many hands-on activities* in the learning of science *and that they talk about what they do.* Working in collaborative groups facilitates this. Each child should have many opportunities to describe observations and to explain what he or she did and why. With the exception of recording observations, these activities usually do not require extensive writing, but that, too, is a skill that can be enriched through interest and involvement in science.

There is an ancient Chinese saying: "A journey of a thousand miles begins with a single step." May these ideas and activities help to provide that first step—or the appropriate next step—for all who use this book and are traveling the road of lifelong learning and discovery.

Marvin N. Tolman

Correlation with National Standards Grid

Grades K–4	Section	Pages
A. Science as Inquiry		
1. Abilities necessary to do scientific inquiry	Living Through Adaptation	1–46
2. Understanding about scientific inquiry	Animals	47–114
	Animal Life Cycles	115–148
	Plants and Seeds	149–230
	Body Systems	231–280
	The Five Senses	281–357
	Health and Nutrition	359–396
B. Physical Science		
1. Properties of objects and materials		
2. Position and motion of objects		
3. Light, heat, electricity, and magnetism		
C. Life Science		
1. Characteristics of organisms	Living Through	
2. Life cycles of organisms	Adaptation	1–46
3. Organisms and environments	Animals	47–114
	Animal Life Cycles	115–148
	Plants and Seeds	149–230
	Body Systems	231–280
	The Five Senses	281–357
	Health and Nutrition	359–396
D. Earth and Space Science		
1. Properties of earth materials		
2. Objects in the sky		
3. Changes in earth and sky		
E. Science in Personal and Social Perspectives		
1. Personal health	Health and Nutrition	359–396
2. Characteristics and changes in populations		
3. Types of resources		
4. Changes in environments		
5. Science and technology in local challenges		

Key to Icons

Whole class

Group/Partner

Home

Individual student

Younger/Less advanced

Older/More advanced

Listing of Activities by Topic

Animal Adaptations

Topic	Activities
Color/Camouflage	1.6, 1.7, 1.8, 1.9
Communication	1.15
Design a Bird	1.18
Eating	1.10, 1.11
Feathers	1.3, 1.4, 1.5
Movement/Control	1.13, 1.14
Seasonal Adaptations	1.16, 1.17
Teeth	1.12
What Is Adaptation?	1.1
Where Animals Live	1.2

Animals

Topic	Activities
Animal Characteristics	2.1
Aquarium	2.21
Bird Characteristics	2.19
Bird Feeders	2.18
Bird Homes	2.20
Creating Animals	2.8, 2.9
Earthworms	2.23
Living/Nonliving	2.26, 2.27
Nature Squares	2.13, 2.14, 2.15, 2.16, 2.17
Pets	2.2, 2.3, 2.4, 2.5, 2.6
Play Animals	2.7, 2.8
Snails	2.24
Terrariums	2.22
Tiny Living Creatures (Not Animals)	2.25
Tracks	2.10, 2.11, 2.12

Growing and Changing Animal Life Cycles

Topic	Activities
Butterflies	3.9
Growing and Changing	3.1, 3.2
How Life Begins	3.3
Length of Life	3.11
Mealworms	3.10
Some Animals Hatch from Eggs	3.4, 3.5, 3.6
Tadpoles	3.7, 3.8

Plants

Topic	Activities
Geotropism	4.13
Growing Plants	4.8, 4.9, 4.10, 4.11, 4.14
Growing Plants Without Seeds	4.5, 4.6
Mold (Not a Plant)	4.27, 4.28, 4.29, 4.30
Phototropism	4.12
Plant Parts	4.15, 4.16, 4.17, 4.18, 4.19, 4.20, 4.21
Plants for Food	4.22, 4.23, 4.24
Seeds	4.1, 4.2, 4.3, 4.4
Transplanting	4.7
Trees	4.25, 4.26

Body Systems

Topic	Activities
Blood Pressure and Pulse	5.3, 5.4
Bones	5.9, 5.10, 5.11, 5.12, 5.13, 5.14, 5.15, 5.16
Fingerprints	5.21
Hair	5.22
Lungs	5.6
Muscles	5.17, 5.18, 5.19
Nails	5.21
Reactions	5.20
Size	5.2
Skin	5.7, 5.8
Systems	5.5

The Five Senses

Topic	Activities
Hearing	6.22, 6.23, 6.24, 6.25, 6.26, 6.27, 6.28
Sight	6.1, 6.2, 6.3, 6.4, 6.5, 6.6, 6.7, 6.8, 6.9, 6.10, 6.11, 6.12, 6.13, 6.14, 6.15, 6.16
Smell	6.17, 6.18, 6.19, 6.20, 6.21
Taste	6.20, 6.21, 6.29, 6.30, 6.31
Touch	6.5, 6.32, 6.33, 6.34, 6.35, 6.36, 6.37, 6.38

Health and Nutrition

Topic	Activities
Body Makeup	7.1
Calories	7.10, 7.11
Cleanliness	7.2
Common and Popular Foods	7.4
Fat	7.9
Food Groups	7.3, 7.5
Protein	7.6
Starch	7.8
Sugar	7.7
Teeth	7.12, 7.13, 7.14, 7.15

Living Through Adaptation

To the Teacher

The following activities focus on some specific ways animals (including humans) adapt to their environment. Feathers and birds are used frequently in these activities because they are common even in large cities and suburban areas, and many types of adaptations are evident. Feathers collected from wild birds should be carefully examined before use. Check on laws pertaining to the possession of feathers before collecting any of them. Like other animals, humans have many ways of adapting to various conditions and changing circumstances.

A picture collection is an important resource in the teaching of science. This section relies heavily on the use of pictures. Older students might be interested in starting picture collections of their own.

Some household tools used in some of these activities are sharp and potentially dangerous. Careful discretion and close teacher supervision are recommended.

1

People are the most adaptable animals on earth. Teachers have a frequent need to adapt. As you read and prepare to teach this section, feel free to adapt it in any way you choose to meet the needs of your students and the conditions of the environment in which they live. Most important, adapt this study according to your needs, special skills, and knowledge.

The following activities are designed as discovery activities that students can usually perform quite independently. You are encouraged to provide students (usually in small groups) with the materials listed and a copy of the activity from the beginning through the "Procedure." The section titled "Teacher Information" is not intended for student use, but rather to assist you with discussion following the hands-on activity, as students share their observations. Discussion of conceptual information prior to completing the hands-on activity can interfere with the discovery process.

Regarding the Early Grades

With verbal instructions and slight modifications, many of these activities can be used with kindergarten, first-grade, and second-grade students. Some of the activities were written specifically with the primary grades in mind. In others, procedural steps that go beyond the level of the child can simply be omitted and yet offer the child experiences that plant conceptual seeds for concepts that will germinate and grow later on.

Teachers of the early grades will probably choose to bypass many of the "For Problem Solvers" sections. That's okay. These sections are provided for those who are especially motivated and want to go beyond the investigation provided by the activity outlined. Use the outlined activities and enjoy worthwhile learning experiences together with your young students. Also consider, however, that many of the "For Problem Solvers" sections can be used appropriately with young children as group activities or as demonstrations. Giving students the advantage of an exposure to the experience can often lay groundwork for connections that will become more meaningful at a later time.

Correlation with National Standards

The following elements of the National Standards are reflected in the activities of this section.

K–4   Content Standard A: Science as Inquiry

As a result of activities in grades K–4, all students should develop

1. Abilities necessary to do scientific inquiry
2. Understanding about scientific inquiry

K–4   Content Standard C: Life Science

As a result of activities in grades K–4, all students should develop understanding of

1. The characteristics of organisms
2. Life cycles of organisms
3. Organisms and environments

5–8   Content Standard A: Science as Inquiry

As a result of activities in grades 5–8, all students should develop

1. Abilities necessary to do scientific inquiry
2. Understanding about scientific inquiry

5–8   Content Standard C: Life Science

As a result of activities in grades 5–8, all students should develop understanding of

1. Structures and function in living systems
2. Reproduction and heredity

What Is Adaptation?

(Small-group discussion)

Materials Needed

- Pictures of people living, working, and playing in different climates
- Newsprint
- Pencils

Procedure

1. Adaptation in plants and animals refers to the way they can adjust or change to be able to live where and how they do. Many animals and plants can live only in certain places. People have made adaptations so they can live for periods of time almost anywhere. Discuss with your teacher some of the adaptations (adjustments) that have been made by you and others to enable you to be comfortable in your classroom today. List a few of these on the board.

2. Divide into groups of four or five and look at the pictures of ways people adapt to live, work, and play all over the world. Make a list of some ways humans are different from other animals in their ability to adapt.

3. From your pictures, choose the most interesting adaptations and share them with the class.

For Problem Solvers

Select two animals that are quite different from each other and write their names in the blanks at the top of the Animal Needs Venn Diagram (see Figure 1.1–1). In the middle section of the Venn Diagram, list some things or conditions you think both of these animals need. In the remaining part of the circle, under the name of each animal, write some of the things or conditions you think are needed by one but not the other. Share your information with your group, comparing and contrasting the needs of the two animals, as you consider the additional thoughts of others.

From resources you have available, including the Internet, learn what you can about plans for current and future space exploration. What adaptations are required for humans to live for an extended time in space stations?

Hands-On Life Science Activities

Figure 1.1-1. Animal Needs Venn Diagram

Animal #1 _____   Animal #2 _____

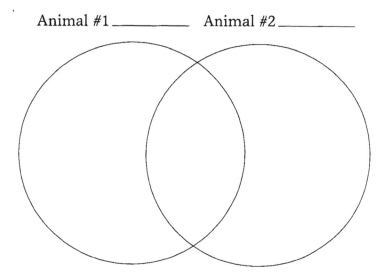

Teacher Information

This can be a very simple activity related to seasons for younger children.

With older students you may want to relate this activity to your social studies lessons and include historical adaptations, such as those of Eskimos, Native American Indians, pioneers of the past, and primitive people of today. Geography, weather, climate, and food offer almost limitless possibilities for illustrating the human ability to adapt.

For centuries people have dreamed of exploring and colonizing outer space. That dream is beginning to unfold. Students who have a background in the study of the solar system may choose to explore this topic for enrichment.

Try to have fifty or more pictures showing homes, food, transportation, recreation, clothing, and everyday activities.

Integrating

Reading, language arts, social studies

Science Process Skills

Observing, inferring, classifying, communicating, comparing and contrasting, using space-time relationships, formulating hypotheses, identifying and controlling variables, researching

How Do Adaptations Affect Where Animals Live?

Materials Needed

- One or more partners
- Animal pictures
- Map of the selected region
- Copies of the "Scientific Investigation Journaling Notes" for this activity (one per student)
- Paper
- Pencils
- Art supplies

Procedure

1. Select a picture of an animal (or draw your own picture and write the name of the animal on the picture) and place it on the area of the map where you think it would most likely live.

2. Write about the animal you chose, including how big it is, where the animal lives, what the environment is like there, what your animal does to survive in its environment, and adaptations that help it to do these things. (See the Journaling Notes.)

3. Describe your animal to your partners and listen to what they say about the animals they chose.

4. Each of you now place your animal in a different area of the map.

5. Using another copy of the same form, write about the adaptations your animal will need in order to survive in the new environment. Draw your animal, showing these adaptations.

6. Discuss your new animal with your group.

7. After your discussion, you might want to make changes or draw it again.

8. When you are finished, put your animal on the bulletin board along with those that were drawn by others who did this activity.

9. Choose a populated area on the map that is at least 500 miles north or south of where you live. Think about what changes you would make in what you do if you lived there. Share your ideas with your group.

Hands-On Life Science Activities

For Problem Solvers

Do some research about animal adaptations, using the Internet and books that are available. Find or draw pictures of the animals, showing or describing the adaptations. Make a journal featuring one important adaptation for each animal.

Teacher Information

Adaptations are specialized structures (wings, claws, tail, and so on) and variations (size of the wing, sharpness of the claws, length of the tail) that develop over time and allow the animal to live where it lives and do the things it does.

Your choice of a map will depend on your circumstances. You might choose to use local animals, those from throughout your state, your nation, or the world, according to the interest and maturity level of your students.

Integrating

Math, reading, language arts, art

Science Process Skills

Observing, inferring, classifying, communicating, comparing and contrasting, researching

Scientific Investigation
Journaling Notes for Activity 1.2

Animal:

_____

Where it lives:

_____

_____

What the environment is like:

_____

_____

_____

What the animal does to survive in its environment:

_____

_____

_____

Adaptations that help it to do those things:

_____

_____

_____

Why Are Feathers Special?

(Take home and do with family and friends)

Materials Needed

- Bird flight feathers (one per student)
- Hand lens (one per student if possible)

Procedure

1. Use the hand lens to examine your feather. Notice that it is made up of a strong shaft or spine, with many small threadlike pieces or filaments attached on either side of the spine.

2. Examine the shaft. Hold it by the thicker end and carefully bend the opposite end a little bit. What happens when you release the bent end?

3. Carefully separate the threadlike filaments near the middle of your feather. Notice they seem to stick together. Although you probably will not be able to see them with a small hand lens, each filament has hundreds of tiny hooks, called barbules, that hold the filaments together to make a long, flat surface called a vane.

4. Beginning at the shaft, use your fingers to gently stroke the area where you separated the filaments. Can you describe what happens and why? Can you think of man-made devices similar to this?

Teacher Information

Before you use feathers, certain precautions should be taken. Be certain they are clean and free of dust and tiny insects such as fleas and lice. Most feathers can be rinsed in warm water (no soap), and when dry, placed in a microwave oven for a few seconds.

Feathers are remarkable examples of animal adaptation. People have not been able to produce any material or system to match them, weight-for-weight, for strength, insulation, or air-foil qualities.

The substance of which feathers are made is called keratin, similar to the material in human fingernails. The tiny barbs on the filaments allow them to be separated and rejoined, much as we use zippers or Velcro® fasteners.

The filaments of flight feathers lock together in an overlapping pattern, providing extra strength. If you have a large feather and a strong magnifier, you may be able to see the overlapping by looking along the shaft from a nearly horizontal angle. Many of the following activities use birds as examples of adaptation.

Science Process Skills

Observing, inferring, classifying, communicating

Living Through Adaptation

What Purposes Can Feathers Serve?

Materials Needed

- Flight feathers
- Downy feathers
- Hand lens (one per student)
- Pictures of penguins in natural habitat
- Pictures of people in heavy winter clothing
- Man-made insulation from a coat, sleeping bag, or ski parka

Procedure

1. Use your hand lens to compare your flight feather with your new downy feather.
2. Locate shaft and filaments. How are they alike? How are they different?
3. Can you think of reasons for why birds have downy feathers?
4. Because they are warm-blooded and must use energy to produce heat, both birds and people keep warm by using protective coverings. Use your hand lens to examine man-made synthetic materials. Compare these materials with your downy feathers. How are they alike? How are they different?
5. Compare the penguins with the people dressed in winter clothing. Although penguins do not fly, their outer feathers serve as a protective waterproof covering for an inner lining of downy feathers. They are the only warm-blooded animals that can survive year-round in the severe cold of the Antarctic. Without extra heat and shelter, humans would perish in a few hours or days. Some of the warmest coats people can make are made from downy feathers.

Teacher Information

Down from the eider duck has long been prized as the best insulation for coats and parkas. Fur and wool are inferior if heat retention alone is desired.

Hands-On Life Science Activities

It is important for students to understand that downy feathers and penguins are only one example of adaptations to a particular environment. It is equally important to point out that people continually improve their ability to adapt through the use of intelligence and technology. In the extreme temperatures of outer space, for example, astronauts have bulky heaters and air conditioners built into their space suits.

Integrating

Language arts, social studies

Science Process Skills

Observing, inferring, classifying, communicating

Can You Make a Feather?

Materials Needed

- Flight feathers
- Downy feathers
- Light-colored construction paper
- Thin plastic drinking straw (not hinged)
- Strong glue
- Scissors
- Pencil

Procedure

1. Place your flight feather on a piece of construction paper. Outline it with your pencil.
2. Use your scissors to cut the outline of the feather from the construction paper.
3. Cut the straw so it is approximately the same length as the shaft of your flight feather.
4. Glue the straw on the paper feather in approximately the same position as the shaft of the real feather.
5. Compare the feather you have constructed with the real feather. Test the weight, strength, and resiliency (ability to bounce back when bent). What happens if you get it wet? Torn?
6. Would a bird like to have feathers like the one you made?

Teacher Information

True feathers are unique to birds. Although all birds have feathers, many do not fly. The oldest known fossil of a bird, archaeopteryx, had feathers, but probably could not fly because it appears to have had solid bones that would have made it too heavy. Small and apparently simple as it appears, the unique design of the feather has not been improved on by modern technology.

Usually birds shed and replace their feathers annually through a process called molting. Animals with hair and fur (including humans) also shed and replace their covering on a regular basis.

Hands-On Life Science Activities

Birds regularly use their beaks to groom and repair their feathers (zip them back together) and keep them in place so that they function properly. The word *preen* is used to describe this instinctive, necessary behavior in birds, and is sometimes applied to vain humans. Many birds have an oil gland located near their tails that secretes a natural protective substance that is applied to their feathers with their beaks.

Most birds are attracted to water. A large clear plastic bowl filled with water may attract as many birds as a feeder. Be sure the bowl is suspended or placed in an area that is cat-proof.

Integrating

Math, art

Science Process Skills

Comparing and contrasting, identifying and controlling variables

How Can We Be Tricked by Color?

(Teacher-directed activity)

Materials Needed

- Colored cereal
- Baggies®

Procedure

1. Count out fifty pieces of each color of cereal.
2. Without students present, scatter the cereal randomly on a section of the playground. This needs to be timed in such a way that you can have your students out for the activity before other students in the school will be using the area where the cereal is located.
3. Tell students that a swarm of insects came into the area (explain the boundaries of the area involved). Students are to pretend to be birds that like to eat insects, and find as many as they can in a very short period of time. Provide small plastic bags and instruct students not to eat the insects, but to collect them in the bags. It is important that they stop and return to the group when time is called. Allow less than ten seconds.
4. Return to the classroom, separate the cereal by color, and count the number of each color. Record these on the board.
5. After reviewing the number of pieces of each color found in the time allowed, disclose that the numbers of each color scattered on the playground were equal.
6. Discuss any differences in the number of each color found, and possible reasons for the differences.
7. Discuss the meaning of "camouflage" (blending into the surroundings).

Teacher Information

If students cannot refrain from eating the "insects," switch to colored toothpicks. The cereal has the advantage that birds will eat the leftovers and you don't need to worry about going back on clean-up detail.

Integrating

Math, physical education, language arts

Science Process Skills

Observing, inferring, classifying, communicating, comparing and contrasting, identifying and controlling variables

Hands-On Life Science Activities

How Is Color Used by Living Things?

(Small groups)

Materials Needed

- Pictures of brightly colored male and drab female common birds (pheasants or robins)
- Pictures of brightly colored and drab fish
- Pictures of humans dressed in bright colors and camouflage
- Pictures of butterflies and insects that resemble a leaf or bark
- Pictures of does and fawns

Procedure

1. Color is important to many living things. Look at the pictures. Classify them according to bright and drab colors.

2. In many species of animals, the female is not as brightly colored as the male. Try to match the male and female of each species. Some male animals use bright colors to attract the female. The drab colors of the female help to protect her while she is caring for her young, by making her less noticeable.

3. Some animals and plants on both land and sea are adapted to protecting themselves by resembling their natural surroundings. This is called camouflage. Can you find animals that use this method of protection? One of the best examples of camouflage is the chameleon, a lizard that changes its skin color to resemble its surroundings. Some birds and fur-bearing animals (rabbits, for example) change color with the seasons.

4. Look at the pictures of humans. How have they used color? Why?

For Problem Solvers

Older students may be interested in studies of the psychological effects of color on animal and human behavior. Consult your encyclopedia and any other sources you have for additional information. Do bulls really react to the color red? Do hummingbirds?

Living Through Adaptation

Two particular colors show up frequently in poisonous animals. If we know what they are, we might be able to avoid danger. Find out what these colors are.

In what other ways does nature seem to use color?

Teacher Information

Color plays such an important part in nature that it could occupy a portion of almost any area of study. People appear to be unique in using color for purely aesthetic purposes. Because the basic physical appearance of humans is quite drab, they have again adapted widely from nature. From earliest times feathers, furs, jewelry, and dyes have all been used as adornments by people, and from prehistoric times people have also used color in art.

Since this activity mentions color in our lives, you may want to discuss the use of color in regulatory signs and advertising, just as color is often used in the animal world to advertise and communicate with others.

Many poisonous snakes and poisonous spiders have bright yellow or bright red, or both, on their bodies. Consider, for instance, the red mark on the female black-widow spider, and the red and yellow rings of the coral snake. We mustn't over-rely on these warning colors, however; the diamondback rattlesnake has neither bright yellow nor bright red, and this is true of some other poisonous animals as well. Still, these two colors show up often enough to be worth knowing about them.

Integrating

Reading, language arts, social studies, art

Science Process Skills

Observing, inferring, classifying, predicting, communicating, comparing and contrasting, researching

What Happens When the Camouflage Is Gone?

(Teacher-directed activity)

Materials Needed

- Green paper
- Pencils or markers
- Scissors
- Two sets of paper wings and bird beaks

Procedure

1. Explain to students that they will each make a butterfly. These butterflies live on the leaves of a particular type of tree—just like the one on the wall of our classroom.

2. Give each child green paper to draw and cut out a butterfly.

3. Students should cut out the green butterflies, write their names on the butterflies with pencils, and tape them on the tree. If some of them are placed on the trunk of the tree, let them stay; it will help to make the point of the activity.

4. Discuss the meaning of camouflage, and note that the color of the butterflies helps them to blend in with their environment.

5. The birds come in, hunting for something to eat, and do not see the butterflies very well (unless some are on the trunk of the tree).

6. Explain that the butterflies go out for a flight around the forest, and tell students to go to the tree and get their butterflies.

7. Now explain that a disease comes through the forest and causes the trees to lose their leaves. Remove the leaves from the tree.

8. The butterflies return and land on their tree. Students all put their butterflies on the bare branches of the tree.

9. Discuss what is different now. What will happen when the birds come back?

10. Invite the "birds" back in. It's very easy now for the birds to see the butterflies, and the birds have a feast!

11. Discuss what happens to insects and other animals that are protected by camouflage when the environment changes.

Living Through Adaptation

Teacher Information

Prepare for this activity by having students create a large tree for a bulletin board or just to put on a blank wall. The tree should have a large brown trunk and branches and be heavily covered with green paper leaves. You could have students each make several leaves, or simply make one bushy green tree top.

You could provide butterfly patterns or allow students to create their own, allowing for greater variety of size and shape. All of the butterflies will be green and will blend in with the leaves of the tree. Use the same paper for the butterflies as for the leaves, to assure the blending of the butterflies with the leaves.

Assign two students to be birds, to come in when the butterflies are all nesting in the tree. These students wear the paper wings and beaks, or simply a sign that says "bird." The birds like to eat butterflies, but they have a hard time seeing them when they blend in with the environment.

Integrating

Art

Science Process Skills

Observing, inferring, classifying, predicting, communicating, comparing and contrasting, using space-time relationships, formulating hypotheses, identifying and controlling variables, experimenting, researching

What Happens to Camouflage When the Environment Changes?

Materials Needed

- Nature square [multi-colored carpet or fabric, 1 sq. meter (or 1 sq. yd.) or larger]
- Construction paper (ten colors)
- Eleven bowls
- Paper punch
- Group of five students

Procedure

1. With the construction paper and paper punch, make a supply of punch-outs of each color, separating the colors into different bowls. These are your "insects."
2. Place ten insects of each color in the extra bowl, and mix them up (total of one hundred mixed-up insects).
3. Now scatter the counted insects over the nature square. The bowl should now be empty.
4. Make a graph that shows the number of each color of insects on the nature square.
5. Have each person in the group of five stand with his or her back to the nature square.
6. The five should turn around all at the same time, and each of them pick up the first two "insects" he or she sees. If someone else takes one that you had picked, take another of the same color.
7. Repeat this four more times, until each person has picked up ten insects.
8. Count the number of each color of insects that were picked up by the group, and from that compute the numbers of each color that are left on the nature square. Write the number of each color left in the nature square.

9. Predators ate the insects that were picked up. Place these in the empty bowl. The only insects that can reproduce are the ones remaining in the nature square.

10. For each insect left on the nature square, take one insect of the same color from the supply bowls and toss it onto the nature square, representing the next generation of insects. Prepare a new graph showing the number of each color of insects now on the nature square. There should again be a total of one hundred insects on the nature square.

11. Repeat steps 5 through 7, with each person in the group picking up ten more insects.

12. Repeat steps 8 through 10, recording and replacing ten insects each. These are the third generation. Again, prepare a new graph showing the number of each color of insects now on the nature square. Again there should be one hundred insects on the nature square.

13. Examine the graphs that now show three generations of insects living in this habitat. Note that for each generation we kept the total numbers the same (one hundred).

14. Compare and contrast the numbers of insects of each color from one generation to the next. What trends are showing up? Discuss your observations.

15. Predict what the results would be if we continued the activity for two more generations.

16. Extend the activity for two more generations and compare your predictions with the actual results.

For Problem Solvers

Do some research on the ideas of *natural selection* and *adaptations*. Write about what you learn from your research and the insights you gained from the above activity. Considering your own pet, or the pet of a neighbor or friend, what adaptations for survival does that animal have?

Try to arrange a visit with a forest ranger or other employee of the Division of Natural Resources in your state. Ask them what implications the process of natural selection has on the public lands. Ask also for examples of adaptations that help local wild animals to survive. Think about predators as well as prey; both need to survive.

What behaviors or body structures do humans have that help them to survive?

Hands-On Life Science Activities

Teacher Information

Adaptations are behaviors or structures that help animals to survive in a given environment. Such adaptations can result from natural selection over a very long period of time. Animal habitats are altered by long-term changes in conditions, such as in temperature, supply of water and food, and disease. As changes become severe, the affected animals must adapt, move, or die.

Camouflage is an example of adaptation. Members of a species whose coloring favors them for survival in a given habitat, either as predator or prey, will pass on the favored trait to offspring, thus leaning the species toward that particular color pattern. Those without this trait are less likely to survive, and therefore less likely to perpetuate the species.

The trait involving body color in this example could be mixed with an inherited behavioral trait as well. In order for color to favor survival, we must assume the animal remains in the habitat that provides the background (plants, rocks, soil) with which the animal blends well. If for any reason (food supply, for example) the animal moves to a new habitat, it might sacrifice the advantage of camouflage.

Considering the "nature" of this activity, a piece of carpet or fabric with a pattern of flowers and/or other plants would add a nice touch, but certainly is not necessary for the success of the activity. If the classroom carpet is suitable, you could simply tape off the area to be used for the activity. If convenient, use a larger area, even up to two meters (six feet) on each side.

For obvious reasons, using carpet for the nature square is an advantage if the classroom carpet is suitable for the activity. Using multi-colored fabric instead of separate carpet squares would make it fairly easy to involve multiple groups of students simultaneously while requiring relatively little storage space. If you use multiples, consider selecting each piece of fabric in a different design, thus representing different environments and producing varied results as to which color offers the greater chance for survival. The variance can then be compared and discussed by the class. If you do not do this activity with multiple groups, the group doing the activity should repeat it with a different background so the differences can be observed and discussed.

Discuss also whether the advantage favors predator or prey. Are we biased for one or the other? Why? They both must survive. In what cases might some people favor the predator? The prey?

Integrating

Math, physical education, reading, language arts, social studies, art

Science Process Skills

Observing, inferring, classifying, measuring, predicting, communicating, comparing and contrasting, using space-time relationships, formulating hypotheses, identifying and controlling variables, researching

How Do Birds Adapt to Eating?

(Teacher-supervised total-group activity)

Materials Needed

- Variety of pictures of birds with many kinds of beaks (names of food they eat written on back)
- Household utensils and tools, including scissors, two-tined fork, linoleum cutter, sieve, knives (serrated and plain), wooden spoons, nutcracker, salad tongs, tweezers, tea ball, eye dropper, needle-nosed and standard pliers, hammer, ice pick or punch, chopsticks, grater, ear syringe

Procedure

1. Arrange the pictures of birds on a large table. Carefully study their beaks. What type of food do you think their beaks are best designed for?
2. Look at the household tools. Do any of them remind you of bird beaks? Be sure you know how each one works.
3. Examine each household implement and put it next to the bird whose beak it most closely resembles. Can you think of other objects around your home or school that work much the same as bird beaks?
4. Test yourself by turning the bird pictures over. On the back is a list of foods they eat.

Teacher Information

Since some implements are sharp, this activity should be carefully supervised. (To avoid the risk of having the sharp instruments, pictures of them could be used instead of the instruments themselves.) Birds do not have teeth, but some of their beaks or bills are highly specialized, depending on the food they usually eat. The terms *beak* and *bill* are generally used interchangeably. Some ornithologists reserve the term *beak* for the sharp, hooked beaks of hawks, eagles, owls, and other birds of prey.

The most common beaks among land birds are varieties of the short, strong seed eaters. If you have a canary or parakeet visiting in your

Hands-On Life Science Activities

classroom, notice that before it eats some types of seeds, it uses its beak to split and remove the outer covering or husk.

Ducks and many other birds with flat bills often use them in water as strainers or sieves to draw in plants, snails, and small aquatic animals. The varieties, range, and eating habits of ducks make them easily available for study throughout the moderate climates of the world.

Some birds (for example, grebes and cormorants) with long scissor-like bills catch small fish by diving and swimming under the water for short periods of time. Other fishing birds (herons and egrets) stand on long legs and fish near the shore.

Marsh and shore birds (for example, sandpipers) have long, often curved bills to catch shrimp and other crustaceans in marshlands and at the seashore.

Some birds (terns, pelicans, kingfishers) circle in the air above the water and dive under to catch fish with their scissor-like bills.

The bills of woodpeckers are mostly long and sharp, with which they chisel out tree bark for insects and construct nest holes. Some woodpeckers also eat acorns and other nuts, often drilling holes in trees as storage bins for their food.

Some birds (pigeons, jays, gulls) eat a wide variety of foods and may become bothersome intruders at picnics and campsites.

The tiny hummingbird uses its very long bill much like an eye dropper to draw in nectar and pollen. Despite its small size, the hummingbird is an excellent flyer and can hover, dart at high speeds, and even fly backward. Hummingbirds are highly territorial, somewhat aggressive, and usually friendly and curious.

Adaptations of birds are almost unlimited. Probably the most feared and respected are the predatory birds (eagles, hawks, ospreys, falcons, owls) with sharp, hooked beaks and powerful claws. Although of different scientific classifications, these birds are often referred to as raptors. They have strong, sharp beaks and claws, superior flying ability, and excellent eyesight.

Integrating
Language arts

Science Process Skills
Observing, inferring, classifying, predicting, communicating, comparing and contrasting

What Are Some Other Eating Adaptations?

(Teacher-supervised total-group activity)

Materials Needed

- Household utensils from Activity 1.10, plus picture of hypodermic needle
- Pictures of animals with mouths open showing mouth parts. Write the name of the principal food they eat on the back. Try to include animals that live almost entirely in the water, such as shark and whale, squid, octopus; other types of animals, such as reptiles (crocodile, alligator, rattlesnake, constrictor, lizard with long tongue); common mammals (rodents, dogs, wolves, bears, sheep, cows, horses, cats, bats, shrews, beaver, and deer); and representative dinosaur pictures. Try also to include enlarged insect mouth parts (mosquito, flea, ant, bee, grasshopper, praying mantis) and enlarged spider mouths.

Procedure

1. In Activity 1.10 we found that birds' beaks are often adapted to eating certain kinds of foods. Study the pictures on the table and try to arrange or classify them into different groups whose open mouths look similar.

2. Look at the household utensils. Try to find some that resemble the mouth parts in the animal pictures. Put the utensils near the pictures. You may find some animal mouth parts that have several utensils in them.

3. Look at the pictures of the dinosaurs. The Brontosaurus had a long neck and small mouth. Compare it with the picture of Tyrannosaurus Rex. Compare the mouths of these giants from the past with the mouth parts of a spider or praying mantis. Can you tell how large the animals are by looking at their mouth parts?

4. One way of classifying animals is by the kind of food they eat. Some animals eat plants, some prefer meat, and some eat both. Arrange your animal pictures into these three groups according to the food they eat. Turn the pictures over and see whether you were right. What were the clues that helped you decide?

Hands-On Life Science Activities

Teacher Information

As with birds, mouth parts of different species of animals vary greatly. Sharp, curved, tearing teeth (similar to eagles' beaks) usually indicate meat eaters. Cutting and grinding teeth (or the absence of teeth) usually suggest plant eaters. Animals that eat both usually have some combination of tearing, grinding, and cutting teeth.

There appears to be no simple relationship between the size of animals and the food they eat. Quantity and availability of food seem more significant. The largest of the dinosaurs were plant eaters, and so are elephants today.

When the giant lizards ruled the earth, mammals were very small and not plentiful. Today, some mammals are very large. Some species of whales are much larger than any other animal that has ever lived.

The traditional terms *herbivore* (plant eaters), *carnivore* (meat eaters), and *omnivore* (both plants and meat) have not been used in this section. Bears, pigs, people, birds, bats, and many other animals feed in such a variety of ways that the terms may become quite confusing. Your students may also have house pets (cats and dogs) that are basically meat eaters but have become so domesticated that they will eat anything people do, even French fries!

Integrating

Language arts

Science Process Skills

Observing, inferring, classifying, predicting, communicating, comparing and contrasting

What Are Human Teeth Like?

Materials Needed

- Dentures
- Tooth model
- Ear syringe
- Picture of mother dog or pig nursing her young
- Picture of typical six- or seven-year-old child with front teeth missing
- Picture of horse or mule showing its teeth

Procedure

1. What does the saying "Don't look a gift horse in the mouth" mean? Look at the picture of the smiling horse. How does it make you feel? If you were a horse dealer, you might react in a different way. Horses eat hay, grass, and some other plants. Over the years their teeth gradually wear down. Looking in a horse's mouth is one way to tell its age. Until recently, looking in a human's mouth might tell the same story. Why is this no longer true?

2. In Activities 1.10 and 1.11, you learned some ways mouth parts are important to animals in getting and eating food. Many of the mouth parts were developed for one kind of food. A few had parts for eating a variety of foods. Examine the dentures (false teeth). They are very similar to the ones you have in your mouth. Find teeth that look like the beaks, bills, and specialized mouth parts of other animals. From looking at their teeth, can you tell what humans eat?

3. How many teeth are in the set of dentures? How many do you have? How many do your classmates have? Are they all the same?

4. Try to find out how many teeth adults usually have. Is it the same for everyone?

5. Baby mammals, including humans, usually don't have teeth when they are born. They get their food in the form of milk by sucking on the soft nipples of their mother. Examine the ear syringe. Put some water in your hand and draw it up with the syringe. You can draw milk or water into it without damaging the surface it touches. Mammal babies seem to be born with an instinct for sucking.

6. Sometimes at birth, but usually after a few months, human babies begin to develop teeth. The first ones are small but allow babies to

Hands-On Life Science Activities

begin eating soft food other than liquids. These first teeth are temporary and usually fall out. Do you have temporary teeth in your mouth? Find a picture of young children who are losing their temporary teeth.

7. Look at the set of false teeth. By the time you are a young adult (sixteen to twenty years old), you will have a permanent set of teeth, usually twenty-eight to thirty-two in number. With care, they will serve you well for the rest of your life.

8. If you haven't figured out what "Don't look a gift horse in the mouth" means, discuss it with your teacher.

Teacher Information

Dentures, real teeth, charts, and models may be obtained from a local dentist. The American Dental Association also provides pamphlets and information about teeth and their care.

"Don't look a gift horse in the mouth" may have originated at the time when horses were as common in everyday life as cars are today. An experienced person can tell a lot about the age and condition of a horse by examining the teeth and mouth. If someone gave you a horse as a gift and you looked in its mouth to see how old it was, it would be as rude as to look for a price tag or brand name on an item received as a gift. Today we often use the expression to describe someone who has had good (unexpected) fortune or received a gift and looks for an underlying or selfish motive behind the gift.

Humans are very adaptable, and their teeth and mouths reflect this pattern. We have fairly good cutting teeth (not as good as those of a beaver) and grinding teeth (but not nearly as good as those of a cow). Our mouths can be shaped for sucking (but not nearly as efficiently as that of a hummingbird, mosquito, spider, leech, or lamprey).

Where food is concerned, the size of our mouths and the limited operations of our jaws keep us from being the best at anything, but because they are so generalized we do pretty well at most things, and we are able to handle a wide variety of food.

Human age can sometimes be determined by counting permanent teeth (six- and twelve-year molars). For many years, the presence of dentures was associated with old age.

Integrating

Math, language arts, social studies

Science Process Skills

Observing, inferring, classifying, communicating, comparing and contrasting

How Important Is Your Thumb?

Materials Needed

- Chalkboard or whiteboard
- Chalk or whiteboard marker
- Partner
- Tape

Procedure

1. Using the hand you write with, fold your thumb over into the palm of your hand and have your partner wrap tape around your hand, enclosing the thumb so it cannot be used.

2. Now do the same for your partner, disabling the thumb of the writing hand.

3. Each of you take a piece of chalk (or marker) with your taped hand and make a list of animals—any animals. Make your lists at the same time, but try not to look at each other's lists.

4. Talk about the task of writing the words on the board. Why was it more difficult than usual?

5. Examine both lists of animals. Put a star by each one that has an opposing thumb, enabling the animal to grab something with its hand.

6. If there are no animals in your list that have an opposing thumb, try to think of one or more to add to your list.

7. Discuss the advantage humans have over most other animals, simply because of the opposing thumb.

8. In what other ways is the human body designed differently from those of most other animals?

9. Which of these differences give humans an advantage, and which of them give other animals an advantage? What can certain other animals do better than humans can do?

For Problem Solvers

Do some research and see how many animals you can list, along with at least one significant strength or advantage each animal has in the way it is designed. What are some things humans do to compensate for weaknesses and adapt to new situations, including harsh environments?

Teacher Information

The opposing thumb is a great advantage favoring humanoids. Their ability to think and reason is another characteristic that gives humans an advantage in the world of animals, enabling them to compensate for many weaknesses. Polar bears have warm coats that protect them in harshly cold climates, for example. Humans are able to invent ways to compensate for the lack of a home-grown coat.

Your young researchers will find fascinating information about the adaptations that enable different animals to do strange and wondrous things.

Integrating

Math, physical education, reading, language arts, social studies, art

Science Process Skills

Observing, inferring, classifying, measuring, predicting, communicating, comparing and contrasting, using space-time relationships, formulating hypotheses, identifying and controlling variables, experimenting, researching

How Do Animals Move?

(Small-group activity)

Materials Needed

- Pictures of animals that move in different ways (swimming, walking, hopping, gliding, crawling, flying, climbing) and of animals that don't move, such as barnacles
- Live animals in aquarium, cages, and terrarium
- Copies of the "Scientific Investigation Journaling Notes" for this activity (one per student)
- Paper
- Pencils

Procedure

1. Look at the live animals and the pictures of animals in your room. Can you tell how each one moves about? Can you find any that don't seem to move?

2. Write the names of the animals down the left-hand column of your copy of the Journaling Notes. In the right-hand column, write the ways they move (remember, some move in different ways). Try to think of more than one word to describe their movement. For example, fish swim, but they also wiggle and swish; snakes crawl, but they also slither and glide; cats walk, run, crawl, creep, climb, stalk, and pounce. How many words can you find for each animal?

3. If you think of still more ways for describing the movements of these animals, write them on your paper.

4. Think of the ways you move. How many did you find?

5. Look at your list of animal movements. Underline the ones you can imitate.

6. Are there any movements you can do as well or better than some other animal (hint: pick up a pencil or tie a shoelace)? Why are you able to do these things better?

7. Have a class discussion about why you think animals move as they do.

Teacher Information

Younger students may enjoy trying to imitate the movements of animals. Older students can play animal movement charades, in which they guess the animal being portrayed. Animal movements may also inspire creative dancing. Some cultures imitate animal movements with costumes, music, and dance.

Animal movements are most often based on their environment (water, land, or both), method of obtaining food, courtship rituals, and defense or protection. Some animals seem to dance or play just for fun.

When size and proportions are taken into consideration, animals that specialize in a particular type of movement can perform that movement far better and more efficiently than people (even remaining still). Thanks to the opposed thumb, the movement people can make better than any other animal is grasping. This has enabled people to be the best tool users and, along with their ability to think and reason, to create many technical and mechanical adaptations to compete with the specialized movements of other animals.

Don't forget the many mechanical robots that are popular as children's toys. You might plan a "robot day" when everyone is invited to bring his or her favorite doll or mechanical animal toy and explain how it works. No matter how well designed, mechanical toys cannot perform animal movements nearly as well as the animal itself.

Integrating

Math, language arts, social studies, art

Science Process Skills

Observing, inferring, classifying, communicating, comparing and contrasting, formulating hypotheses, identifying and controlling variables

Scientific Investigation

Journaling Notes for Activity 1.14

Animal

How It Moves

_____   _____

_____   _____

_____   _____

_____   _____

_____   _____

_____   _____

_____   _____

_____   _____

_____   _____

_____   _____

_____   _____

How Do Some Animals Communicate?

(Partners or small-group activity)

Materials Needed

- Paper
- Pencil

Procedure

1. We usually think of communicating as ways of giving or receiving information or conveying emotions and feelings by talking and listening. Listening and watching (movies, radio, television) or drawing and looking at pictures are also usual ways people communicate. Can you think of any other ways? How many?

2. In step 1, did you add reading, which you are doing now? Did you remember gestures, too? On your paper, write as many ways as you can think of that people communicate.

3. Scientists believe that many animals communicate in different ways, but only people have been able to create a vocabulary of many words to communicate ideas. If you own or know a household pet, discuss the ways it communicates with you without using words. Does it seem to understand what you say? Write down as many of these ways as you can.

4. With partners or in small groups, pretend none of you can hear or speak. Without drawing pictures or making any sound, take turns describing your favorite game or toy.

5. You probably found your best way of communicating without making sound was with gestures. Many people who cannot speak or hear learn gestures called sign language or "signing" to communicate. List on your paper some animals that use gestures or signals to communicate (hint: How does a dog show it is friendly?).

6. What are some ways people communicate today that they could not do before the invention of the computer? How many can you name?

For Problem Solvers

Much research has been done, and is being done, on ways various forms of animals communicate with each other. Use your references and learn all you can about what has been discovered through such research. What about the monkey family and the whale family? What about ants, bees, and other insects? Other animals?

Teacher Information

In addition to the opposed thumb, the abilities to create and use oral language and pictures seem to be unique to people. There seems to be little doubt that other higher animals such as apes can reason and think, but only people are known to have developed a complex language with which to express ideas.

Apes and chimpanzees have been successfully trained to use symbols and sign language (see *National Geographic,* January 1985).

Most other animals seem to use communication instinctively to express warning, fear, anger, recognition, and food gathering, or as mating calls and signals. The famous "bee dance" is described in your encyclopedia. Ants also have methods for communicating the location of food. Most insect communities provide studies of specialization and ways animals within a species are adapted to specialized roles. Some sea mammals, such as porpoises and whales, seem to have complex communication systems that scientists have, so far, been unable to decode.

Language has enabled people to use the environment to adapt, create, and express as no other animal can. As people continue to adapt the computer to every phase of life, the implications for computers seem endless. For sheer joy of expression, however, many people believe that the infinitely varied song of the humpback whale has no equal.

Integrating

Math, reading, language arts, social studies

Science Process Skills

Observing, inferring, classifying, communicating, comparing and contrasting, using space-time relationships, formulating hypotheses, identifying and controlling variables, experimenting, researching

How Do Seasons Affect Animal Adaptations?

Materials Needed

- Pictures of a butterfly, migratory bird (Arctic tern, Canada goose), local year-round bird, squirrel, rabbit, earthworm, snake, bear, deer, elk, whale, and pictures of people living, working, and playing in different climates
- Map of the world
- Globe
- Cards labeled "Hibernate," "Migrate," "Adapt"

Procedure

1. Place the three cards at the top of the table. Discuss the meaning of each word with your teacher.

2. Look at the map and the globe of the earth. Usually there is less seasonal change near the middle, or the equator. As you travel north or south toward the poles, seasonal changes become greater. Find the place where you live. How far (in miles or kilometers) are you from the equator and from the North Pole or South Pole?

3. Oceans and other large bodies of water affect land temperature. Water does not change in temperature as rapidly as land does. If you live near an ocean, changes in seasons may not be as great. Does a large body of water affect your climate? How?

4. Study the pictures of animals. See how many pictures you can match with the three cards to show how these animals adapt to seasonal change.

5. With your teacher and other members of the group, discuss your reasons for grouping the pictures the way you did. Why do you think some animals migrate, while others stay and adapt to seasonal change?

For Problem Solvers

Do people migrate? Think about people you know who move from one place to another throughout the year. Write a list of examples of people you know or can find out about.

Teacher Information

Animals have different ways of adapting to seasonal change, mostly due to the availability of food. Some hibernate in a completely resting stage. Some animals, such as bears, increase their rest and reduce their level of activity, but do not completely hibernate.

Many animals remain active in the same area year-round and utilize whatever food is available.

Animal migration is a fascinating area of study. You may find high student interest and extend your study beyond the information introduced here.

In past times caribou, buffalo, and reindeer existed in great numbers. As these animals migrated with seasonal change, people who depended on them for their existence (food and clothing) also migrated.

Integrating

Math, language arts, social studies

Science Process Skills

Observing, inferring, classifying, measuring, predicting, communicating, comparing and contrasting, using space-time relationships, formulating hypotheses, experimenting, researching

How Do Animals Adapt to Seasonal Change?

(Small-group activity)

Materials Needed

- Pictures, map, and globe from Activity 1.16
- Picture of Arctic tern (if not in above collection)
- String
- Masking tape
- Scissors

Procedure

1. Find the picture of the Arctic tern. It is most famous as a world traveler. Locate Greenland on the globe. Many baby terns are hatched here in late June or early July. Place a piece of masking tape there.

2. Within a few weeks, the terns are ready to begin their migration. Use the globe, a 50-cm (20-in.) piece of string, and a piece of masking tape to mark their journey.

3. After leaving Greenland, they fly to the west coast of Europe. Stretch your string and tape it from Greenland to the west coast of France, Spain, or Portugal.

4. From this point, they fly down the west coast of Africa. Stretch your string and tape it to at least two points near the top and bottom of Africa's west coast.

5. From a point near the southwest part of Africa, they make a long journey over the south Atlantic and the Antarctic Oceans to the crusted ice of Antarctica. Stretch your string across the oceans to Antarctica and tape it there. Because the seasons are opposite in the Northern and Southern Hemispheres of our earth, it is summer in the south when it is winter in the north.

6. Terns spend several months in Antarctica, during which they may circle the entire continent. Make a circle with your string around Antarctica.

7. Look at the string path from Greenland to Antarctica on your globe. This marks half the distance a tern flies each year. By May, winter is beginning in Antarctica and the tern returns to Greenland over approximately the same route. Mark or cut the string where the tern's

journey ends in Antarctica. Remove the string from the globe. Measure the length of the string and cut another piece twice as long. This represents (stands for) the total distance a tern may travel each year.

8. Wrap the longer piece of string around the globe at the equator. Then wrap it around the globe crossing both the North Pole and the South Pole. Can you see why we call terns world travelers?

9. Find the Scale of Miles on your globe and compute the number of miles the tern flies in a year.

10. Other animals in the pictures travel shorter distances, and for different reasons. Some birds in the United States and Europe migrate east and west rather than north and south. Why do you suppose this is?

11. Do you know someone who "migrates" with the seasons? People who move to warmer climates for the winter months and back to cooler climates for the summer are often called "snowbirds." Visit a relative or friend of the family who does that, and ask him or her to explain the reasons. Write a short report of your interview and share with your teacher and your class.

For Problem Solvers

Choose a picture of one animal that migrates. Use your resources, including the Internet, to find out as much as you can about the animal you chose. Share your investigation with the class.

Find out about animals that migrate very short distances.

Teacher Information

Availability of globes may limit the size of groups. Try to borrow as many globes as possible so students can work out the problems themselves.

Some birds in Europe, North America, and other parts of the world migrate east and west rather than north and south because they "summer" inland and "winter" near the coast, where it is warmer. Ornithologists are not certain how birds navigate or "home." Theories include the use of stars, the earth's magnetism, landmarks, and combinations of these. Their ability to find a specific location on the earth is amazing, and they do it even in great numbers without the help of air traffic controllers!

Integrating

Math, reading, social studies

Science Process Skills

Observing, inferring, classifying, measuring, predicting, communicating, comparing and contrasting, using space-time relationships, formulating hypotheses, identifying and controlling variables, researching

Hands-On Life Science Activities

Can You Design a Better Bird?

(Teacher-assisted small groups or partners)

Materials Needed

- Pictures of birds in flight, on land, on water
- Paper and straw feathers constructed in Activity 1.5
- Balloons of different sizes and shapes
- Small plastic foam balls
- Plastic drinking straws
- Household utensils
- Colored construction paper
- Cloth or nylon stockings
- String
- Strong white glue
- Pencils and crayons
- Scissors
- Newsprint
- Wire coat hangers and tape (optional)

Procedure

1. Choose a picture of a bird you like. On the table are materials to construct a bird of your own.

2. With your partner or group, make a plan for a bird made of balloons, plastic foam balls, paper, straws, and household utensils.

3. On a sheet of newsprint, draw and color a picture of what you think your bird will look like. This will be your construction plan. Be sure to decide whether your bird will be flying, standing, walking, sitting (perching), or swimming.

4. Balloons and plastic foam balls will make good bodies and heads. Straws can be used for feather parts, legs, and feet. If a household utensil is not satisfactory, you may want to make the beak or bill out of something else. Remember, you will need to make many feathers of different colors. You may want to share your plan with your teacher before you begin.

5. After your bird is finished, share it with the class.

6. Give your bird a name. On a piece of paper write its name, what it eats, where it lives, how big (how long and how tall, and its wingspan) it is, and why it is special.

7. Make an "aviary" for all the birds in your class. Invite visitors to see it.

Teacher Information

This activity could be used at the end of your study of animal adaptation. You will need many paper feathers. If different sizes and colors are cut out from a pattern in advance, much time can be saved. Students may need help in forming the tail, as its shape and construction are often not as obvious as they are for wings.

Coat-hanger wire can be used as rigid supports for the wings of flying birds. If you use coat-hanger wire, be sure to cover the sharp ends with tape (saves on balloons).

No matter how tightly you seal them, balloons will gradually lose air. Inflate them last and plan to have your birds on display for only a few days. If you care to invest the time, the balloons can be covered with papier-mâché to increase the longevity of your birds.

Integrating

Math, art

Science Process Skills

Observing, inferring, classifying, measuring, communicating, comparing and contrasting, identifying and controlling variables

Can You Solve This Animal Adaptations Word Search?

Try to find the following Animal Adaptations terms in the grid below. They could appear in horizontal (left to right), vertical (up or down), or diagonal (upward or downward) position.

adaptation	wetland	animal
environment	habitat	biome
clothing	camouflage	desert
mountain	adapt	change
design	seasons	

```
P  O  I  U  Y  T  C  H  A  N  G  E
D  E  S  I  G  N  R  E  W  S  M  A
C  A  M  O  U  F  L  A  G  E  O  S
L  N  D  S  D  F  G  H  J  A  U  T
O  I  L  A  D  A  P  T  K  S  N  R
T  M  M  N  P  B  A  V  C  O  T  E
H  A  X  A  Q  T  W  S  X  N  A  S
I  L  C  V  I  F  A  R  T  S  I  E
N  Y  U  B  I  W  E  T  L  A  N  D
G  O  A  P  L  K  J  H  I  G  F  D
N  H  B  V  C  D  F  B  I  O  M  E
M  E  N  V  I  R  O  N  M  E  N  T
```

Can You Create a New Animal Adaptations Word Search of Your Own?

Write your Animal Adaptations words in the grid below. Arrange them in the grid so they appear in horizontal (left to right), vertical (up or down), or diagonal (upward or downward) position. Fill in the blank boxes with other letters. Trade your Word Search with someone else who has created one of his or her own, and see whether you can solve the new puzzle.

_____   _____   _____

_____   _____   _____

_____   _____   _____

_____   _____   _____

Answer Key for Animal Adaptations Word Search

```
P  O  I  U  Y  T  C  H  A  N  G  E
D  E  S  I  G  N  R  E  W  S  M  A
C  A  M  O  U  F  L  A  G  E  O  S
L  N  D  S  D  F  G  H  J  A  U  T
O  I  L  A  D  A  P  T  K  S  N  R
T  M  M  N  P  B  A  V  C  O  T  E
H  A  X  A  Q  T  W  S  X  N  A  S
I  L  C  V  I  F  A  R  T  S  I  E
N  Y  U  B  I  W  E  T  L  A  N  D
G  O  A  P  L  K  J  H  I  G  F  D
N  H  B  V  C  D  F  B  I  O  M  E
M  E  N  V  I  R  O  N  M  E  N  T
```

Do You Recall?

Section One: Animal Adaptations

1. Explain the meaning of "adaptation" and give one example of an adaptation for a plant or an animal.

2. Give two examples of ways feathers help ducks to live where and how they do.

3. Name two animals that use color to their advantage, and explain the advantage color provides each of them.

4. What does a pelican eat, and how does the beak help this to happen?

Do You Recall? *(Cont'd.)*

5. What does the eagle eat, and how does the beak help this to happen?

6. Do the feet of the pelican help it with its diet? If so, how?

7. How important is the human thumb? Why?

8. Name one animal that migrates. Tell where it migrates, when it migrates, and whatever you can say about why it migrates.

9. Name an animal that in some way adapts to change of seasons. Describe the adaptation and one of the benefits the adaptation provides for the animal.

Answer Key for Do You Recall?

Section One: Animal Adaptations

Answer	Related Activities
1. The way they adjust to live where and how they do. Examples will vary.	1.1, 1.2
2. Waterproofing, warmth, flight	1.3, 1.4, 1.5
3. Answers will vary.	1.6–1.9
4. Fish; Long, large pouch	1.10, 1.11
5. Meat; Short, strong, sharp for tearing	1.11, 1.12
6. Webbed feet help it to swim and dive	1.14
7. Grab and hold with the hand	1.13
8. Answers will vary.	1.16, 1.17
9. Answers will vary.	1.16, 1.17

Animals

To the Teacher

The study of animals is so broad that it can, and often does, encompass a lifetime. In this section we have tried to limit our study to some of the animals in our immediate environment. We have focused on the following general areas:

- Pets and Imaginary Animals
- Relatives of Pets (Animal Tracks)
- Animals in Our Neighborhood (Nature Square)
- Animals Outside Our Window (Birds)
- Animals in Our Room (Aquariums; Terrariums)

Many broad categories such as domesticated animals, animal colonies, animals of the zoo, and exotic animals have been omitted. You are encouraged to study these areas, using the skills and resources developed in the following activities.

This section places a strong emphasis on the use of books, the Internet, other media, and resource persons. Before you begin, read through the materials lists so you can begin organizing, collecting, and arranging for future activities.

The nature square requires outside activities and field trips.

There are also several simple construction projects such as bird feeders, birdhouses, and butterfly nets. Enlist the help of parents and others.

To complete some activities, small costs may be involved. Inexpensive hand lenses, animals, and plants may need to be purchased. In some cases, orders may have to be sent to science supply houses, and delivery time will be a factor.

We urge you to use resource people whenever possible. There are amateur and professional naturalists everywhere.

The main purpose of these activities is to help students develop respect and appreciation for the variety, beauty, and wonder of the animals around them.

Be as creative as you can. Wander and explore in any direction you choose. These activities could be starting points for lifelong interests and hobbies.

All of the following activities can be adapted for use with young children. Occasionally, specific suggestions for adaptation are made, but usually we have attempted to present ideas that are flexible enough to be used with a broad range of age groups.

Perhaps to prepare yourself for this adventure you could read Robert Frost's poem "The Vantage Point." You can find a vantage point wherever you are.

The following activities are designed as discovery activities that students can usually perform quite independently. You are encouraged to provide students (usually in small groups) with the materials listed and a copy of the activity from the beginning through the "Procedure." The section titled "Teacher Information" is not intended for student use, but rather to assist you with discussion following the hands-on activity, as students share their observations. Discussion of conceptual information prior to completing the hands-on activity can interfere with the discovery process.

Regarding the Early Grades

With verbal instructions and slight modifications, many of these activities can be used with kindergarten, first-grade, and second-grade students. Some of the activities were written specifically with the primary grades in mind. In others, procedural steps that go beyond the level of the child can simply be omitted and yet offer the child experiences that plant conceptual seeds for concepts that will germinate and grow later on.

Teachers of the early grades will probably choose to bypass many of the "For Problem Solvers" sections. That's okay. These sections are provided for those who are especially motivated and want to go beyond the investigation provided by the activity outlined. Use the outlined activities and enjoy worthwhile learning experiences together with your young students. Also consider, however, that many of the "For Problem Solvers" sections can be used appropriately with young children as group activities or as demonstrations. Giving students the advantage of an exposure to the experience can often lay groundwork for connections that will become more meaningful at a later time.

Correlation with National Standards

The following elements of the National Standards are reflected in the activities of this section.

K–4   Content Standard A: Science as Inquiry

As a result of activities in grades K–4, all students should develop

1. Abilities necessary to do scientific inquiry
2. Understanding about scientific inquiry

K–4   Content Standard C: Life Science

As a result of activities in grades K–4, all students should develop understanding of

1. The characteristics of organisms
3. Organisms and environments

Who Are the New Members of Our Class?

(Total-class activity)

Materials Needed

- Two or more animals of different kinds, properly caged for a two- or three-week stay in the classroom (birds, fish, turtles, frogs, gerbils, or guinea pigs are good candidates)
- Pencils
- Copy of "Animal Characteristics" form for each student (found at the end of this activity)

Procedure

1. Today we have several animals in our room. Observe them carefully. Make a list of everything you can about each animal.
2. What kind of animal is it? How big is it? How many legs does it have? What is its outer covering like? What kind of mouth does it have? How does it move about? Can you tell what it eats? Is there anything strange or surprising about this animal?
3. Your teacher will give you a paper with some questions on it. Observe each animal and see how many of the questions you can answer. Save your paper so you can report your findings to the class.

Teacher Information

This activity is planned to help children begin to develop a systematic awareness in their observations of animals. From the group discussion, children should be able to identify similarities and differences in some kinds of animal life. An outcome from the group discussion should be the planning of care for the animals while they are in the room.

It is not recommended that strange, unusual, or potentially dangerous animals be introduced at this time. Snakes, spiders, and wild animals should be reserved for study later on.

The "Animal Characteristics" form shown here can be reproduced in quantity and used throughout the time animals are being studied. You can modify this sheet according to the ages of the children, geographical regions, and animals you choose to study. In early childhood education,

a simplified version of this sheet can be developed in chart form for large group use.

Before beginning a study of animals, be certain to check with your library and/or media center for books, stories, filmstrips, pictures, and so forth. Many books and pictures about the specific animals you introduce should be available in the classroom.

Integrating

Math, language arts, social studies

Science Process Skills

Observing, inferring, classifying, communicating

Animal Characteristics

Name of animal: _____

Type of animal: _____

Size in centimeters or inches: Height: _____ Length: _____

Color(s): _____

Outer covering: _____

Locomotion (How does it move?): _____

_____

Number and kinds of appendages (legs, arms, wings, fins, tail):

_____

_____

Type(s) of food(s) eaten: _____

_____

Habitat (Where does it usually live?): _____

_____

Sounds it makes: _____

Tell as many special things as you can about this animal:

_____

_____

_____

_____

_____

_____

How Can We Keep Our Pets Healthy?

(Teacher-directed activity)

Materials Needed

- Large chart paper
- Marking pen
- Completed "Animal Characteristics" from Activity 2.1
- Copy of "Animal Needs" form (found at the end of this activity)

Procedure

1. You now know the kinds of pets with which you are going to share your classroom. Your "Animal Characteristics" form, which you filled out for each pet, should help you decide what your pets need in order to be well and comfortable during their stay with you.

2. With the help of your teacher, see whether you can find answers to the following questions:

   a. What kind of housing is best for each pet?

   b. What kind of food does each pet need? How much? How often?

   c. What kind of environment does each pet need or like best (water, dirt, rocks, grass, perches)?

   d. Can more than one pet live in the same area?

   e. What temperature does your pet need or like best?

   f. All living things must get water in some way. How does your pet get its water?

   g. What are other special needs you think your pet has?

3. Make a chart for each pet, answering the questions listed above.

4. Divide the class into groups, and, using the chart as a guide, care for each pet for a week.

Animals

Teacher Information

A form is provided here if you care to make copies of it. Some teachers prefer to have children prepare their own, for the added learning experience.

Many of the activities in this section begin with total-group planning or discussion, but in each case they should lead to individual participation. Through caring for classroom pets, children should become acquainted with the needs of specific animals and be able to generalize their experiences to the needs of many animals. This activity is intended to introduce the concept of responsibility, which will be emphasized throughout the study. Animal ownership implies responsibility for the care, welfare, and behavior (control) of the pet. Later, the big idea of responsibility will be extended to include all kinds of wildlife in our nation and the world.

Integrating

Math, language arts, social studies

Science Process Skills

Observing, inferring, classifying, communicating

Animal Needs

Kind of pet: _____

Best housing: _____

Food the animal likes or needs: _____

How much and how often does it need to eat? _____

_____

Environment: _____

Can the animal live with others of its own kind? _____

Best temperature: _____

Water source: _____

_____

Other special needs: _____

_____

_____

_____

_____

_____

_____

_____

_____

_____

_____

_____

_____

_____

How Many Pets Can You Find?

(Total-class activity)

Materials Needed
- Paper
- Pencils

Procedure

1. Many people have pets. A pet can be any animal that lives around your home and that you care for. Some of the most common pets are dogs, cats, birds, and fish, but many people have pets that are more unusual.

2. With your group, try to make a list of all the kinds of animals people might have for pets.

3. Decide which of the pets on your list would be the most practical to keep in your area. Draw a line under those animals and be prepared to report to the whole class. Choose someone from your group to report.

4. Your group leader should report to the class the animals you have chosen. Your teacher will list them on the board.

5. How many pets are on your list?

6. How many of the pets listed on the board does someone in your class have? Try to plan a time when each of these pets could come to school for a short visit.

Teacher Information

We suggest you divide the class into groups of five or six to do steps 1 through 3. Then have group leaders report to the whole class.

This activity should be conducted early in the study so that pets can be scheduled throughout the time you are working with animals. Care should be taken to ensure that the animals are not dangerous and are properly housed or controlled by a restraint. A responsible individual should accompany each animal. Prepare the class for the animal visitor so they won't frighten or disturb it.

Integrating
Math, language arts, social studies

Science Process Skills
Classifying, communicating

How Many Other Pets Can You Find?

Materials Needed

- Paper
- Pencils
- Calendar
- Drawing paper
- Crayons
- Cassette player
- Camera

Procedure

1. By now you probably have a good idea of how many kinds of pets people in your class have. In this activity you will see how many more you can find.

2. Choose a group of students to make a survey of your entire school. Make a form that can be passed out (with permission of your principal and other teachers) to all students in your school. Ask whether the other person has a pet or knows of anyone else, not a student at your school, who does. You might mention that you are interested in unusual pets. Be sure to get the names, addresses, and phone numbers of the people who own the pets.

3. When the questionnaires are returned, develop a system for classifying or grouping them.

4. As a class, make a list of all the pets owned by people in your class, plus the ones recommended in your questionnaires.

5. How many pets are on your list?

6. Look at a calendar and estimate the number of days you are planning to spend studying animals. From the list you developed, choose the pets you would most like to have visit your class. You may be able to have more than one a day if you choose carefully. Also, if you find many unusual or interesting pets, they could be scheduled for visits throughout the year. It is assumed that all of your guest pets will be brought to class by their owners.

7. Contact the owner and arrange to have the pet come on a specific day. Ask the pet's owner to be prepared to tell the class about the pet.

Animals

8. Before your "guest" pet comes, and while it is there, use your library and other resources to find out as much as you can about it. Record all the information you can. Make drawings and pictures. Invite other classes to visit and tell them about the pet. Make a photograph of each pet. If your guest pet makes sounds, record them.

9. Make a scrapbook of your guest pets for the year.

10. Be sure to write thank-you notes to people who share their pets with you.

11. Which pets would you most like to have? Why?

For Problem Solvers

Write a creative story about your favorite pet. This could be an animal that you have had as a pet or an animal you would like to have as a pet. Include in your story the unique characteristics and habits of your pet—the things you think other people could learn from and would most like to read about.

Share your story with the class.

Teacher Information

This activity requires careful coordination and planning. Be sure to consult the principal of your school in the early stages of planning. If more than one class will be studying animals during the year, be sure to involve those teachers in the planning.

Don't forget to contact pet store owners and veterinarians if they are available in your area.

If you live near a zoo, docent services are often available to bring unusual animals to the classroom. It is recommended that exotic animals be scheduled late in the study, after the children become comfortable with animal visitors.

Adequate housing and control of the animals are essential. Children should understand that animals become frightened easily in strange surroundings.

You may be surprised about some of the pets you find.

If you record sounds from the animals that come to class, use the recording later as an exercise in auditory discrimination. Let the children try to identify which animal made each of the sounds.

Integrating

Math, reading, language arts, social studies, art

Science Process Skills

Observing, inferring, classifying, communicating, researching

What Kind of Pet Would You Like to Own?

Materials Needed

- Drawing paper
- Pencils
- Crayons

Procedure

1. Choose a pet you would like to own.
2. Make a picture of this pet. Draw a picture of the place your pet would need to live.
3. Write about, or draw a picture of, the food and water your pet would need each day and how you would provide it.
4. Write in one column the advantages (good things) of owning the pet you have chosen.
5. In another column, list the disadvantages (problems) of keeping this particular pet.
6. Show your picture and read your lists to your group or to the whole class. Perhaps they can help you decide whether this is a pet you should have.

Teacher Information

People occasionally acquire pets they cannot care for properly. This activity attempts to introduce the idea of responsible pet ownership. If you live in an incorporated area, there may be laws regulating the ownership and care of animals. Animal ownership may also be regulated because of possible disease transmission or other potential health problems.

Children need to understand that wild animals generally do not make good pets.

Integrating

Language arts, social studies, art

Science Process Skills

Communicating, comparing and contrasting

What Can Hair Tell You?

Materials Needed

- Large, gentle dog
- Newspapers
- Markers
- Clean, wire pet brush
- Small plastic bags
- Small labels

Procedure

1. Have your teacher or a parent help you find a large, very gentle, well-trained dog with a shaggy coat. A dog who lives outside most of the year is best. Do not use a stray.

2. Spread newspapers on the floor. Use a clean, wire pet brush to brush the dog ten times (strokes). Remember the exact area you brushed. Make a drawing of the dog and mark that spot to help you remember.

3. Collect all the dog hair from the newspaper and wire brush. Store the hair in a small plastic bag. Put a tag on the bag telling the day, date, and time of the brushing.

4. Brush the dog in exactly the same place, in the same way, four times during the school year. October, January, April, and late June might be best.

5. Examine and compare the hair you collected with each brushing. You need to decide what is the best way to measure the amount of hair you brush out. Will you measure it by the size of the pile? Will you weigh it? Will you count the hairs? What do you think will work best?

6. Make a graph that shows how much hair you collected with each brushing.

7. Try to explain the reasons for the differences. Discuss your ideas with your group.

For Problem Solvers

Examine various types of human hair under a microscope, including cross-sections of the hairs (ask your teacher to help you cut the hairs diagonally). Be sure to include both straight hair and curly hair, and see

whether you can detect any differences in them. Before you examine them under a microscope, predict what differences you might find. Make a drawing of what you see with each hair, and label the drawings so you will remember which person the hair for each drawing came from. Compare your information with that of others who did this activity, and share what you learned with your group.

Figure out a way to determine how many hairs you could lay side by side in a space of 2.5 centimeters (1 inch). Do this for each type of hair you examine and use this information to compare the size of the hairs.

Teacher Information

Before you brush the dog, it might be well to have it visit several times to get acquainted with the class. This activity is most effective in climates with pronounced seasonal changes. However, most dogs will undergo seasonal changes in the thickness of their coats, even in mild climates.

Animals with hair shed constantly (humans included). Animals that normally live outdoors often develop a thick undercoating in winter. The condition of the hair of a mammal is often an indicator of the animal's health (including humans).

Students might notice that they lose hair regularly. Unless the loss of hair is extreme or in patches, it is part of the normal hair-growth pattern. At any one time, nearly one-third of a person's hair is typically in the "resting" stage; that is, the hair is gone but the follicle will remain and in a few months will grow a new hair. Baldness, which occurs mostly in males, is hereditary. Certain diseases also cause baldness.

The fur of many mammals serves the dual purpose of warmth and protection. Human hair mostly provides protection. Hair on our head insulates somewhat, but mostly protects the skull. Eyebrows help to shade our eyes from the sun. Eyelashes and hair in the nose and ears help to keep out dust and insects. Some scientists believe the tiny sensitive hairs around our mouths serve the same purpose as feelers on insects.

All hair is not the same shape. If you examine different types of hair under a low-power microscope or hand lens, you will find that straight hair is round. Curly hair is flat.

Integrating

Math, language arts, art

Science Process Skills

Observing, inferring, classifying, measuring, predicting, communicating, comparing and contrasting, formulating hypotheses

Animals

How Many Play Animals Can You Find?

(Lower-grades activity)

Materials Needed

- Stuffed animals
- Animals made of other nonliving materials

Procedure

1. Many of us have animals in our homes that are not living. Some of these animals are used for decorations, some just for fun or play. Do you have a stuffed animal or some other kind of nonliving "friend" you play with?

2. With your teacher, choose a day when some of these nonliving friends can come to school.

3. Introduce your friends to the class and tell about them. What are their names? Where did they come from? Why are they special?

4. Think of as many ways as possible to tell a living animal from a nonliving animal.

Teacher Information

One purpose of this activity is to encourage language experience through sharing. Another purpose is to introduce the idea of living and nonliving things. Young children often associate living things with movement or some observable change in behavior. Life processes, needs, and changes are best understood if developed through concrete experiences and observations.

Science today is studying the basic building blocks or substances of life. There is much debate as to what constitutes living and nonliving material and what the necessary characteristics of life really are.

For pre-operational and concrete operational children, generalizations about basic needs of life such as food, water, shelter, and reproduction seem to be sufficient for a study of the life sciences. Specific characteristics of plants and animals are introduced when appropriate.

Integrating

Language arts, social studies

Science Process Skills

Observing, inferring, classifying, communicating

62

How Can You Make a New Animal for a Funny Zoo?

Materials Needed

- Art paper
- Watercolors
- Paintbrushes
- Crayons
- Water

Procedure

1. Use your paintbrush to get your paper wet.
2. Put three or four watercolors on your paper. Let them run together.
3. After your paper is dry, look at it carefully. Try to imagine there are strange animals on your paper. How many can you find? What else do you see?
4. Use your crayons to outline (draw around) the animals and other things. Have you ever seen anything like them before?
5. When you have finished, try to think of names for your animals.
6. Find a place in your classroom to hang your funny-zoo pictures.

For Problem Solvers

Go outdoors on a partly cloudy day and look for animal shapes in the clouds. Do this with other children and see how many "animals" you can find together in the sky.

Teacher Information

This activity can be adapted in many ways. Large pieces of butcher paper may be substituted, with several children working together. Thin poster paint could take the place of watercolors.

In addition to being a form of creative art, this activity should help children to review body parts and animal anatomy informally.

Although many children will be able to find only "real" animals such as birds, fish, and so forth, in their pictures, they should be encouraged to imagine, explore, and create as much as possible.

Animals

Before introducing this activity, you might take the children outdoors on a partly cloudy day and have them look for animal shapes in the clouds. Read or show some children's stories that use imaginary animals, such as the Dr. Seuss stories.

Integrating

Math, language arts, art

Science Process Skills

Observing, classifying, communicating, comparing and contrasting

Hands-On Life Science Activities

How Can You Make a Bony Animal?

Materials Needed

- Large box of dried, clean bird bones from turkeys, chickens, or other larger birds
- Plastic foam squares 25 cm × 25 cm (10 in. × 10 in.) for bases
- Light, soft wire (tie wire)
- Strong glue
- Cardboard box
- Masking tape
- Newspapers
- Pictures of dinosaurs and other animal skeletons (including birds)
- Plastic foam balls of various sizes
- Colored plastic clay
- Pipe cleaners
- Wood dowels (miscellaneous lengths)
- Crayons

Procedure

1. Choose several friends and look at the pictures. Could you create and build your own bony animal?

2. Draw a picture of your imaginary animal. Remember, it should have the same basic parts (feet, legs, other parts) as other bony animals do. Label the parts.

3. From your teacher's collection of bones, choose the ones you think you can use to build your animal. If you can't find the right bone, perhaps a piece of clay, a pipe cleaner, or a dowel will do.

4. Lay the bones and other parts on a newspaper as if your animal were lying on its side. Remember, you may need two or more of some bones for arms or legs.

5. After laying your animal out on its side, begin to put it together from the bottom up. Use a plastic foam square as a base. Build the feet first, then the legs. Use glue and wire to hold the bones

together. You may need to wrap the joints in masking tape until they dry.

6. If your animal has only two feet, you may need to use something to hold it up as you add the backbone and upper body parts.

7. If you have trouble finding bones for the head, consider using plastic foam balls or clay.

8. When your animal is finished, you may need to use dowels or coat hanger wire to help it stand. Be sure to wire or glue its feet to the plastic foam base.

9. Think of a name for your animal.

10. Write information about your animal on a piece of paper. Tell how big it was, what it ate, where it lived, and how it moved about. Be sure to include a picture showing how the animal looked when it was alive.

11. Invite other people to look at your class museum.

For Problem Solvers

Make a list of all of the skeletal parts you can think of, such as head, neck, spinal column, arms, hands, fingers, wings, and so on. In a second column, mark the ones that are human parts. Then, in additional columns, mark those that are true parts for dogs, cats, birds, fish, and so on. Which parts are shared by most of the animals you know? Are there any parts that only one type of animal has?

Teacher Information

The purpose of this project is to increase children's understanding of the bony skeletons of animals, to encourage creativity, and to give practice in constructing three-dimensional figures from two-dimensional pictures or plans. Encourage children not to reconstruct turkeys or chickens. Instead, ask them to use the bones to build what they think would be an "ideal" animal.

Before children begin the procedural steps, use a picture to review the names and basic functions of a typical skeleton in general terms, that is, feet, legs, hips, backbone, ribs, neck, and head.

This activity could be done any time, but after Thanksgiving would be a good time for availability of bones. Bird bones are recommended because of their light weight and because they can be easily cleaned and dried. Before Thanksgiving send a note to parents asking them to contribute bones. Before they are sent to school, the bones should be stripped of flesh and then dried thoroughly in a hot oven. Check the bones the children bring to be sure they have been prepared properly; otherwise, odors

may develop. If children want to add wings, tails, eyes, or other non-bony parts, suggest colored paper.

If you teach young children, you may want to simplify the construction by using small bones, pipe cleaners, and plastic foam balls.

Integrating

Math, physical education, art

Science Process Skills

Observing, inferring, classifying, measuring, communicating, comparing and contrasting

What Can Footprints Tell Us?

Materials Needed

- Dark-colored finger paint
- Newsprint

Procedure

1. Clench one hand into a fist. Use the fingers of your other hand to lightly coat the bottom side of your fist (opposite the thumb) and the outside of your little finger with paint.
2. Press the painted side of your fist on the paper.
3. Open your fist and put a light coat of paint on the tips of each finger (not the thumb) of the same hand.
4. Gently press the painted fingers about 1 cm (1/2 in.) above the widest part of the impression you made with your fist.
5. What does the print look like?

Figure 2.10-1. Sample Fist Print

Teacher Information

The impression should resemble a baby's footprint.

Newborn babies are sometimes footprinted for positive identification. Most students may have heard of using fingerprints for identification, as each person has a unique set. Footprints serve almost as well and are used with babies because their fingers are so tiny. Point out to the children that although all human footprints have the same basic shape, each one has unique swirls.

Integrating

Art

Science Process Skills

Observing, classifying

68

Hands-On Life Science Activities

What More Can Footprints Tell Us?

Materials Needed

- Sample bird tracks (Figure 2.11-1)
- Photograph of Neil Armstrong's footprint on the moon (see Figure 2.11-2 on page 71)
- Crayons
- 9 by 12-inch sheet of newsprint for each student

Procedure

1. Look at the picture your teacher gave you. Many would say it is the most famous animal track ever made. Can you guess what it is?

2. Look at the footprint you made with your hand in Activity 2.10. Watch your feet as you take several steps. On a piece of paper, draw a picture of what your bare footprints would look like if you walked four steps in sand or mud.

3. The tracks of animals can tell us many things. Study the chart below that shows the tracks of three birds standing and walking in the sand. Carefully examine their tracks and see how much you can tell about the birds as they near the edge of a freshwater pond.

Figure 2.11-1. Bird Tracks

Read from Bottom Up

At the Lake	↯	?	?
Moving Toward Lake	(tracks)	↯ ↯ / ↯ ↯ / ↯ ↯	(tracks)
Standing	↯ ↯	↯ ↯	♥ ♥
Bird No.	1	2	3

Animals

For Problem Solvers

Make some true-size drawings of the tracks of a particular animal. Trade drawings with someone else who is doing this activity and analyze each other's tracks. What is the animal? How big is it? What was it doing when it made these tracks?

Teacher Information

As students begin this activity, you will need to give them an unlabeled copy of Figure 2.11–2. For discussions that are generated from this photo, you might want additional information about the famous Apollo 11 moon landing. You could also obtain a copy of the lunar-landing article in the December 1969 issue of *National Geographic*. Your library or media center will likely have other pictures of the astronauts' footprints on the moon. The Internet is another good source. In snow or sand, "moon boots" will make similar imprints.

Before the students do step 2 under "Procedure," you may want to have a student walk and point out the heel-toe rolling motion of our feet inward as we walk. Our feet usually turn outward. If we walk with our feet turned inward, it is called "pigeon-toed." If pigeons are common in your area, have students observe them and describe how they walk.

By carefully reading the tracks in Figure 2.11–1, your students may reach some of the following conclusions:

1. Bird 1 is larger than birds 2 or 3 (biggest feet).
2. Bird 3 swims in water (webbed feet).
3. Birds 1 and 3 walk. Bird 2 hops.
4. Bird 1 has longer legs than bird 3 (longer strides).
5. At the edge of the pond, bird 1 is standing on one leg, so is possibly a crane, heron, or other large shorebird. Bird 3 is swimming away in search of food; it is probably a duck or goose. Bird 2 is probably a perching, hopping, land bird who stopped for a drink and is now perched in a nearby tree.

Activities using animal tracks or signs can help children develop skills of observation and inference.

Integrating

Art

Science Process Skills

Observing, inferring, classifying, communicating, comparing and contrasting, using space-time relationships, identifying and controlling variables, researching

Figure 2.11–2.

What Clues Can Help Us Read Tracks?

Materials Needed

- Drawings of common animal tracks of dog, cat, squirrel, deer (numbered but unnamed)
- Paper
- Crayons

Procedure

1. Study the animal tracks in the picture. You have probably seen one or two of these tracks before in dust, dirt, sand, or snow.

1   2   3   4

2. Compare the tracks. How many toes can you count on each? Which have claws? Can you tell how many have foot pads? What is different about track 4?

3. The tracks belong to the following animals: squirrel, dog, cat, and deer (not necessarily in that order). Think of each animal. On your paper write those four animal names and write the number of the track above the name of each animal.

4. Compare your answers with others in the class.

5. Animals that belong to the same family make similar tracks. If you changed the size and the shape slightly, you could rename the tracks: mountain lion, wolf, elk, chipmunk. Match these four animals with the animals and tracks that you already have on your paper.

6. Compare your animal pairs with those of others in your group. Ask your teacher for the correct information.

Hands-On Life Science Activities

For Problem Solvers

Using the encyclopedia and other books that you have available, along with your own experience, add at least one animal to each of the four groups that match the animal tracks used in this activity.

Select another type of animal, draw its tracks, and make a list of the animals you think might make that shape of track. Share your work with others in your group, check each other's work, and learn from each other.

Why was it important for the early settlers to recognize the tracks of wild animals? Discuss this question with your group.

Teacher Information

The drawings in the figure are tracks of a dog (1), cat (2), squirrel (3), and deer (4).

Other members of the same family whose tracks are similar are:

Dog	Cat	Squirrel	Deer
Wolf	Mountain Lion	Chipmunk	Elk
Coyote	Bobcat	Groundhog	Moose

The purpose of this activity is to help children understand that, although animal tracks are different, members of the same families make similar-shaped tracks. Thus the track of a dog accompanying a hunter may make a track similar to that of a wolf or a coyote. There may be several varieties of squirrels and chipmunks in the park whose tracks look alike. Tracks give only one clue to the identification and behavior of animals.

For cats, many students will probably choose a track with claws because of the association of cats with being scratched. Members of the cat family, with one exception, have retractable claws that are usually drawn into a sheath when they walk and extended when they climb, attack, or defend. The cheetah, the fastest runner on earth for short distances, is the only cat that does not have retractable claws.

Integrating

Math, reading, language arts, social studies, art

Science Process Skills

Observing, inferring, classifying, communicating, comparing and contrasting, researching

What Animals Live Around You?

Materials Needed

- Paper
- Pencils

Procedure

1. Animals live almost everywhere on the earth. There is a place near your home or school where many animals live. You may not have noticed them because they are small or shy, or they live under some kind of cover. Think of your school grounds, backyard, empty lot, park, or even an alley near you. It should be a place that has dirt, rocks, green plants, shade, and some source of moisture. A pond, pool, standing water, or regularly sprinkled area is best. On your paper write the name of the place you have chosen.

2. Describe the area you have chosen as you remember it. Write all the details you remember. Draw a picture if you can.

3. Describe your special place to the other class members and your teacher.

4. Make a plan to visit your area and study it. Work alone or choose a friend to join you.

Teacher Information

This is the first of a series on the study of a nature square. The initial study should be conducted during mild weather in the spring or early fall if your climate has distinct seasons. In the following activities, the children will be asked to visit the square regularly, observe the environment, collect samples, and observe changes.

Since the kind of nature squares that are available will be determined by your location (climate; geography; urban, suburban, or rural area), you will need to approve and perhaps suggest locations if the children have difficulty choosing a place.

The major purpose of the nature square activity is to help children become aware of the many forms of animal life that exist around us. Skills of observation, organization, and classification will be emphasized.

If you have a large, landscaped school ground that is several years old, or a large vacant lot adjacent to the school, the entire class could set up nature squares in the same area under your supervision. Although you will have less supervision, there are advantages to having other squares scattered over a wider variety of areas. A compromise might be to choose an area close to the school, where you can help the children learn observation and collection skills that they can apply to the place they have chosen.

Nature square activities are easily adapted for teaching younger children. Choose one or two areas near your school and adapt the following activities and suggestions for use with the total group.

Integrating
Language arts, art

Science Process Skills
Observing, inferring, classifying, measuring, predicting, communicating

What Do You Need in Order to Study a Nature Square?

Materials Needed

- Meter stick or string 10 meters (10 yards) long
- Wooden stakes or markers to show borders
- "Observation Chart for Nature Squares" (at the end of this activity)
- 9 by 12-inch heavy white paper (for mapping)
- Crayons

Procedure

1. Study the list of materials on the Observation Chart. This is the beginning of a list of things you will be looking for when you visit the special place you have chosen, which will be called a "nature square." Notice there are extra spaces at the bottom for you to add unusual or different things you find.

2. When you first visit your square, use the string or meter stick to make approximate measurements of its size. Remember, your square does not have to be a real square shape. It could be long, round, or kidney-shaped. Put wooden stakes or markers around the border.

3. On your first visit to the square, make a picture-map of the distinctive features (things that stand out) such as rocks, trees, bushes, or water areas.

4. Report your initial (first) findings to the class.

Teacher Information

In the following activities, students will be expected to make periodic visits to the places they have selected. Try to help them select areas that will be inviting to as many forms of wildlife as possible.

Areas should be large enough to include many of the features mentioned in step 1 of the preceding activity, but not so large as to be unmanageable. Shape is important only if it can be altered to include special features such as a tree, pond, or shaded area.

If digital cameras are available, actual photographs could be included but should not replace the picture-map suggested in this activity.

Activity 2.15 gives specific instructions for using the Observation Chart.

Integrating

Math, language arts, art

Science Process Skills

Observing, inferring, classifying, measuring, communicating

Observation Chart
for Nature Squares

Date of visit:	General conditions: climate, wind, temperature, precipitation, and so on	Vegetation: trees, shrubs, weeds, flowers, grass, and so on	Small underground animals: ants, worms, beetles, bugs, and so on	Small animals on the ground and under rocks, leaves, or other ground cover: spiders, ants, and so on	Small animals on or in vegetation: aphids, caterpillars, larvae, eggs, bugs, beetles, and so on	Small flying insects: bees, beetles, gnats, butterflies, mosquitoes, grasshoppers, dragonflies, and so on	Larger underground animals: gophers, chipmunks, moles, and so on	Larger animals flying, nesting, perching, walking (tracks), or crawling	Animals in standing water, pond, or lake: tadpoles, frogs, fish, snakes, salamanders, insects, and so on	Other observations:

Observations, Discoveries, and Conditions

How Can a Chart Help Us Make Observations?

Materials Needed

- "Observation Chart for Nature Squares" (see Activity 2.14)
- Pencils

Procedure

1. This chart is designed to help you study your nature square.
2. The column on the far left suggests specific things you should watch for and record each time you visit your square.
3. The other smaller columns with boxes are places for you to record words to report each observation.
4. The bottom space is blank all the way across. Use it to record and report things you find that are special about your square.
5. With your teacher and other students, discuss the areas listed in the far left column. Leave out anything that does not apply to your own square.
6. Make visits to your square every other day. Write the date at the top of the column and use the chart as you study your square.

Teacher Information

The Observation Chart is general in nature and may need to be adapted to your particular location.

Discuss each category on the left and be certain students understand the examples. Add and delete items as necessary.

It may be helpful to go through an imaginary visit, step-by-step, to show them how to use the chart.

Activity 2.16 suggests guidelines for equipment to take along on visits to the square.

Integrating

Language arts

Science Process Skills

Observing, inferring, classifying, measuring, communicating, using space-time relationships, researching

What Equipment Can Help Us Study Our Nature Squares?

Materials Needed

- Shoe boxes
- Hand lenses
- Metal spoons
- Dull table knives
- Scissors or garden shears
- Tweezers (or forceps)
- Mosquito netting
- Small-to-large jars with lids or assorted rigid plastic containers with lids
- Small cans with hinged lids
- Small-to-large plastic bags
- Butterfly nets
- Notebook and pencils
- Tape, string, and rubber bands

Procedure

1. Look at the list of materials. You can probably gather most of the equipment around your home and school.
2. Put a mark by the items you think you can find.
3. Discuss the list with your teacher and class. Perhaps you can trade with others to get the things you don't have.
4. After the class discussion, make a list of things you still need and ask your teacher for help in locating them.
5. Gather the materials. Put the smaller items in a shoe box and the larger items in a plastic bag (pack glass in paper).
6. Scientists called naturalists study nature as you are going to do. The simple equipment you have is very similar to the equipment they use.
7. After you have gathered your equipment, you will be ready to begin investigating your nature square, just as a naturalist would do.

For Problem Solvers

Visit with a biologist, forest ranger, or other naturalist. Ask this person to tell you about the equipment he or she uses in studying life forms in an area in nature. Compare their equipment with your list and see how many of their items you can match with items in the list that will accomplish a similar purpose.

Share your information with your group.

Teacher Information

A simple plan for making butterfly nets is shown in Figure 2.16–1. Construction can be done by children individually, or they can work in groups of three or four.

Before you begin studying and collecting specimens, discuss the following simple safety rules:

1. Don't put anything you find in your mouth.
2. Be very careful with insects that sting, such as bees, hornets, and wasps (never disturb their nests).
3. Use a spoon or envelope to scoop crawling insects into containers.
4. If any animals are removed from the nature square, they should have comfortable housing and later be returned alive.
5. Always wash your hands as soon as possible after visiting the nature square.
6. Attend to accidental cuts, scratches, or bites as soon as they occur.

Figure 2.16–1. Constructing a Butterfly Net

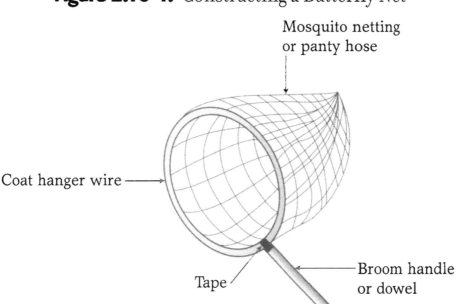

Mosquito netting or panty hose

Coat hanger wire

Tape

Broom handle or dowel

If you are using public lands, check out the regulations governing the collection of specimens, both plant and animal (even rocks), before removing them from the property.

If there are poisonous plants or animals common to your region of the country, such as poison ivy, poison oak, ticks, or chiggers, be sure the children can identify and avoid these specimens.

High-quality hand lenses are not necessary for field study. Lenses molded from plastic are sold in the school equipment or stationery departments of most general merchandise (variety) stores. You will, however, need several high-quality hand lenses for classroom use.

Items not included in the kit are insect-killing jars and materials to preserve and mount specimens. The focus of this section is on the observation and study of nature as it exists. If specimens are brought to school, every effort should be made to put them in a suitable container, and when appropriate try to include a portion of their immediate surroundings—twigs, leaves, soil. A small, moist sponge or piece of apple, pear, or peach, and plenty of fresh air should be provided for insects. Jars with small holes punched in the top do not provide enough air circulation. Use a piece of mosquito netting held with a rubber band over the top of the container. After study, all live specimens should be released where they were collected. Caution students not to bring injured or baby birds to the classroom.

This could be an excellent opportunity to involve parents and other groups. They can help in collecting and organizing equipment.

Integrating

Language arts, social studies

Science Process Skills

Observing, inferring, classifying, measuring, communicating, using space-time relationships, researching

How Can We Report Our Findings?

(Class discussion with older students)

Materials Needed

- Paper
- Pencils
- Calendars (optional)

Procedure

1. Visit your nature square about every other day for a period of two or three weeks. Use a calendar to write the specific dates you plan to go. When you sign your name to this paper and give it to your teacher, it will mean that you agree to visit your square on the days listed, spend at least thirty minutes, make observations, collect specimens when possible, and keep a record on your Observation Chart. When your paper is accepted, it will mean that your teacher agrees to assist you in your study and in the evaluation of what you have done. This then becomes a contract.

2. Plan with your teacher and other members of the class as to how your study will be shared. Scientists hold conferences to share their ideas with each other. They often give oral reports from notes. Sometimes they meet in small, informal groups to share and compare their important discoveries. Some get together to write books or magazine and newspaper articles. They usually find some way to communicate their important findings to others. As a group of naturalists, how will you report your findings so others will know what you have observed and discovered?

For Problem Solvers

Compare the types of plants and animals found in all areas used by the class for nature squares. In cases for which there are differences in the types of plants and animals, discuss possible reasons. Analyze the nature squares in terms of location, moisture, amount of sunlight, nearness to traffic or homes, and other characteristics that might explain the differences in life forms found there.

Teacher Information

Omit step 1 if you have made the study during class time on the school grounds or a nearby vacant lot. Contracting is a technique some teachers have found helpful in encouraging responsibility and independent work. Parents are sometimes asked to sign a contract, too.

The length of time students spend studying their squares will vary according to the situation, but stating a specific minimum time is usually helpful.

Students may need help in developing skills of observation. Remind them to move slowly and quietly and sit for lengths of time. Shy animals will reveal themselves only if they think they are alone. Encourage children to use their senses (except taste). Listening is often as important as looking.

A study of a nature square will provide many opportunities for the use of books and other media as they are available. Handbooks and field guides for identification of insects, spiders, birds, snakes, flowers, and plants will be especially helpful.

If they are available, videos and CDs can be of great help in supplementing this area of study.

As you identify insects and spiders of different kinds, classify them into harmful, coexisting, and helpful categories as they relate to humans. Although many people dislike them, spiders are usually harmless and are very valuable in the control of harmful insects.

Figures 2.17–1 through 2.17–3 show an insect, a spider, and a mouse. These should be helpful for quick classification so children can pursue further identification in field books.

Integrating

Math, reading, language arts, social studies, art

Science Process Skills

Observing, inferring, classifying, communicating, researching

Figure 2.17-1. Dragonfly

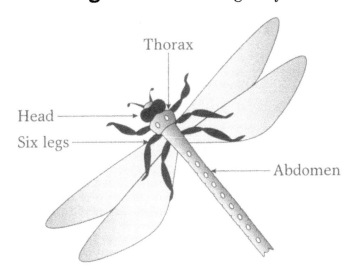

Figure 2.17-2. Spider

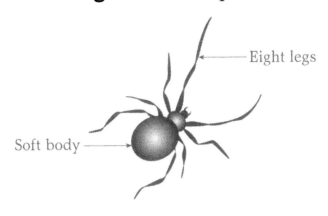

Figure 2.17-3. Mouse

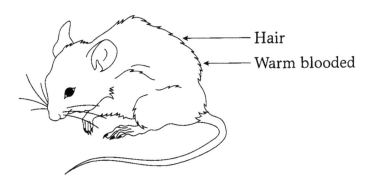

How Can We Attract Wild Birds?

(Take home and do with family and friends.)

Materials Needed

- Wooden board 40 cm long by 15 cm wide by 2.5 cm thick (16 inches by 6 inches by 1 inch)
- Two wood slats 40 cm (16 inches) long
- Five wood slats 15 cm (6 inches) long
- Small nails
- Hammer
- Bird seed, bread crumbs, breakfast food, grains, or other items birds eat

Procedure

1. The following instructions will help you make a feeder to attract different kinds of birds. Use the two long slats and two of the shorter slats to enclose the long wide board with a rim.

2. Arrange the remaining three slats inside the enclosed space about 10 cm (4 in.) apart so they form partitions to divide the large board into four sections. Use two nails on each end to hold the slats in place. If you live in a rainy climate, you may want to construct a roof of heavy plastic and coat-hanger wire. When you finish, your project should look something like Figure 2.18–1.

3. Find an isolated place near a window of your school building or home. Try to find a place near trees and shade. The feeder must be near a tree or large shrub and some safe place (ledge or rooftop) so birds will have some place to go for shelter if they are startled.

4. Locate your feeder off the ground (hanging from a tree limb, pole, or wooden base), low enough so it can be refilled. Be sure to put it in a place where you can observe it from a window.

5. Wait a day or two for your scent to leave the feeder. A shallow bowl with water might be included. Because you will leave a human scent, try not to handle the food more than necessary.

Figure 2.18-1. Bird Feeder

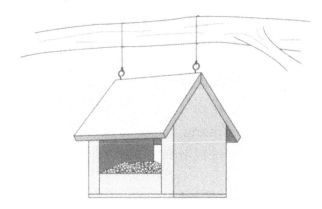

6. Observe your feeder as much as possible for two weeks. When you see a bird, make a quick sketch of it, noting color and size. The next activities will help you identify some of the birds your feeder attracts.

7. How many birds were attracted to your bird feeder?

For Problem Solvers

Design and conduct an experiment to find out what types of feeders, types of food, and locations of feeders are more attractive to different kinds of birds. Work together with others who are interested in doing this activity. After deciding how to carry out this investigation, make predictions of what you will learn before you actually place the feeders for birds to use.

Teacher Information

Birds are everywhere. Even large cities and arid desert regions have many species. Bird watching is inexpensive, entertaining, and rewarding.

Note: Do not use glue on bird feeders or birdhouses. Some birds might avoid the odor.

Integrating

Math, language arts, social studies, art

Science Process Skills

Observing, inferring, classifying, measuring, predicting, communicating, comparing and contrasting, using space-time relationships, formulating hypotheses, identifying and controlling variables, experimenting, researching

What Is a Bird?

Materials Needed

- One drawing of a typical bird per student
- Pictures of many varieties of birds
- Caged live pet bird

Procedure

1. Figure 2.19–1 shows a typical bird.

2. All birds have these same basic parts, but some appear to be different in ways that help the bird to survive in its particular environment. Refer to the typical bird parts as you read steps 3 through 6.

3. Notice the short, pointed beak. This could tell us the bird eats certain things for which a short beak is helpful. If the beak is slightly longer, it might belong to a woodpecker. Fishing and shore birds usually have very long beaks. Ducks have wide, flat beaks for sifting water on and below the surface in search of vegetation. Birds of prey often have very sharp, curved (hooked) beaks. A beak is often called a bill. The pelican is famous for its long bill and pouch.

4. The feet and legs of birds often tell much about them. Short legs and feet with short claws usually belong to a land-perching bird (such as the one in the picture). Fatter feet with longer toes often suggest a ground-nesting bird. Most swimming water birds have webbed feet, while birds of prey have powerful curved feet with long, sharp claws. Shore and marsh birds usually have longer, thin feet and very long legs. Many birds have a characteristic of standing or resting on one leg.

5. The environment and feeding habits of birds are affected by their wings. Our typical bird has a wingspan (open wings) of more than twice the length of its body. Some soaring birds have very wide wingspans, while birds of prey have flatter, wider wings that permit them to both soar and hover.

6. Although our typical bird is not shown in color, colors are very important for bird study. Males usually have brighter colors than females. Female birds are colored less brightly, which makes it easier for them to remain hidden when they are nesting. Different species of birds have distinct markings. Ornithologists (scientists

Hands-On Life Science Activities

who study birds) use colors and markings as a major means of identifying birds.

7. Choose a bird picture from your teacher's collection. Put it on your desk beside the drawing of the typical bird. Can you find the same parts? From what you have learned about birds, tell all you can about the bird you have chosen, by the characteristics you see.

8. Study the live bird in the cage. In what ways is it different from the ones in the pictures? Tell all you can about the live bird.

9. You are now ready to begin your observation of wild birds.

Figure 2.19-1. Typical Bird

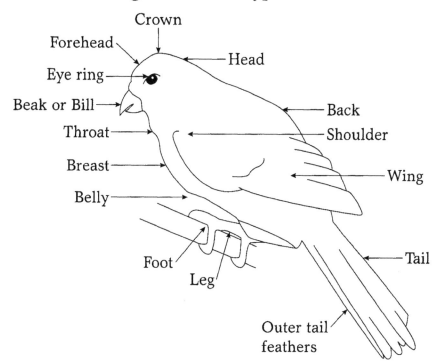

Teacher Information

A high-quality field book for bird identification is essential. Binoculars are helpful, especially if your bird feeder is located some distance from the classroom. A notebook and sketch pad should be available at all times.

These activities are designed to introduce children to bird study. Your library or media center can provide many other materials and suggestions. Depending on where you live (most of your students will likely move several times in their lifetimes), bird watching can become an exciting and interesting lifelong hobby. If your school is not a member, we strongly suggest that you join the National Audubon Society, Membership Data Center, P.O. Box 51005, Boulder, CO 80323-1005. There may be a local chapter in your community.

Integrating

Reading, language arts, art

Science Process Skills

Observing, inferring, classifying, measuring, communicating, comparing and contrasting, formulating hypotheses, identifying and controlling variables, researching

Hands-On Life Science Activities

How Can You Make a Birdhouse?

(Construction project under teacher supervision)

Materials Needed

- Assorted pieces of wood
- Saw
- Hammer
- Plastic and paper milk cartons
- Assorted nails
- Dowels
- Paper

Procedure

1. Figures 2.20–1 and 2.20–2 show pictures of simple birdhouses.
2. If you would like to construct one, make a drawing (plan) and show it to your teacher.
3. Your teacher will help you gather the materials and build a birdhouse, or take your approved plan home and have someone help you.
4. Share your birdhouse with the class.

Figure 2.20–1. Two Birdhouse Designs

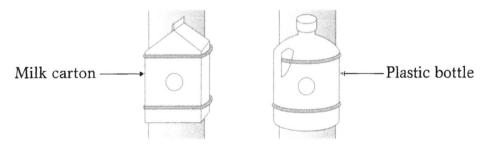

Milk carton ⟶   ⟵ Plastic bottle

Animals

Figure 2.20–2. Birdhouse Design with Cat Guard

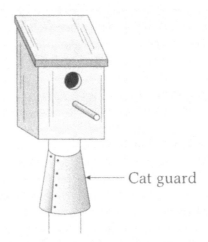

Cat guard

For Problem Solvers

Do some serious observation and research and find out what kinds of birds are in your area and what types of birdhouses they seem to prefer. With others who are interested in this activity, build several types of bird-houses. Predict what kinds of birds will be attracted to each, then test your predictions by frequent observation. Also find out which locations birds prefer by placing the same type of birdhouse in two or more locations. In each case, before you actually set out a birdhouse for occupancy, write your predictions of the kinds of birds that will be attracted to each type of birdhouse and which location that bird will prefer. Keep accurate records of your observations. Can you outguess the birds?

Share your observations with one another as you complete the activity.

Teacher Information

If there is enough interest, this could become a project for everyone in the classroom. If so, you will need parents or aides to assist.

Don't feel limited to the birdhouses in the pictures. Urge students to be creative in their designs. Remember that birdhouses need to be durable and weatherproof. Also, different styles of birdhouses will attract different birds. The size of the hole, for instance, will help determine the type of bird attracted to the birdhouse. Consult a bird book for specifics. Birds may not move into the houses for some time due to season, scent, location, or other factors.

Commercial bird feeders and birdhouses are available, but should be purchased only if students are unable to construct them. Kits from which birdhouses can be constructed are often available.

If birds are plentiful in your area, birdhouses make wonderful gifts.

Hands-On Life Science Activities

Integrating
Language arts, math, art

Science Process Skills
Observing, inferring, classifying, measuring, predicting, communicating, comparing and contrasting, using space-time relationships, formulating hypotheses, identifying and controlling variables, experimenting, researching

What Do We Need in Order to Keep Pets in an Aquarium?

(Total-group project)

Materials Needed

- 10-gallon (or larger) aquarium, glass cover, and stand
- Heater
- Thermometer
- Air pump
- Clean gravel
- Sand
- Water plants
- Water
- Snails
- Fish
- Fish food
- Rocks of various sizes and shapes
- Small fish net

Procedure

1. An aquarium is a place in your classroom for aquatic animals. With your teacher's help, you can make the aquarium into a comfortable home for these animals. Place the aquarium in a sunny, protected place in the room.

2. Decide on the variety of fish you will want to have in your aquarium. Freshwater fish (goldfish varieties) can usually live comfortably without a special heater in most classrooms. Tropical and exotic fish need a carefully controlled environment, so you will need a heater and thermometer. If you choose saltwater fish and don't live near an ocean, your pet store may have salt you can add to fresh water, but it is more difficult to maintain.

3. Put about 2.5 cm (1 in.) of clean gravel in the bottom of the aquarium. Add assorted rocks near the back.

4. Spread about 2.5 cm (1 in.) of clean sand over the gravel slope.

Figure 2.21-1. Aquarium with Heater and Air Pump

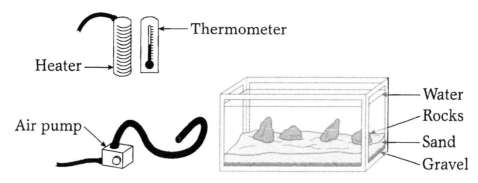

5. Slowly add water (so as not to stir the sand) up to about 5 cm (2 in.) of the top. For freshwater fish, pond water or well water is best. If you use city water, let it stand in open containers for at least 24 hours before adding it to the aquarium (to allow chemicals to disperse into the air).

6. Add green water plants (a variety of six or more). These can be purchased at a pet store and will depend on the kind of fish you choose to keep.

7. If you have chosen to make a freshwater aquarium, all you need to do is add several fish and freshwater snails to keep the tank clean. Put the lid on top. If you have chosen tropical fish, you will need to continue with the following steps.

8. Install the heater and thermometer and wait for the water to stabilize at the desired temperature. (*Note:* Some heaters come with thermostats, but a thermometer is still helpful as a safety check.)

9. Secure the hose from the air pump to a rock on the bottom of the aquarium. Turn it on.

10. Put the tropical fish in your aquarium. Instead of snails, you may need to purchase special fish with suction mouths to keep the tank clean. The pet store can provide special instructions for testing the water and feeding fish.

11. You now have a type of "aquatic nature square" in your classroom.

Teacher Information

If you have never constructed an aquarium before, talk to a pet store owner or someone else about the special needs of tropical fish. You may need additional equipment to maintain it properly.

Aquariums with tropical fish are very attractive and interesting, but freshwater or saltwater aquariums (if you are near the ocean) are more representative of water life as it exists. There are several additional advantages

to a freshwater aquarium. If it is 10 gallons or larger, it will be nearly balanced and will not require an air pump. "Balanced" means that the plants produce about the same amount of oxygen as the animals use. The animals in turn release enough carbon dioxide for the plants. If you match your fish, snails, and plants properly (this usually takes time), the fish will get food from the plants. The plants will use the waste products of the fish for food to produce new growth, and the snails will keep the whole area clean and tidy.

Occasionally, you should remove the glass lid to permit air to get in (or leave a ventilating space), and you may want to add a little fish food to give your pets a treat. An aquarium that is nearly in balance will need a change of water about twice a year (add pond water occasionally to replace evaporated water). When the water is changed, you will need to start at the beginning with fresh, clean gravel, sand, and rocks. Again, use fresh pond water if you can—if you use tap water, be sure to let it stand for at least 24 hours. The same plant and animal life can be retained.

Periodically have the students assist you in checking the "health" of your aquarium. Usually conditions will let you know when you need more plants, animals, or snails.

Don't be concerned if a green slimy film develops on the top of the water. This is a sign of a healthy aquarium. Probably plants and animals too small to see with the naked eye are also living in the tank.

Freshwater aquariums can also provide a home for tadpoles. When they begin to grow legs, simply transfer them to a combined environment of pond water and land and watch them develop into frogs. Use shallow water and tilt the tank so part of the tank floor is not covered with water. This will assure that the tadpoles can get air when their lungs begin to develop, in case they are not transferred quite soon enough.

Integrating
Math, language arts, social studies

Science Process Skills
Observing, inferring, classifying, measuring, predicting, communicating, using space-time relationships, identifying and controlling variables, researching

Hands-On Life Science Activities

How Can We Keep Small Animals in Our Classroom?

(Total-group project)

Materials Needed

- Aquarium or terrarium (at least 20 gallons)
- Clean gravel
- Clean sand
- Potting soil
- Plants
- Assorted rocks, small pieces of wood
- Small, shallow plastic pan
- Heavy wire screen
- Small reptiles or other small animals

Procedure

1. You can keep small animals in your classroom if they have a comfortable place to live. Find a warm, sunny, protected place in your room as a permanent location for your terrarium. Although you may be using the same container, aquarium means water home, and terrarium means land home. Be sure it is clean.

2. With your teacher and other class members, choose the kind of animals (reptiles, amphibians, or mammals) you would like to have. If you have enough containers, you could make homes for each variety.

3. Use library books to learn about the animals you have chosen and plan a comfortable environment for the animals.

4. Put about 2.5 cm (1 inch) of gravel in the bottom of your terrarium. Add about 2.5 cm (1 inch) of sand on top. Arrange the rocks and pieces of wood throughout the container to provide privacy and shade.

5. Locate the plastic pan near one side. If you have chosen desert animals, they will need very little water. If you have chosen turtles or amphibians, you should use a water container somewhat deeper that will cover about one-third of the bottom. Put several flat rocks in the amphibian or turtle container so the animals will have a place to climb out and "sun."

6. Be sure the pan is easy to remove, as you will need to clean it regularly. Depending on the variety of animal you have chosen, you may need to add a small tray for food.

7. From the study of the animal you have chosen, select small plants that naturally occur in its environment. If you are housing animals that like a moist environment, mix about 2.5 cm (1 inch) of potting soil in the sand.

8. Before you put your animals in their new home, be sure you have a heavy wire covering over the top so your animals cannot climb or jump out.

9. Your terrarium cannot be "balanced" as a freshwater aquarium can be; therefore, your animals will need fresh food and water regularly. The plants will need varying amounts of moisture, too.

10. Put your animals in their new home and watch their behavior. Can you design an Observation Chart to help study them?

Teacher Information

Resource people can be of great help in this study. If aquariums are not available, cardboard or wooden boxes with the top and one side covered with heavy plastic can be used for insects, reptiles, and amphibians. Be sure to provide plenty of air holes covered with screen. Mammals, especially rodents, will gnaw through cardboard or wood and must be housed in glass or metal cages. Use a sieve to clean the sand in the bottom of the cage about once a week. Commercially purchased cages are excellent for temporary housing. They are easy to clean and they reduce the amount of care required.

Housing male and female mammals together can become a problem. If the female becomes pregnant, she will need to be separated from the male. Pregnant rodents are not recommended for classroom care and study. During gestation they should not be disturbed for cleaning (especially their nests); and after birth, if frightened or molested, they may eat their young.

Turtles, newts, and frogs make very good amphibian-reptile pets. Horned lizards, common lizards, tortoises, and small snakes will live together in a desert environment.

Usually, it is best to have only one species of mammal. Gerbils, hamsters, and guinea pigs are clean and easy to care for. Wild mice, rats, or mink are not recommended.

Many insects will live together. Spiders (including the gentle tarantula), beetles, and crickets can share the same cage. Praying mantises are very interesting but should be housed alone, as they are voracious eaters and also cannibalistic. Books and resource persons can help in your selection of animals.

Hands-On Life Science Activities

When your terrariums are complete, have the children list the "daily care" tasks and organize groups with specific time, day, and date assignments.

Live specimens and food can be obtained by collecting and from pet stores and science-supply houses.

If animals are kept in the classroom, some are likely to die there. Teachers need to be aware of the sensitivity of this issue with children. Insects have a short life span. Insects and spiders eat other insects and spiders. Tadpoles have a high mortality rate from egg to frog. Handled properly, these can be valuable learning experiences for children as they observe life's natural processes.

Integrating
Math, reading, language arts, social studies

Science Process Skills
Observing, inferring, classifying, measuring, predicting, communicating, using space-time relationships, formulating hypotheses, identifying and controlling variables, researching

Figure 2.22-1. Desert Terrarium

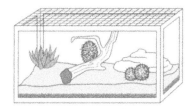

Figure 2.22-2. Woodland Terrarium

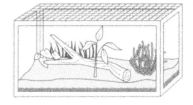

Figure 2.22-3. Pond Terrarium

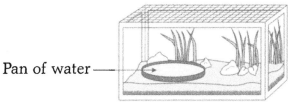

Pan of water

How Do Earthworms Live?

Materials Needed

- One-quart or larger wide-mouthed clear jar
- Tall, narrow metal can with one end closed
- Rich, moist soil and sand
- One sheet of heavy black paper
- Earthworms

Procedure

1. Study your earthworms. Can you tell which end is the head and which is the tail? Does it matter?
2. How do the worms move? What surfaces do they seem to like best? Do they like water? Do they like light? What else can you discover about your worms?
3. Put the metal can, closed end up, in the large jar. Fill the large jar with soil, level with the top of the can. Add a thin layer of sand.
4. Put your earthworms in the jar.
5. Cover the outside of the jar with black paper.
6. Leave the jar covered for at least 24 hours.
7. Uncover the jar and examine it.
8. Can you see evidence that the earthworms have been at work?
9. Study the sand on top of the soil. Earthworms take soil through their bodies, removing nutrients, and deposit a substance called castings.
10. Cover your jar for another 24 hours. Repeat your study of your worms.
11. Write or tell everything you can about earthworms.

For Problem Solvers

Do some research about worms. Are they good for the soil, do they damage it, or neither? Would you want them in your garden? Why? What do they do that is either good or bad for the soil? Discuss your information with your group.

Figure 2.23-1. Earthworm Bottle

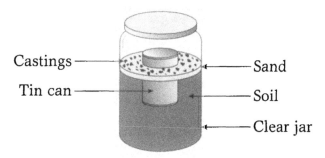

Get together with at least one other person who has a worm and have a worm race. See whose worm can move a certain distance first. What can you do to cause your worm to move? What seems to attract them?

Do large worms move faster than small worms? Make your prediction, then test your prediction.

Teacher Information

Earthworms will not tunnel near the surface of the jar until it is covered with heavy black paper to make it dark. The can is used to make the layer of soil inside the jar thinner and force the earthworms to tunnel near the surface of the glass jar. If you decide to continue the activity for several days, the soil should be kept moist. Take care not to over-water.

Integrating

Math, reading, language arts

Science Process Skills

Observing, inferring, classifying, measuring, predicting, communicating, using space-time relationships, formulating hypotheses, identifying and controlling variables, experimenting, researching

Why Is the Snail So Unusual?

Materials Needed

- Snails (one per student)
- Black construction paper (one per snail)
- Flashlight
- Newsprint
- Hand lenses
- Small pieces of lettuce

Procedure

1. The snail is a most magnificent animal. It is shy, yet curious, calm, quiet, usually helpful, and it doesn't disturb others. It is creative and artistic, slow but hard working, and tidy; it doesn't depend on others for its home or food (some even carry their homes around with them on their backs). Snails glide through life as vagabonds. Sometimes they become too plentiful, but when that happens, nature reduces their numbers.

2. Choose a snail and put it on a piece of black paper. Give it a name so you can talk to it. Study your snail and compare it with Figure 2.24–1. Can you find the same parts?

3. Because snails are shy, you may have to wait a little while for it to come out of its shell and begin moving about.

4. Notice its head with the round-tipped feelers or tentacles sticking out. Land snails have two long tentacles with eyes at the ends, and two short, stubby ones that some scientists believe help them smell. Carefully touch one of the feelers and watch what happens.

5. Examine the underside of your snail. The whole bottom is a large foot. The front of the foot secretes a slippery substance called mucus, on which it can slide. Since the mucus is also sticky, the snail can go straight up or down, even on slick surfaces such as glass, without a problem.

6. When your snail begins to come out of its shell, put a small piece of lettuce about 15 cm (6 in.) away. Be sure the lettuce is on the black paper.

7. Watch your snail to see whether it can see or smell the lettuce. If it begins to move toward it, measure how far it can travel in one minute. Look at its "glide" path on the paper.

Hands-On Life Science Activities

Figure 2.24-1. Snail with Feelers, Head, and Foot Extended

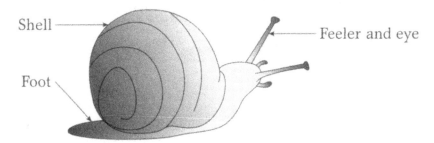

Shell

Foot

Feeler and eye

8. Make a wet spot on the paper. Is the snail attracted to it? Snails must have moisture in order to survive. They prefer a shady, moist environment. On hot, dry days they go into their shells and wait for moisture.

9. Darken the room and shine a flashlight near your snail. Does it move toward the light or move away from it?

10. Share your findings with the class.

For Problem Solvers

Who has the fastest snail? How can you find out? Predict the speed in centimeters (inches) per minute before you begin the race.

Think of other investigations to conduct with your snail. Don't do anything that might harm it. Share your findings with your group.

Teacher Information

Snails are plentiful in many parts of the country. Many of the same activities can be adapted for earthworms or mealworms. The snail completely fills its shell, and as it grows larger it adds additional swirls. Slugs are "naked" snails, with the same characteristics, but they usually need more moisture because moisture evaporates from them more readily.

An average snail, under "full steam," travels about 5 cm (2 inches) in a minute.

Although they are sometimes considered pests, snails eat decaying vegetation and can improve the soil in a garden.

Water snails eat decaying vegetation, which helps in the balance of a pond ecosystem. They will keep your aquarium clean without asking for a thing in return.

Integrating

Math, language arts

Science Process Skills

Observing, inferring, measuring, predicting, communicating, using space-time relationships, formulating hypotheses, identifying and controlling variables, experimenting

What Organisms Live Around Us That Are Too Tiny to See?

Materials Needed

- Common microscopic organisms, such as euglena and paramecium
- Microscopes
- 9 by 12-inch drawing paper
- Pencils

Procedure

1. There are many tiny living things, too small to see with the naked eye, that live around us. You have already used magnifying lenses to examine some small insects and plants. In your study of birds, you might use binoculars. Today we are going to see tiny living things—so tiny that they cannot be seen without microscopes. Figure 2.25–1 shows some of the most common organisms you may see.

2. Across the top of your paper, draw pictures of the organisms in the figure. As you see other organisms in the microscope today, try to make drawings of them. Put your pictures under the drawings of the ones in the figure they most closely resemble. You are now ready to conduct your inquiry.

3. After you have seen and made drawings of the tiny living things you see, share your findings with the class. How are they alike? How are they different? Which did you like best?

Figure 2.25-1. Drawings of Four Microorganisms

| Euglena | Paramecium | Hydra | Planaria |

For Problem Solvers

Do some research on microorganisms. Get some water from a pond and with just a drop of water at a time see whether you can find some tiny living things in it. Find out what a hay infusion is and prepare one. Using a microscope, see how many different kinds of tiny organisms you can find in your hay infusion. Use an encyclopedia or other reference books and identify as many of them as you can.

Can you figure out a way to measure the length of one of your tiny organisms? Consider this question with others who are interested in these tiny creatures, and discuss your plan with your teacher.

Teacher Information

These tiny creatures are no longer classified as animals, as they once were. For our purposes, it is sufficient to use the generic term "microorganisms," although some students might enjoy the research challenge of finding more specific classification terminology.

Microorganisms are usually present in pond water, the surface of your freshwater aquarium, or in a hay infusion, which you can make or purchase from a science-supply house. A video on organisms of a pond may be helpful.

Some of the microorganisms you find might move around so fast that it's difficult to keep them in view in the microscope. Try putting a tiny bit of cotton in the drop of water. This will usually corral the little varmints long enough to get a good look at them.

If you invite a specialist to help you, be sure to explain that you are interested only in a simple, general introduction with many visuals. The purpose of this activity is to develop awareness of these tiny creatures, not to learn all about them. The students will encounter courses in later years in which they will be able to explore in depth.

An in-depth study of microorganisms could be an enrichment activity for highly motivated students.

Integrating

Math, language arts, art

Science Process Skills

Observing, inferring, classifying, measuring, communicating, comparing and contrasting, using space-time relationships, identifying and controlling variables, researching

Is It Alive or Not?

(Teacher-directed activity)

Materials Needed

- Tweezers
- Lenses
- Small plastic bags
- Paper plates
- Trays (or large paper plates)
- Plastic hoops (or loops of string)

Procedure

1. With students in small groups, give each group a lens, a plastic bag, a pair of tweezers, and a hoop. [If you don't have plastic hoops, 3 meters (10 feet) of string, with the ends tied together will make a loop with a diameter slightly less than 1 meter (about 3 feet).]

2. Identify boundaries for the activity and instruct each group to lay out their hoop somewhere in that region.

3. Students should now gather objects (including live objects!) they find within their hoop. This is their territory. Encourage them to get down close and look carefully. They are to pick up their "treasures" carefully with the tweezers and collect them in the plastic bags. They will likely return with some sprigs of grass, plus small twigs, rocks, and perhaps even a soil sample, a worm, or insect.

4. Back in the classroom, give each group a tray on which to spread their treasures for examination, both with and without the lens.

5. Ask students to separate their treasures into two groups:

    a.   Those that are alive.
    b.   Those that are not alive.

6. Instruct students to make lists of their treasures on paper, on the chalkboard, or on chart paper. A simple form like the following can be used for students to write on, either independently or as the words are written on the board or chart. Children who cannot yet write the words could draw pictures.

Living	Nonliving

7. A comprehensive list could be created, making tally marks for the duplicated items.

8. Let students share their ideas about things on the list that were once alive but are not alive any more. It's okay if they don't all agree, but coach them in their reasoning.

9. Graph the results from the comprehensive list. Which things did the class find the most of? The fewest? Write the number of items in the space with each group.

10. Give each group (or each person) a paper plate and have them section it off for the different kinds of treasures they found as a class. Make this into a pie graph, similar to the following, allowing larger spaces on the plate for things they found the most of. In each space, have them write the word and draw the item represented by the space. It's okay if the spacing is shown differently for each person.

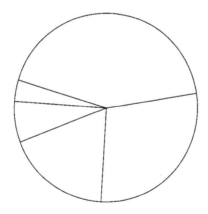

Teacher Information

Of course, if you prefer not to use the hoops, you can let students roam freely within any boundaries you set. When confined to the more limited space, children tend to focus more carefully on the small, hidden creatures and objects that are otherwise missed.

With this activity, you are likely working with children who are too young to distinguish accurately between nonliving and once-living organisms. However, after they sort their treasures into groups of "living" and "nonliving," you could ask them whether they think there are any items in the "nonliving" group that they think were alive at one time. This will help to build experiences and thought processes to expand on later.

Integrating

Math, physical education, language arts, art

Science Process Skills

Observing, inferring, classifying, measuring, communicating, comparing and contrasting, using space-time relationships

Is It Living, Once-Living, or Nonliving?

Materials Needed

- Paper
- Pencils

Procedure

1. Go outdoors or look out the window and make a list of things you see, either on the ground or in the air.

2. Put the following three headings across a new sheet of paper, like this:

Living	Once-Living	Nonliving

3. Look at your list of things and write each one under the heading you think fits best. Do this before you read any further.

4. Now that you have made your lists, think about these examples:

   Green grass is a living thing. It grows.

   Dead grass is no longer alive; it is a once-living thing because it once lived.

   Insects you see crawling along are living things.

   A dead insect is once-living, because it was once alive.

   A brown twig from a tree is once-living because it was once a part of a living tree.

   A rock is nonliving. Rocks neither walk nor grow, nor have baby rocks. A rock was never a living thing.

5. Now look at your three lists again. Do you need to change any of them?

Animals

6. Exchange lists with someone else who did this activity. Look at each other's lists, then discuss your ideas and see what you can learn from each other.

7. Take your paper to your teacher for more information. Perhaps your teacher would like to discuss your work with the class.

For Problem Solvers

Make a graph that shows the number of living, once-living, and nonliving things that are on your list. Design your list in such a way that you can add the numbers from the lists of other boys and girls who did the same activity.

Make a new list of living, once-living, and nonliving things you can find at home. Compare this list with the list you made at school.

Teacher Information

The living/nonliving status of many things in a child's environment is obvious. We need to begin with these things as children develop the concept of living/once-living/nonliving things.

The difference becomes less obvious as we compare things that are nonliving with things that are dead. A rock is not living, but neither is it dead. To describe an object as being dead is to say that it was once alive. Water is a nonliving substance, but a stain of dried blood is once-living because it was once a part of a living thing. An automobile is a complex system that is made mostly of nonliving materials, such as iron, aluminum, and copper. Some parts, however, were living at some earlier time. These might include a wooden dashboard panel (from trees), plastic fenders (from oil—a once-living substance), leather seat covers (from animals).

Integrating

Math, physical education, reading, language arts

Science Process Skills

Observing, inferring, classifying, communicating, comparing and contrasting, using space-time relationships

Can You Solve This Animal Word Search?

Try to find the following animal terms in the grid below. They could appear in horizontal (left to right), vertical (up or down), or diagonal (upward or downward) position.

animal	bird	living
nonliving	fish	feather
environment	bony	tracks
hair	skeleton	observe
mammal	warm-blooded	wild
snail		

```
F  E  A  T  H  E  R  D  W  E  R  T
M  I  Y  U  S  K  E  L  E  T  O  N
I  A  S  O  P  A  N  I  M  A  L  L
K  J  M  H  G  N  V  W  B  O  N  Y
Z  X  C  M  V  O  I  B  N  B  M  L
K  J  H  G  A  N  R  F  D  S  A  W
W  A  R  M  B  L  O  O  D  E  D  U
E  R  L  I  V  I  N  G  R  R  T  Y
U  I  H  O  P  V  M  A  I  V  S  D
S  N  A  I  L  I  E  F  B  E  G  H
J  K  I  Z  X  N  N  X  C  V  B  N
M  Q  R  W  E  G  T  R  A  C  K  S
```

🪑 Can You Create a New Animal Word Search of Your Own?

Write your Animals words in the grid below. Arrange them in the grid so they appear in horizontal (left to right), vertical (up or down), or diagonal (upward or downward) position. Fill in the blank boxes with other letters. Trade your Word Search with someone else who has created one of his or her own, and see whether you can solve the new puzzle.

_____   _____   _____

_____   _____   _____

_____   _____   _____

Answer Key for Animal Word Search

```
F   E   A   T   H   E   R   D   W   E   R   T
M   I   Y   U   S   K   E   L   E   T   O   N
I   A   S   O   P   A   N   I   M   A   L   L
K   J   M   H   G   N   V   W   B   O   N   Y
Z   X   C   M   V   O   I   B   N   B   M   L
K   J   H   G   A   N   R   F   D   S   A   W
W   A   R   M   B   L   O   O   D   E   D   U
E   R   L   I   V   I   N   G   R   R   T   Y
U   I   H   O   P   V   M   A   I   V   S   D
S   N   A   I   L   I   E   F   B   E   G   H
J   K   I   Z   X   N   N   X   C   V   B   N
M   Q   R   W   E   G   T   R   A   C   K   S
```

Growing and Changing: Animal Life Cycles

To the Teacher

This section, "Growing and Changing," should follow or be integrated into the preceding section, "Animals." Depending on where you live, the Animals section may be taught in early fall, but in locations where distinct seasons occur, Growing and Changing is best taught in the spring months.

Several of the activities involve the use of live specimens. If you live in an area where you cannot collect caterpillars or tadpoles, you will need to place orders with pet stores or biological science–supply houses in January or February. If you order early and specify a later shipping date, most supply houses are happy to cooperate, and they are very good at getting your orders to you at the right time. Be aware that some states require USDA permits for interstate shipment of live animals. The supply catalog will advise you if this is necessary. Animals purchased in local pet stores will already have been approved.

Obtaining, organizing, and filing a wide variety of pictures is essential to quality teaching in the elementary school. In addition to the journals that you may find in the school library, old biological science supply catalogs obtained from a local high school or college should be of great help. Many are filled with high-quality photographs. Obsolete science textbooks and library books can often be obtained from your school district free of charge. The text material may be out-of-date, but the pictures usually are not. Some organizations, such as the Audubon Society, sponsor junior organizations for young people.

In some activities in this section, animals that lay eggs with the young hatching and developing outside the female's body are studied. Others utilize animals that retain the fertilized egg inside the mother's body. The terms "hatch" and "born alive" are used in some manner to make this distinction.

Instructions are included for hatching eggs in the classroom. Attempting to show live birth at the elementary level is not recommended. Smaller mammals, such as mice or gerbils, should not be disturbed during the gestation time, even for cage cleaning. After birth, if mothers are frightened, they might eat their young.

Integrated creative learning activities are suggested throughout this section. Try to include as many as possible.

The following activities are designed as discovery activities, which students can usually perform quite independently. You are encouraged to provide students (usually in small groups) with the materials listed and a copy of the activity from the beginning through the "Procedure." The section titled "Teacher Information" is not intended for student use, but rather to assist you with discussion following the hands-on activity, as students share their observations. Discussion of conceptual information prior to completing the hands-on activity can interfere with the discovery process.

Regarding the Early Grades

With verbal instructions and slight modifications, many of these activities can be used with kindergarten, first-grade, and second-grade students. Some of the activities were written specifically with the primary grades in mind. In others, procedural steps that go beyond the level of the child can simply be omitted and yet offer the child experiences that plant conceptual seeds for concepts that will germinate and grow later on.

Teachers of the early grades will probably choose to bypass many of the "For Problem Solvers" sections. That's okay. These sections are provided for those who are especially motivated and want to go beyond the investigation provided by the activity outlined. Use the outlined activities and enjoy worthwhile learning experiences together with your young

students. Also consider, however, that many of the "For Problem Solvers" sections can be used appropriately with young children as group activities or as demonstrations. Giving students the advantage of an exposure to the experience can often lay groundwork for connections that will become more meaningful at a later time.

Correlation with National Standards

The following elements of the National Standards are reflected in the activities of this section.

K-4   Content Standard A: Science as Inquiry
As a result of activities in grades K-4, all students should develop
   1. Abilities necessary to do scientific inquiry
   2. Understanding about scientific inquiry

K-4   Content Standard C: Life Science
As a result of activities in grades K-4, all students should develop understanding of
   1. The characteristics of organisms
   2. Life cycles of organisms
   3. Organisms and environments

5-8   Content Standard A: Science as Inquiry
As a result of activities in grades 5-8, all students should develop
   1. Abilities necessary to do scientific inquiry
   2. Understanding about scientific inquiry

5-8   Content Standard C: Life Science
As a result of activities in grades 5-8, all students should develop understanding of
   1. Structures and function in living systems
   2. Reproduction and heredity

What Is Growing Up?

(Teacher-directed total-group activity)

Materials Needed

- Chart or chalkboard with the following terms listed: newborn infant, baby, toddler, young child, youth, adolescent, teenager, young adult, grown-up, adult, mature adult, senior citizen, and old person
- Lined paper
- Pencils

Procedure

1. On the chart or chalkboard are some words we often use to describe humans of different ages. Discuss each word with your teacher and the class. Do some words refer to the same age group? If so, choose one word for each group.
2. Write the words down the left side of your page.
3. Put numerals by the words to show how old you think people must be to be classified with a certain group.
4. Next to the words write the name of someone you know in each age group. Share your list with others in the class.

Teacher Information

During the group discussions you will need to add and change terms until students are able to associate someone they know with each age group. If you have not done this before, be prepared for some surprises. Young children's concept of age is similar to their concept of time; it develops as they mature. Because they are "today" oriented, infancy seems long ago, and "When I grow up" can mean almost anything. As they grow older, students develop a greater awareness of their progress into the next age group and some feelings for the expectations of adult life.

You may discover that young children will recognize only four or five categories: babies, children, adolescents, adults, and old people. They may decide adults and old people are the same. The concept of growth and change can be developed with four basic categories. Aging is common in natural animal populations. Old age is rare.

Integrating

Math, language arts, social studies

Science Process Skills

Observing, inferring, classifying, communicating, using space-time relationships, formulating hypotheses

Hands-On Life Science Activities

How Much Do People Change?

(Teacher-directed activity)

Materials Needed

- Baby pictures of several class members (preferably large pictures)

Procedure

1. Those who brought pictures of themselves must not tell anyone which picture is theirs. This is a good time to practice keeping secrets!

2. Have all students who brought pictures come to the front of the room.

3. Divide the rest of the class into small groups.

4. Give one or two pictures to each group, then allow a few minutes for the groups to compare their pictures with the people at the front of the class and decide which person is in each picture. Instruct the groups to be prepared to defend their decisions by noting similarities in hair, shape of mouth, or other visible characteristics.

5. Have each group announce its decisions and explain their reasons for choosing as they did. Those at the front of the room should not give clues as to correctness yet.

6. After all groups have made their selections and explained why they chose as they did, the group at the front could reveal whether they were correctly matched with their pictures.

7. Discuss clues that were used and ways that humans change as they grow. Note some of the characteristics that aided identification and some that seem to have fooled the groups.

8. Compare the changes we undergo with those of other mammals, as well as with animals that go through metamorphosis.

9. Discuss: Do you think baby pictures would be any help to the FBI in identifying a suspect? Why or why not?

Teacher Information

This activity needs to be done with a fairly large group of students in order to offer the intended challenge. Giving each group of students only a few of the photos helps to assure the challenge. If you receive only a few pictures, you could increase the challenge by selecting one or more students who did not bring a picture, but who are good at keeping secrets, to join the group at the front of the room.

This experience gives students an opportunity for some good detective work, as well as greater recognition that humans, too, change as they grow, and that the changes we undergo are quite like those of some animals but very unlike those of others.

Integrating

Social studies

Science Process Skills

Observing, inferring, predicting, communicating, comparing and contrasting, formulating hypotheses, identifying and controlling variables

How Does Growing Up Begin?

Materials Needed

- Pictures of humans, both male and female, of all age groups, especially mothers with babies
- Pictures of pregnant women
- Pictures of mammals of all kinds (some pregnant females if possible)
- Pictures of mammal babies being cared for by their mothers
- List of age groups developed in Activity 3.1

Procedure

1. Study the pictures of humans. Group them according to the age classifications you chose in Activity 3.1. You should have at least one picture for each group.

2. Can you find women in the pictures who will have babies soon? How can you tell?

3. Look at the pictures of animals that are not humans. Put them in the age classifications with the people. Do you have an animal picture in each group?

4. The animals you have classified are called mammals. Like humans, the females all carry their babies inside them until the babies are ready to be born. Then they give birth to living young. Can you find pictures of animals you think will soon give birth to babies? How can you tell?

5. Compare the pictures of human babies and other animal babies. Notice that they need their mothers' care.

6. With your teacher and other members of the group, discuss how humans and other mammals care for their young.

For Problem Solvers

Make a list of many animals that you know. Put them into two categories—those that hatch from eggs and those that are born alive. Compare your list with the lists of others who are doing this activity. If there are any animals that you don't agree on, search for the correct answer. Read and ask questions until you are sure.

Teacher Information

This activity begins with an overview of humans and alludes to a relationship with other mammals. The focus then narrows to their common method of giving birth and their extended care of the young. It is not intended to introduce a study of reproduction except as it applies to the beginning growth process. Reproduction is essential to the perpetuation of the species. All types of living things have the ability to reproduce themselves.

Mammal babies are born in a relatively helpless condition and require care from their mothers or some other mature adult.

Concepts to be emphasized in this activity are

1. Human and other mammal young begin as eggs and grow and develop inside their mothers. They are quite small at birth.
2. When compared to most other animals, human and other mammal babies are quite helpless at birth and require care for longer periods of time.

The role of the male in caring for the young has been intentionally excluded, as it varies so greatly from species to species.

An interesting extension of this activity is the study of marsupials. Live young are born in an early stage of development and spend time in a special pouch in their mothers' abdomens, consuming milk until they are fully developed. Although students may be more familiar with kangaroos, the opossum is the only native marsupial found in the United States.

Integrating

Language arts, social studies

Science Process Skills

Observing, inferring, classifying, communicating, using space-time relationships, formulating hypotheses, researching

What Is a Chicken Egg Really Like?

(Teacher-supervised small groups)

Materials Needed

- Hard-boiled chicken eggs (one per group)
- Squares of paper towel (one per group)
- Plastic knife (or dull metal knife)
- Drawing of cross section of a chicken egg (Figure 3.4–1, one per student)

Procedure

1. Eggs that hatch outside the mother's body are a part of the reproductive process of many animals. Study your diagram of an egg. Use it to locate the parts in a real chicken egg.

2. Your chicken egg has been hard-boiled so the contents will not run out. Place the egg on the square of paper towel and gently crack it in many places by tapping it on a table or desk.

3. Carefully peel the hard outer shell from the egg. Be sure to keep the shell on the paper towel.

4. Look at the egg without a shell. Can you find the thin membrane?

5. Use the diagram to help find the place where there was an air space between the shell and the soft white part of the egg. How did you find it?

6. Use the knife to carefully cut the egg in half.

7. Compare your diagram with the chicken egg. Did you find all the parts?

8. Discuss your findings with your teacher and with other class members.

Growing and Changing: Animal Life Cycles   **123**

Teacher Information

The egg diagram has been simplified to show basic parts that students can easily identify. For this activity, unfertilized eggs are preferred.

Many of us are familiar with an egg as food but have never carefully examined its parts. The hard outer shell serves as a protective covering. Some animal eggs do not have protective outer coverings, or if they are present they may appear in a different form, such as the soft leather-like shells of reptiles.

A thin membrane encloses the albumen and yolk. If the egg is fertilized, material in the albumen will form the embryo. The yellow yolk provides food for the embryo until some time (at least 24 hours) after it hatches. Birds hatching from hard-shelled eggs have a special "egg tooth" on their beaks to assist them in getting out of the egg.

Although they appear to be solid, egg shells are porous to allow the exchange of oxygen and carbon dioxide necessary for a developing embryo. Chalaza are whitish spiral bands extending from the yolk to the membrane at each end of the egg. You may not be able to identify them in a hard-boiled egg. You may substitute a raw egg in a small bowl. The parts shown in Figure 3.4–1 will then be easier to observe. Be careful of spills.

Integrating

Math, language arts

Science Process Skills

Observing, communicating

Hands–On Life Science Activities

Figure 3.4-1. Cross Section of a Chicken Egg

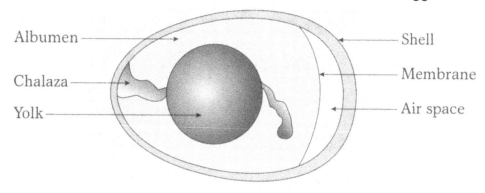

Albumen

Chalaza

Yolk

Shell

Membrane

Air space

What Are Some Other Animals That Hatch from Eggs?

(Groups of four or five)

Materials Needed

- Pictures of many different animals in the process of hatching from eggs: fish, amphibians, tadpoles, reptiles (snake, crocodile), insects (grasshopper, caterpillar), spiders, and birds
- Pictures of adult metamorphosed animals: butterfly or moth, and frog

Procedure

1. Look at the pictures of different kinds of animals hatching from eggs. Many look somewhat like their adult parents. Some do not.
2. Classify the pictures into two groups: (a) those that look like their parents and (b) those that do not.
3. Ask your teacher to check your groupings.
4. When certain animals hatch, they go through several changes before they become adults. This process is called metamorphosis. One group of pictures should include some of these animals in various stages of development.

For Problem Solvers

Animals that do not experience metamorphosis still change as they grow through the developmental stages to adulthood. Find pictures of several animals that do not go through metamorphosis. Read about them in the encyclopedia and in other references. Check the Internet. Select one or more of these and make a list of ways they change as they grow. These changes could be in what they do as well as in physical characteristics.

Humans also change as they grow up. Make a list of ways you have changed since you were born. Find a baby picture of yourself to help you notice ways you have changed physically, but also consider your abilities, your interests, and the ways you think.

How much taller have you grown in the past year? Predict how tall you will be six months from now and one year from now. Keep your predictions and compare them with your actual growth as the months go by.

Teacher Information

The major purpose of this activity is to introduce the concept of growth and change through metamorphosis.

It is also important to observe that many insects, fish, reptiles, and other animals that resemble their parents when they hatch also possess instinctive behaviors that resemble those of the adult.

Many adult animals lay their fertilized eggs in a place where food will be available to the hatching young and then abandon them. The term "baby" is most often applied to humans and other mammals. To many children, "baby" also implies the presence of a mother. Since mothering is not instinctive among some animals, scientists use many different terms to identify and classify immature and mature animals. For example:

kit (immature)—beaver (mature)

calf (immature)—cow (mature)

elver (immature)—eel (mature)

whelp (immature)—otter (mature)

cub (immature)—wolf (mature)

Integrating

Language arts, physical education

Science Process Skills

Observing, inferring, classifying, predicting, communicating, comparing and contrasting, using space-time relationships, formulating hypotheses, researching

How Can You Hatch Eggs in the Classroom?

(Teacher-directed total-group activity)

Materials Needed

- Fertilized chicken eggs
- Garden spider eggs
- Praying mantis eggs
- Incubators

Teacher Information

Hatching eggs in the classroom can be an interesting and exciting first-hand experience for students. However, there are problems involved. Following are two examples of egg-hatching activities. Please read carefully before you begin.

Hatching Chicken Eggs

A major problem with hatching bird eggs is the 21-day incubation period. Several biological supply houses offer incubators, but costs are fairly high. Several science textbooks provide plans for building simple incubators using boxes, wire, and incandescent lights. Plan to use an incubator large enough to accommodate several (up to twelve) fertilized eggs, as usually some will not hatch. Tiny incubators that hold only one or two eggs are not recommended.

You will need a thermostat to ensure a constant temperature in the incubator throughout the 21-day period. Be sure the electrical power in your school is not turned off overnight or on weekends.

Eggs must be turned several times (three or four) every 24 hours. Some commercial incubators do this automatically. If you are planning to do it manually, be sure to mark the eggshell so students will know how far to turn it. This must be done on weekends as well as on school days.

The eggs will hatch when the chick is ready; they will not wait for science class. Your eggs may not take a full 21 days to hatch, as they were probably fertilized and laid a day or two before you obtained them. Incubating a large number of eggs increases the possibility of having some hatch during the school day.

Fertilized eggs may be obtained from hatcheries or biological supply houses. As an alternative to chickens, quail or pheasant eggs may also be available.

If lengthy incubation is not practical, some hatcheries may be able to provide eggs that are ready to hatch within a day or two. You will still need an incubator, but the time involved is much less.

Be sure to prepare the students for the experience in advance. Your library or media center can provide books and pictures.

If you live in or near a rural area, you may be able to borrow a mother hen with fertilized eggs. She is a natural incubator. She will turn the eggs, keep them warm, and provide care for the chicks after they hatch. If you get a "setting" hen, be sure to have an adequate cage and preparations for feeding and cleaning.

Young chicks hatched in an incubator can remain in it for several days. They will require warmth, water, and food. As they become larger, they will need to be transferred to a larger warm space called a brooder. If possible, this is the time to return them to the hatchery or farm. It is not recommended that baby chicks be sent home with children, especially in urban or suburban areas.

Cautions
a. Not all eggs will hatch, and some chicks may not survive the hatching process or may die soon after. Students should be prepared for this eventuality. Under no circumstance should you "help" the chick during the hatching process. The struggle it goes through is part of its beginning life process, and it is important to the strength and well-being of the chick.

b. A few older science books suggest incubating a larger number of eggs and opening one every other day to observe the development of the chick embryo. This is generally considered inappropriate for elementary-school-age children and is not recommended. It will kill the chicks, of course.

Watching Insect or Spider Eggs Hatch
Clusters of eggs of the praying mantis may be ordered from biological supply houses. Spider eggs can be collected in the spring. Although neither type of egg requires particular care during incubation, problems may occur after hatching.

Spider eggs should remain attached to the object (branch, leaf, or stick) on which they are found. If you bring them into the classroom, be sure to provide a secure cage of tightly woven mesh, as some species of spiders are extremely tiny when they hatch. You may need hand lenses even to find them. It is not necessary to have a female adult spider with the eggs. Release the young spiders in a day or two near the location where the eggs were collected. Most spiders do not or cannot bite humans. A few species can and do (for example, black widows). Such species should never be allowed in the classroom. Spider bites are rarely fatal, but they can be irritating and painful. For most spiders, cotton or leather gloves will provide adequate protection. The book *Charlotte's Web*, available in most libraries, could be used to develop positive attitudes toward spiders.

Praying mantis egg clusters may be ordered from late winter through spring. Plan to put them outside in a shady, protected area and check them daily. As the eggs hatch, you will probably be able to catch the small nymphs and cage them in the classroom. They should be housed separately and fed according to the instructions that accompany them. They cannot bite humans, even when they grow to a large size, 5 cm to 8 cm (2 in. to 3 in.); however, they are voracious eaters and are cannibalistic.

Local variety stores and biological supply houses often stock craft kits with parts to construct cages for adult animals, including the praying mantis.

Spiders and predatory insects such as the praying mantis, ladybird beetles, and dragonflies are valuable in controlling harmful insects. They should not be killed or disturbed.

Integrating
Math, language arts

Science Process Skills
Observing, inferring, predicting, communicating, using space-time relationships, formulating hypotheses, identifying and controlling variables, experimenting, researching

Hands-On Life Science Activities

What Is a Tadpole?

(Individual and group activity)

Materials Needed

- Hand lenses
- Pencils
- Crayons
- Newsprint
- Tadpoles

Procedure

1. Frogs belong to a family of animals called amphibians. They hatch from eggs and begin the first active phase of their lives in water.

2. There are tadpoles in your room. Use a hand lens to examine them.

3. Make a drawing of a tadpole on your paper. With your drawing try to show the following:

   a. How does it move about?

   b. Can it see? How do you know?

   c. What body parts can you identify? Use words such as head, tail, legs, fin, body, abdomen, and gills.

4. Use your crayons to show the color of the tadpoles.

5. Just like other animals, tadpoles need a good environment in order to grow and remain healthy. With your teacher and other class members, plan the type of environment your tadpoles will need.

Teacher Information

In early spring, frog eggs and tadpoles can be collected from ponds and marshy areas around lakes. If you live in a geographic area where live collection is possible, students may be able to gather their own specimens. They may need the help of parents and other adults. A local high school or college biologist could be of great help in locating and identifying your specimens.

Tadpoles may be ordered from biological supply houses or local pet stores that sell fish. Place your order in early spring. Allow four to six weeks for delivery. Be sure to order a rapidly developing variety such as Xenopus, as some tadpoles may require several months to develop into

young frogs. Order thirty or more, as the mortality rate is high. Plan this activity for early spring.

Expense, time, and other problems in your particular school may make it impossible to carry out this and certain other activities as outlined. Kits containing eggs, plastic aquariums, food, and instructions are available from commercial sources such as Delta Education and Carolina Biological.

Integrating

Language arts, art

Science Process Skills

Observing, inferring, communicating, using space-time relationships, formulating hypotheses, researching

What Is a Good Environment for Tadpoles?

(Teacher-directed individual or group activity)

Materials Needed

- Transparent shoe box
- Block of wood 5 cm (2 in.) tall or wide strip of corrugated cardboard folded as a wedge 5 cm (2 in.) high
- Pencils
- Pond water (needed every other week) (If you must use tap water, be sure to let it stand for at least 24 hours.)
- Dipping net
- Tadpoles (at least five)
- One copy of Figure 3.8–1 per student
- One copy of Figure 3.8–2 per student

Procedure

1. In the "Animals" section, you learned about aquariums and terrariums for small land animals and fish. Review the illustrations of the aquarium and pond terrarium used in those activities.

2. Tadpoles begin their lives resembling fish in many ways and gradually develop into adult land animals. To do this, they must have an environment that combines land and water. Figure 3.8–1 shows the change from egg to tadpole to frog. Compare your live tadpoles with the ones in the drawing. Circle the animal that most closely resembles the live tadpoles. Try to decide whether they are very young or are starting to change. This will help you decide what to feed them.

3. Remove the lid from a plastic shoe box. Most regular shoe boxes are about 35 cm long by 12 cm deep (14 in. by 4½ in.). Place the box on a flat surface and use a wedge made of corrugated cardboard or wood to raise one end about 5 cm (2 in.).

4. Add pond water until more than half of the bottom is covered, but not all of it. Your pond water may have a green scum and tiny pieces of material in it. These are healthy for your tadpoles and should not be removed.

Growing and Changing: Animal Life Cycles   **133**

5. Compare your shoe box aquarium with Figure 3.8–2. If it is similar, use a dipping net to add several (five to eight) tadpoles.

6. You will need to change the pond water about every other week. If they are very young, tadpoles will eat small amounts of boiled spinach. After a few weeks, they eat spinach without boiling. Don't overfeed! Once or twice a week is enough.

Figure 3.8-1. Metamorphosis of a Frog

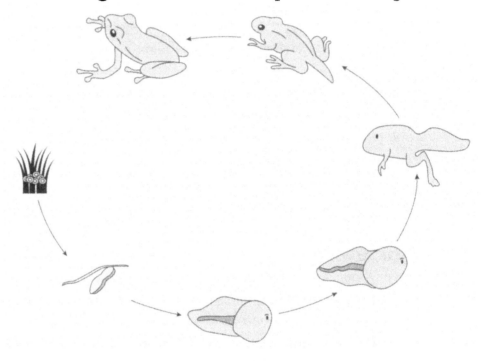

Figure 3.8-2. Shoe Box Aquarium

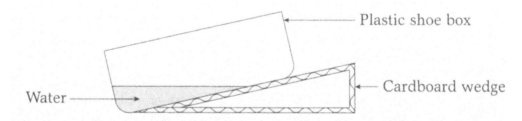

Hands-On Life Science Activities

For Problem Solvers

Do some research and learn what you can about different kinds of frogs. See how many of the following questions you can answer.

- How big is the largest frog? The smallest? Where do they live?
- In what ways are different types of frogs really different?
- Where do most frogs usually live at different stages of their lives?
- What do most frogs eat at different stages of their lives?
- Are frogs ever used as food for humans?

Teacher Information

You might want each small group of students to do this activity. You will need a complete set of materials for each group.

In nature, animals often lay many eggs, and a few of them usually survive to adult stage. With careful feeding and excellent care, you can expect some tadpoles to advance through several stages of metamorphosis.

Tilting the shoe box so shallow water and land are available is most important, as the tadpoles lose their gills and become lung breathers. This is usually at about the time the front legs begin to develop. If they can't get out of the water, many will drown.

Remember, depending on the species, complete metamorphosis in an amphibian may take from four months to over a year. This is a very long time, especially for young children who expect immediate results.

After the tadpoles are in the shoe boxes, put them in a shady place in the room and set up a feeding and water-changing schedule. Use the dipping net to remove any dead specimens. Discuss the tadpoles briefly as observable changes appear. Remind the children that they, too, take a long time to grow and change.

Be sure to have books and stories about frogs and toads available. Don't put lids on the plastic shoe boxes, but save the lids to use when you transport the animals to free them in a suitable area.

Integrating

Math, reading

Science Process Skills

Observing, inferring, classifying, measuring, predicting, communicating, using space-time relationships, formulating hypotheses, identifying and controlling variables, experimenting, researching

Where Do Butterflies Come From?

Materials Needed

- Larva, cocoon, or chrysalis of moth or butterfly
- One copy of Figure 3.9–1 for each student
- One copy of Figure 3.8–1 (from Activity 3.8) for each student
- Insect cage (see Figure 3.9–2) or butterfly kit from pet store or supply house
- Hand lenses
- Pencils

Procedure

1. Study Figure 3.9–1. It shows the way butterflies and moths develop.

2. Compare this figure with Figure 3.8–1 of the frog. How are they alike? How are they different? Measure them. Which is largest?

3. There is a new animal in the room in a particular stage of metamorphosis. Look at Figure 3.9–1 and find the stage of development your new animal most closely resembles.

4. If your animal is in the larva or pupa stage, there are usually ways to tell whether the adult will be a moth or a butterfly. Look at Figure 3.9–1 and see whether you can find any differences. Beside the picture of the adult, write the name of the variety of insect (moth or butterfly) you think your animal will become.

5. When your insect becomes an adult, it will soon be able to fly. Do you have a good cage for it? Figure 3.9–2 shows several simple cages you can make. Choose one and form a group to construct it.

6. Give your adult insect a name. Use books, pictures, and your own observations to learn all you can about it. Notice how many beautiful ways butterflies are used in art.

7. After a few days, take your butterfly or moth cage to a sunny place outside near flowers and open the lid. Say good-bye to your butterfly or moth (do not touch its wings) and set it free.

Figure 3.9-1. Butterfly or Moth Metamorphosis

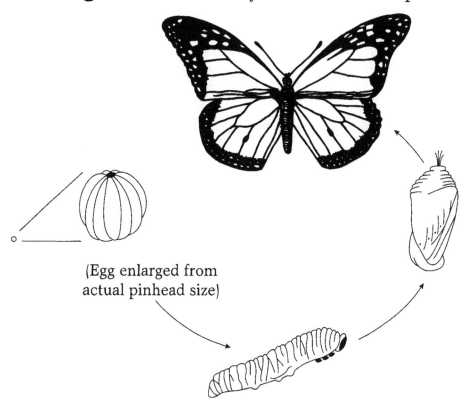

(Egg enlarged from actual pinhead size)

Figure 3.9-2. Homemade Insect Cages

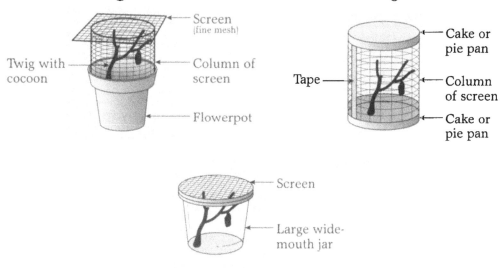

Growing and Changing: Animal Life Cycles

For Problem Solvers

Make a butterfly net. Find ideas in the encyclopedia or, better yet, create your own design. Consider using nylon stockings or panty hose as the net. You will need a ring to mount it to and a handle. Share your ideas with others, and together you should be able to come up with a dandy design.

Teacher Information

This is a middle- to late-spring activity in many parts of the country. Observing the metamorphosis of a butterfly or moth is an exciting, worthwhile experience for students of all ages. The time it takes to develop from larva to pupa to adult is less than that for a frog. Allow 30 to 45 days; however, the larval stage of caterpillars varies in length. Specimens collected locally are best. You will need to provide ample food and moisture for a period. Your encyclopedia or library books will provide detailed instructions.

Occasionally, a student may bring a cocoon or chrysalis to class. If this occurs, you may want to try to find a caterpillar to use for comparisons with Figure 3.9–1, butterfly and moth metamorphosis. In the larva stage, moth caterpillars are usually hairy or "woolly." Butterfly caterpillars are usually smooth-skinned.

Butterflies form a hard, smooth shell called a chrysalis. Pictures from books may help show the differences. Remember, as with egg hatching, your insect may not spin its cocoon or emerge as an adult during the school day. If you have several specimens, the chance of the children seeing the process is greatly increased. Mortality rate is lower than with tadpoles, but occasionally a caterpillar will die or not emerge from its cocoon or chrysalis. Be patient; never try to help the adult emerge from the pupal stage. The struggle to emerge and the drying out of the wings are part of the natural life process and should not be disturbed. Moths spin cocoons.

The development of a butterfly or moth is so exciting, beautiful, and "mysterious" that every child should experience it at some time during his or her school years. Even if the activity is repeated several times over the years, students will view it with different backgrounds of experience, but always with great anticipation and excitement.

If you live in an area where butterflies are not readily available, larva, and even complete kits with cages and food, can be ordered from biological science–supply houses at a very reasonable price. However, we recommend that you collect, house, and care for local insects if possible.

Books, pictures, and stories about butterflies are plentiful. Be sure to use them to enrich this experience. Music, art, poetry, and creative movement can be included in your learning activities.

Collecting, killing, and mounting insects is not recommended for early elementary grades.

Integrating

Math, reading, music, art, dance

Science Process Skills

Observing, inferring, classifying, predicting, communicating, comparing and contrasting, using space-time relationships, formulating hypotheses, identifying and controlling variables, experimenting, researching

What Is Wormy?

(Small-group activity)

Materials Needed

- Mealworms in container labeled "Mealworms"
- Earthworms in container labeled "Earthworms"
- Waxed paper
- Figure 3.9–1 (from Activity 3.9)
- Writing paper
- Pencils
- Hand lenses
- Tablespoons
- Pie tins or small cake pans

Procedure

1. Have you ever heard someone say, "Oh, it has worms in it"? On your paper write the names of things they might be talking about. Most of the items on your list are probably things humans eat. What is similar about them?
2. Line a pie tin or cake pan with waxed paper.
3. Use a spoon to transfer one animal from the container marked "Earthworms" and one from the container marked "Mealworms."
4. Use your hand lens to study both worms. Make a simple drawing of each.
5. On your paper write ways they are alike and ways they are different. Compare such things as size, color, how they move, legs, head, eyes, mouth, and any other similarities or differences you can find.
6. Compare your pictures and descriptions of your worms with the caterpillar in Figure 3.9–1.
7. One of your worms is not a real worm at all. Can you tell which one? How?
8. Share the findings of your group with your teacher and the class.

Hands-On Life Science Activities

For Problem Solvers

Which can move faster—a snail, an earthworm, or a mealworm? How could you find out?

From what you have learned, can you answer this question: Is the silkworm really a worm?

Teacher Information

There are many more known species of insects in the world than all other species of animals and plants combined. Many species go through a complete metamorphosis where the larvae bear some resemblance to true worms.

Many insects lay their eggs on or in living or once-living material, including plants and wool. When the eggs hatch, the larva feed on the material upon which they were laid. "Wormy" apples are actually apples that have housed the larva or maggot stage of an insect.

Maggots are legless, soft-bodied larvae, usually found in decaying material. Larvae from the housefly, the mosquito, and relatives are common throughout the world. We often try to control harmful insects at the larva stage (for example, a lid on a garbage can or treating standing water may kill more flies or mosquitoes than you could swat in a lifetime).

A mealworm is the larva of one of several grain-eating beetles. They are available at most pet stores because they are used as food for larger animals (fish, amphibians, and lizards). They are easily stored in a can with bran flakes or a similar food substance. Add moisture to the can occasionally and dispose of the contents at least once during the school year.

Your earthworm is a true segmented worm and belongs to a completely different group of animals (see your encyclopedia for further information).

Integrating

Math, reading, language arts

Science Process Skills

Observing, inferring, classifying, measuring, communicating, using space-time relationships, formulating hypotheses, identifying and controlling variables, experimenting, researching

How Long Do Animals Live?

Materials Needed

- Chart of animal life spans (see Figure 3.11-1)
- Resource people

Procedure

1. Look at Figure 3.11-1. It shows the average length of life of some common animals. On the left side of the diagram from bottom to top are numbers of years. Across the page are drawings of different animals. Find the animals with the shortest and the longest life spans.

2. Use your chart to discuss with your teacher and the class the following questions:

   a. Why do some animals live longer than others?

   b. How do scientists determine an average age?

   c. Why has people's life expectancy increased in recent years?

3. Invite some older people to visit your class. Find out why they think they have lived as long as they have.

Teacher Information

Animal life spans and cycles vary greatly. Some complete a generation in hours, weeks, or months. Others take many years to mature. Life cycles of many animals are focused on continuation of the species. When the reproductive process is complete, the animal dies. Natural controls such as predators, available food supplies, and other environmental factors also play a part.

Although many animals have different adaptations and use different methods for survival, humans are the only animal to seek consciously to prolong life. For this reason, too, domesticated animals tend to live longer than their "cousins" in a natural or wild state.

Students may want to add animals to their life span chart. An encyclopedia or other reference book will usually give life expectancies. Microscopic organisms are not included in this activity.

Be sure to select the older visitors with care. Conduct a personal interview first and if possible suggest some specific topics to discuss. Children often have more in common with older people than with people in the "middle" years. With care, this activity can be a very rich learning experience, and perhaps form lasting bonds.

Integrating

Math, language arts, social studies

Science Process Skills

Communicating, comparing and contrasting, using space-time relationships, formulating hypotheses

Figure 3.11-1. Animal Life Spans

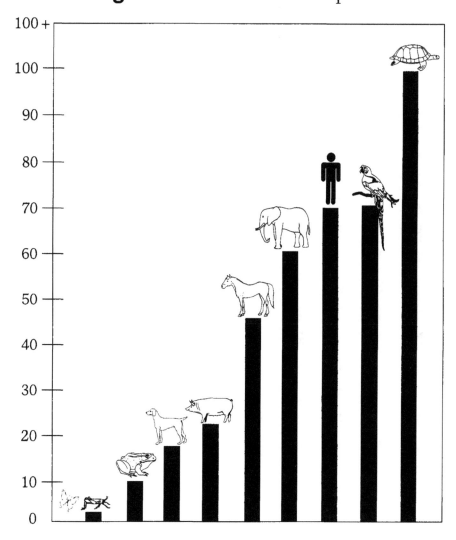

Can You Solve This Growing and Changing Word Search?

Try to find the following Growing and Changing terms in the grid below. They could appear in horizontal (left to right), vertical (up or down), or diagonal (upward or downward) position.

toddler	adolescent	changing
mammal	mother	egg
tadpole	butterfly	frog
cocoon	grow	environment
animal	life	mature

```
M  A  T  U  R  E  M  N  G  B  M  V
C  X  Z  A  E  A  S  D  G  F  O  T
G  A  D  O  L  E  S  C  E  N  T  A
F  H  J  K  D  I  L  P  B  I  H  D
U  R  Y  T  D  C  F  O  U  C  E  P
R  E  O  W  O  O  Q  E  T  H  R  O
A  L  K  G  T  C  J  H  T  A  G  L
E  N  V  I  R  O  N  M  E  N  T  E
G  F  I  D  S  O  A  Q  R  G  W  E
R  T  Y  M  U  N  W  I  F  I  O  P
L  K  J  H  A  W  E  F  L  N  N  M
M  A  M  M  A  L  T  R  Y  G  Y  U
```

Copyright © 2006 by John Wiley & Sons. Inc.

Can You Create a New Growing and Changing Word Search of Your Own?

Write your Growing and Changing words in the grid below. Arrange them in the grid so they appear in horizontal (left to right), vertical (up or down), or diagonal (upward or downward) position. Fill in the blank boxes with other letters. Trade your Word Search with someone else who has created one of his or her own, and see whether you can solve the new puzzle.

_____   _____   _____

_____   _____   _____

_____   _____   _____

_____   _____   _____

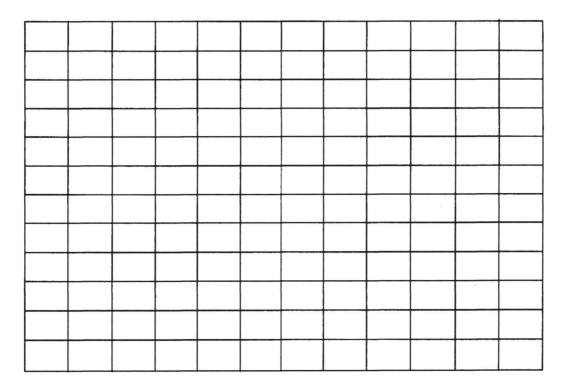

Growing and Changing: Animal Life Cycles

Answer Key for Growing and Changing Word Search

```
M  A  T  U  R  E  M  N  G  B  M  V
C  X  Z  A  E  A  S  D  G  F  O  T
G  A  D  O  L  E  S  C  E  N  T  A
F  H  J  K  D  I  L  P  B  I  H  D
U  R  Y  T  D  C  F  O  U  C  E  P
R  E  O  W  O  O  Q  E  T  H  R  O
A  L  K  G  T  C  J  H  T  A  G  L
E  N  V  I  R  O  N  M  E  N  T  E
G  F  I  D  S  O  A  Q  R  G  W  E
R  T  Y  M  U  N  W  I  F  I  O  P
L  K  J  H  A  W  E  F  L  N  N  M
M  A  M  M  A  L  T  R  Y  G  Y  U
```

146

Do You Recall?

Section Three: Growing and Changing: Animal Life Cycles

1. In what ways do people change as they grow older?

2. How does the hard shell of a chicken egg help the new chick as it grows?

3. Name three animals that hatch from eggs.

4. What kind of animal will a tadpole become?

5. What kind of animal will a caterpillar become?

6. What is the major difference between a mealworm and an earthworm?

Answer Key for Do You Recall?

Section Three: Growing and Changing: Animal Life Cycles

Answer	Related Activities
1. Answers will vary, but might include size, color of hair, and wrinkles.	3.1, 3.2
2. The hard shell protects the chick.	3.4
3. Birds, fish, snakes, frogs, insects, and others	3.5, 3.6
4. Frog or toad	3.7
5. Butterfly or moth	3.9
6. The earthworm is a true worm; the mealworm is an insect larva.	3.10

Plants and Seeds

To the Teacher

A study of plants offers many opportunities for creative imagination. Most of the activities herein are nongraded. Throughout the study, appreciation for the beauty and wonder of life should be emphasized. Language arts, music, art, and other subjects can be easily integrated into these science activities.

Teachers in urban areas may find some difficulty in conducting a few of the field trip activities. Window boxes and other improvised growing areas can work out well as substitutes.

Resource people can be valuable in this area. Many students have mothers or fathers who grow plants as a hobby. Agronomists (soil specialists), horticulturists, florists, botanists, and nutritionists can also be helpful in their areas of specialization. Designing and planting a school garden could be a very worthwhile outgrowth of this study.

Throughout the study, care should be taken to emphasize the danger of eating any unknown substance. Even some parts of plants we eat can be poisonous, such as rhubarb leaves and some varieties of potato plant leaves. Warn children never to eat

149

berries or flowers they find growing wild. On field trips, take into account regional variations to avoid such things as poison ivy and stinging nettle.

Most growing activities suggest the use of potting soil; however, as plants develop they will usually do better in rich, loamy garden soil. Specialized plants such as cactuses and pine trees will need special alkali or acid soils. Be sure to check reference sources before growing specialized plants.

Older children may be interested in solving problems scientifically, as a plant scientist might do. Several plants in the same kinds of containers could be presented with the following statement and question: These are all the same species of plant, planted on the same day from similar seeds. How can you account for the differences?

The plants used will have been grown in different media—gravel, sand, potting soil, or loam. One will have been put in a dark place, one in sunlight. One will have been over-watered or under-watered and one watered properly. As children observe differences in the conditions of the plants, soil, and moisture, they will form hypotheses they can test through replication: identifying a problem (Some plants don't grow as well as others.); stating a hypothesis (This plant is too dry.); testing the hypothesis (If I transplant this plant to soil instead of gravel, it will grow better.); conclusion (What I tried worked or did not work.). This activity is similar to the work of agricultural specialists.

The following activities are designed as discovery activities that students can usually perform quite independently. You are encouraged to provide students (usually in small groups) with the materials listed and a copy of the activity from the beginning through the "Procedure." The section titled "Teacher Information" is not intended for student use, but rather to assist you with discussion following the hands-on activity, as students share their observations. Discussion of conceptual information prior to completing the hands-on activity can interfere with the discovery process.

Final Thoughts

1. Memorizing scientific names of plants is not important at the elementary level.
2. Plant study affords many excellent opportunities for integration of other subject areas, such as language arts, math, art, social studies, music, and health.
3. Our major purpose is to develop understanding, respect, and appreciation for the contributions plants make in our lives.

Regarding the Early Grades

With verbal instructions and slight modifications, many of these activities can be used with kindergarten, first-grade, and second-grade students.

Some of the activities were written specifically with the primary grades in mind. In others, procedural steps that go beyond the level of the child can simply be omitted and yet offer the child experiences that plant conceptual seeds for concepts that will germinate and grow later on.

Teachers of the early grades will probably choose to bypass many of the "For Problem Solvers" sections. That's okay. These sections are provided for those who are especially motivated and want to go beyond the investigation provided by the activity outlined. Use the outlined activities and enjoy worthwhile learning experiences together with your young students. Also consider, however, that many of the "For Problem Solvers" sections can be used appropriately with young children as group activities or as demonstrations. Giving students the advantage of an exposure to the experience can often lay groundwork for connections that will become more meaningful at a later time.

Correlation with National Standards

The following elements of the National Standards are reflected in the activities of this section.

K–4   Content Standard A: Science as Inquiry

As a result of activities in grades K–4, all students should develop

1. Abilities necessary to do scientific inquiry
2. Understanding about scientific inquiry

K–4   Content Standard C: Life Science

As a result of activities in grades K–4, all students should develop understanding of

1. The characteristics of organisms
2. Life cycles of organisms

5–8   Content Standard A: Science as Inquiry

As a result of activities in grades 5–8, all students should develop

1. Abilities necessary to do scientific inquiry
2. Understanding about scientific inquiry

5–8   Content Standard C: Life Science

As a result of activities in grades 5–8, all students should develop understanding of

1. Structures and function in living systems

What Plant Is This?

(Advance teacher preparation needed)

Materials Needed

- Variety of seeds from common garden plants, such as radish, corn, carrot, onion, beans, and other seeds found in your region (see "Teacher Information")
- Small container such as paper, foam, or plastic cup (one per student) filled with moist potting soil containing two or three seeds from one variety of plant listed above
- Library books or seed packages with pictures of the plants that will grow from the seeds
- Masking tape
- Pencils
- Water

Procedure

1. Your container has potting soil and seeds in it. Write your name on a piece of masking tape and put it on your container.
2. Put it in a warm, shady place in the room.
3. Give it a small amount of water daily.
4. In a few days, tiny green plants will come up.
5. When all of the plants for the class have come out of the soil, predict which ones will grow fastest or slowest and which ones will be tallest and shortest after they mature.
6. Move your plant into a sunny spot in the room. Continue to water it sparingly.
7. As your plant grows larger, compare it with the plants of everyone else in the room.
8. Try to find everyone who has a plant that looks like yours.
9. With the other members of your group, use library books to find a picture of your plant.
10. When you think you know the name of your plant, ask your teacher to see whether you are correct.

152

For Problem Solvers

As the plants grow, study the differences in the plants that are being raised by everyone in the room. Try to find pictures of them and learn their names. See how many of these plants you can find in other parts of the school, in your home, or in other buildings and yards wherever you go. As you look for certain types of plants, if there are some that you have not found a name for, ask the people who are raising them. Notice how the plants are alike and how they are different, and learn to identify as many of them as you can.

Which of all the types of plants in your classroom seem to grow fastest? Which ones grow slowest? Measure them and make a graph that shows a comparison of growth patterns.

Think of other questions you could investigate with plants. Write these down, talk about them, and decide which one to investigate first.

Teacher Information

This activity will require several weeks to complete. If it could be started early, it would serve to capture student interest in the topic of plants. Other science activities can be done along with it. Other activities in this section could parallel this activity.

Students may enjoy having a few surprise seeds, such as popcorn (non-popped) or raw peanuts. If you live in an area where a particular plant (corn, wheat, peanuts, or another) is a common agricultural crop known to the students, use it along with less familiar seeds and see how soon in its growth cycle students begin to recognize it.

If space or time is limited, you could have several small plants that are labeled incorrectly and ask the students to help you learn about the plants and label them correctly.

Integrating

Math, reading, art

Science Process Skills

Observing, inferring, classifying, measuring, predicting, communicating, comparing and contrasting, using space-time relationships, formulating hypotheses, identifying and controlling variables, experimenting, researching

How Do Seeds Begin to Grow?

Materials Needed

- Large dry lima bean seeds
- Container of water

Procedure

1. Observe the dry lima bean seeds.

2. Draw a picture of what you think the seeds will look like after they have soaked in water for one full day.

3. Soak the seeds in water for 24 hours. How did they change? Were you right in your prediction?

4. Carefully split one of the seeds in half.

5. Try to find the baby plant and the other parts shown in the picture below.

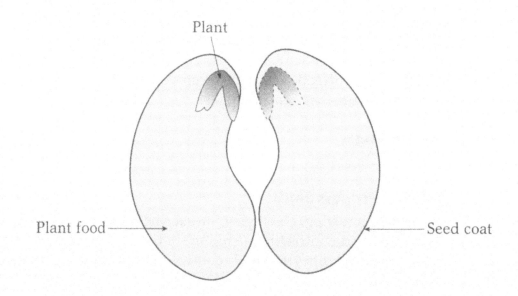

Plant

Plant food

Seed coat

Hands-On Life Science Activities

For Problem Solvers

Fill a milk carton all the way to the top with dry lima bean seeds. Next, fill the carton with water, then close the top of the carton. Wrap masking tape around and around the carton in all directions, taping the carton as tightly as you can.

Set the carton aside. Draw a picture of it. Measure its girth (distance around) and write the number beside the picture you drew. What do you predict will happen in one day? Two days? Three days?

Look at the carton each day for three days. Each day, draw a picture of it. How is it changing? Each day, measure and record the girth of the milk carton. Were you right in your predictions? What is different about the pictures you drew of the milk carton?

Teacher Information

Seeds that produce flowering plants come in many shapes and sizes. They all have three things in common: a protective cover, a food supply, and a baby plant called the embryo. Peas or raw peanuts may be substituted for beans.

This is an excellent individual or small-group activity.

Integrating

Math, art

Science Process Skills

Observing, inferring, measuring, predicting, communicating, using space-time relationships, formulating hypotheses, identifying and controlling variables, experimenting

What Happens to a Growing Plant If It Has No Light?

(Take home and do with family and friends.)

Materials Needed

- Two eight-ounce clear plastic tumblers
- Two 10 by 15-cm (or 4 by 6-inch) sponges
- Dry lima bean seeds
- Water
- A copy of the "Science Investigation Journaling Notes" for this activity for each student

Procedure

1. As you complete this activity, you will keep record of what you do, just as scientists do. Obtain a copy of the form "Science Investigation Journaling Notes" from your teacher and write the information that is called for, including your name and the date.

2. For this activity you will find out whether plants need light. For item 1, the question is provided for you.

3. Item 2 asks for what you already know about the topic. If you have some ideas about whether light helps plants to grow, write your ideas.

4. For item 3, you need to think about what you wrote for item 2 and decide whether you think light helps plants to grow. Write what you know about the topic, and that will be your hypothesis. If you think your plant will grow well without light, write that. If you think it won't grow as well without light, or won't grow at all, write that as your hypothesis.

5. Now continue with the following instructions. Complete your Journaling Notes as you go. Numbers 6 through 10 below will help you with the information you need to write on the form for items 4, 5, and 6.

6. Soak the bean seeds for 24 hours.

7. Put a damp sponge around the inside surface of each tumbler. (See Figure 4.3–1.)

156

Figure 4.3-1. Seeds in a Glass with a Sponge

8. Put eight seeds between the sponge and the side of each tumbler. The seeds should be placed 2 or 3 cm (about 1 in.) apart.

9. Place one tumbler in a dark location and the other in the light of the classroom.

10. Observe your seeds daily. Check the sponge to be sure it is still moist.

11. What happened? Why do you think it was this way? (This is item 6 on the form.)

12. For item 7 on the form, think about your hypothesis (item 3) and write what actually happened. Was your hypothesis correct? Did it turn out the way you expected?

For Problem Solvers

As the seeds begin to sprout, turn one tumbler on its side. Predict any changes you think there will be in the way the plants grow. Observe for two or three days, then turn the tumbler again.

Do the same experiment using a zip-closed plastic bag instead of the tumbler. Find a way to experiment with the plant growing in different positions. Think of other containers you could use to sprout seeds and be able to watch both the roots and the stem grow. Try them and decide which container you like best.

Teacher Information

After several days, the bean seeds will begin to sprout. The seeds kept in the dark place should sprout at about the same time as the ones in the light. Seeds do not need sunlight until they begin to grow leaves. Remind the children that many plants begin their lives in the dark, below the surface of the soil.

As the seeds continue to sprout and your problem solvers turn one tumbler on its side, the sprouts will change their direction of growth, with roots growing downward and stem growing upward. In whatever position the tumbler is placed, the roots will grow downward. This phenomenon is called geotropism.

Integrating

Math

Science Process Skills

Observing, inferring, predicting, communicating, using space-time relationships, formulating hypotheses, identifying and controlling variables, experimenting

Name _____   Date _____

Science Investigation

Journaling Notes for Activity 4.3

1. Question: *What happens to a growing plant if it has no light?*

2. What we already know: _____

_____

3. Hypothesis: _____

_____

4. Materials needed: _____

_____

5. Procedure: _____

_____

_____

_____

_____

6. Observations/New information: _____

_____

_____

7. Conclusion: _____

_____

Copyright © 2006 by John Wiley & Sons, Inc.

How Do Seeds Travel?

(Teacher-supervised activity)

Materials Needed

- Paper bags (or plastic)
- Scissors (or knives)
- Hand lenses
- White paper

Procedure

1. Visit a vacant lot or field in late spring or early fall. Be sure you wear long pants and socks.

2. Explore the field. Try to find plants that have bloomed and are producing seeds or "turning to seed." Walk through the field and examine your pant legs and socks.

3. Look at trees in your neighborhood (especially in the fall). See whether you can find seeds or nuts on or around these trees. Be sure to include a dandelion.

4. From your field trip to the vacant lot and examination of trees, collect as many different kinds of seeds as you can. Be sure to examine your pant legs and socks.

5. Put the seeds you have gathered on a clean white sheet of paper on your desk.

6. How many seeds do you have? Examine them with a hand lens.

7. If you have seeds that look different from each other, separate them into groups. How many do you have in each group?

8. How are the different seeds alike, and how are they different?

9. Seeds are spread or dispersed in many ways. Can you imagine how your seeds might travel?

10. Find a fluffy white dandelion top. (See Figure 4.4–1.) Examine one of the tiny white tufts. Can you find the seed? What does the seed have to help it travel? What makes it travel? Can you find other seeds that might be spread in the same way?

Hands-On Life Science Activities

Figure 4.4 –1. Dandelion Top

11. Did you examine your pant legs and socks after walking through the weeds? If a dog or other furry animal walked through the field, what might happen?

For Problem Solvers

Find an old pair of large socks. Put them on over your shoes and pant legs, and then walk through a vacant lot or other area where there are lots of dried plants. Plant the socks in a planter. Water them. Do you think anything will grow? Draw what you think it will look like in three or four weeks. Maybe you'll grow a new pair of socks!

Some plants have special ways of spreading seeds. Do some research and make a list of many different types of seeds and the ways they travel. Make a pictograph to show how many types of seeds you can find for each method of spreading.

Teacher Information

Your library or media center will have books on plants and seeds. Try to review as many as possible and have them as references for children. Seeds travel most frequently by wind, water, and animals. Help students find some good references on seed dispersal.

It may be that everyone will want to be problem solvers this time. Planting the socks that have wandered through the weeds is an exciting experience that creates lots of anticipation as students predict and wait to see what comes out of the ground.

Integrating

Math, language arts, physical education

Science Process Skills

Observing, classifying, inferring, predicting, communicating, comparing and contrasting, using space-time relationships, formulating hypotheses, researching

Hands-On Life Science Activities

How Can Plants Grow Without Seeds?

Materials Needed

- Small aluminum pie tins or bowls
- Toothpicks
- Eight-ounce plastic tumblers
- Freshly cut carrots, potatoes, sweet potatoes, onions, and beets
- Water

Procedure

1. Choose a vegetable and a container.
2. Put your vegetable in the container exactly as shown in the picture below, using toothpicks for support where necessary.
3. Add water to the container every day for at least two weeks.
4. What happened? How are the plants alike? How are they different?

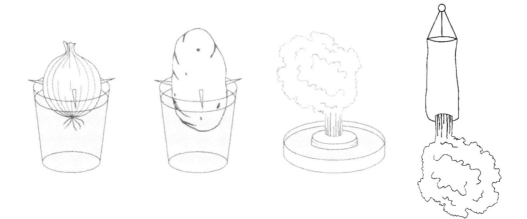

For Problem Solvers

As you investigate with study and trials, find out about some other plants that can be grown without seeds and some that cannot. What about peas? Geraniums? Coleus? African violets? As you select each new plant to try, make a prediction about whether or not the plant will grow without seeds. Make a list of the plants you use, the method you try for each to make it grow, and your prediction of whether it will grow or not.

Methods you could try include growing the plant from a root, from a leaf, a cutting (part of the stem with leaves on it). Try other ideas you might have.

Be sure you keep good records of the type of plant, the part you are trying to get to grow, the date you planted it, and the day-by-day (or week-by-week) progress. Be patient—you might want to start several of these at once, then observe them all and keep notes on the changes that occur.

Teacher Information

This is an excellent individual activity. Be certain to have plenty of materials available so children can try more than one if they wish. Potatoes and sweet potatoes should have several eyes and be freshly cut. The green part of the carrot should not be submerged in water. Avocado seeds can be grown in the same manner as potatoes and will produce beautiful plants, but remember that they *are* seeds, and the objective of this activity is to learn about plants that can be grown *without* seeds. In this case, the seed is very different from most other seeds, however, making it a unique experience.

Onions are bulbs (similar to tulips) and can be easily transplanted. The carrot is a root, and the potato is called a tuber.

Integrating

Math and language arts

Science Process Skills

Observing, inferring, classifying, predicting, comparing and contrasting, identifying and controlling variables, experimenting

What Is Another Way to Grow Plants Without Seeds?

Materials Needed

- Water
- Rubber bands
- Pencils
- Knives
- Eight-ounce glass tumblers
- Aluminum foil
- Philodendron plants

Procedure

1. Fill the tumbler with water.
2. Cover the top of the tumbler with aluminum foil and hold it in place with a rubber band.
3. With your pencil, punch a hole in the center of the foil.
4. Cut a young, leafy stem, at least 20 cm (8 in.) from the plant. (*Caution:* Don't break off the stem. Cut it cleanly.)
5. Trim the leaves from the bottom 10 cm (4 in.) of the stem.
6. Insert the stem through the hole in the foil. Be sure the stem is in water. You might want to punch a second hole in the foil so you can easily add water. (See Figure 4.6–1.)
7. What do you think the plant will do?
8. Observe for at least one week.
9. What happened? What can you say about this?

Figure 4.6-1. Plant Cutting in Jar of Water

For Problem Solvers

Expand your knowledge about ways to start new plants. Do some research on plant grafting, and find a way to try it with a plant at home or at school. Be sure to obtain permission before you begin. Perhaps your parent or your teacher would be willing to help you with this project; you might be teaching him or her how to do it as you go along.

Teacher Information

Keep the plant in sunlight. Many plants are started this way. The part cut away is often called a start, a clipping, or a cutting. This can lead to a discussion of plant grafting, which could be a fascinating project for your young problem solvers. See your encyclopedia for information.

Integrating

Math, language arts

Science Process Skills

Observing, measuring, predicting, communicating, using space-time relationships

What Can You Do with Plants That Become Too Big for Their Containers?

Materials Needed

- Flowerpots and other large plant containers
- Potting soil
- Sand or small stones
- Plant starts
- Water

Procedure

1. Choose a plant you have started.
2. Choose a large pot or other container and cover the bottom with small rocks or sand about 1 cm (1/4 in. to 1/2 in.) deep.
3. Add potting soil until the container is three-fourths full. (Don't pack it down.)

Plants and Seeds 167

4. Make a hole in the center of the potting soil approximately 3 cm (1¼ in.) across and 2 cm (3/4 in.) deep.

5. Remove your plant from its present container and put its roots in the hole you prepared in the potting soil. You might need to make the hole larger if you have many roots.

6. Add potting soil until the roots are covered, leaving only the stem and leaves exposed.

7. Carefully water your plant and put it in a sunny place to grow.

For Problem Solvers

Do plants really need to be transplanted? If so, why? Design an investigation and find out what happens if you don't transplant them. Before you begin, predict what will happen to the plants.

Will plants do better if the soil is packed tightly or left loose, or does it matter? How can you find out? Try it. Before you begin, predict what will happen to the plants. How well do you think they will do in packed soil and in loose soil?

Teacher Information

Plants with strong, hardy root systems will work best. Transplanting should be done without needless delay, so the roots will not be exposed to the air any longer than necessary.

Transplanting fails most often because of damaged root systems and over-watering.

Ask the children to bring pots and containers from home. An interesting variety of plant containers is likely to result.

Integrating

Math, language arts

Science Process Skills

Observing, inferring, measuring, predicting, communicating, using space-time relationships, formulating hypotheses, identifying and controlling variables, experimenting

How Do Containers Make Plants More Interesting?

Materials Needed

- Potting soil
- Variety of seeds
- Plastic egg cartons
- Eggshells
- Seashells
- Grapefruit or orange rinds
- Other assorted planters
- Grapefruit or orange seeds
- Water

Procedure

1. Choose an attractive container.
2. Fill it with potting soil.
3. Plant a seed just below the surface of the soil.
4. Keep the soil moist and watch your plant grow.
5. If you choose a grapefruit or orange rind, you might want to try a matching grapefruit or orange seed.
6. See Figure 4.8–1 for a variety of planters.

For Problem Solvers

What other creative planters can you find or make? As the plants grow, compare them as to what the root systems do. Which ones can you transplant directly, planter and all, into larger pots? Which ones will you need to remove from your creative planter? Make your predictions before you plant the seeds and see which ones you predicted correctly.

Figure 4.8–1. A Variety of Planters

Teacher Information

Seeds will sprout in almost any container that will hold potting soil. Objects that rust or are painted on the inside should be avoided.

With some of the creative planters, the roots might grow right through the planter, allowing the planter to simply be planted, as is, in a larger pot. Some of the planters will need to be cut through or removed before transplanting. Plants in small containers, such as eggshells or egg cartons, will need to be transplanted. When this becomes necessary, you could simply crack the eggshell or cut through the carton and transplant into a larger container without disturbing the root system. Your problem solvers will investigate related questions, and possibly produce new questions to pursue.

This activity provides an opportunity to emphasize creativity and develop an appreciation for the beauty of plants. Any container that is to be used as a planter for an extended period of time must provide drainage.

Integrating

Math, language arts, art

Science Process Skills

Observing, classifying, predicting, communicating, comparing and contrasting, using space-time relationships, formulating hypotheses, identifying and controlling variables, experimenting

170

What Is a Terrarium?

Materials Needed

- Potting soil
- Small plants
- Worms
- Insects that crawl but do not fly
- Wild bird seed
- Various containers (one-gallon clear, wide-mouthed bottle; clear plastic shoe box; one-gallon plastic milk bottle cut in half; fish bowl)

Procedure

1. One kind of artificial home for plants is called a terrarium. Terrariums can be made in a variety of ways. The large ones can be covered so air cannot get in or out, and larger ones may contain both plants and animals.

2. Choose a container and make a terrarium of your own. Use the drawings in Figure 4.9–1 to help you.

Figure 4.9–1. A Variety of Terrariums

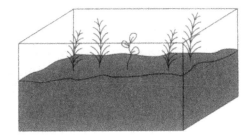
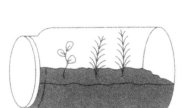
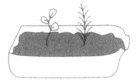

Plants and Seeds

For Problem Solvers

Experiment with three or four terrariums, each a bit different in types of plant and animal life involved. Try to balance each terrarium with the right amount of plant and animal life so that it is self-sustaining. Observe carefully for needed adjustments, and keep a record of the things you do, including dates, to keep your terrariums thriving.

Study about the efforts people have made to maintain a large, self-contained environment.

Teacher Information

Larger terrariums may be sealed and may continue to thrive for many months. The plants will produce oxygen, while any animal life you have will produce carbon dioxide. The terrarium is then balanced. Both the plants and the animals will release moisture into the air, and water droplets will likely form inside the container. As a class project, you might want to convert a ten-gallon aquarium to a terrarium and include animals such as snails, newts, and salamanders. Be sure to check reference sources on terrariums as you plan a classroom project.

It is important in balancing a terrarium that you choose plants that require similar amounts of moisture and sunlight. Small terrariums in unique containers can make attractive gifts or centerpieces. A plastic two-liter soft-drink bottle with tiny plants and ground cover is an example. Do not seal a small terrarium.

Integrating

Reading, social studies

Science Process Skills

Observing, inferring, predicting, communicating, using space-time relationships, formulating hypotheses, identifying and controlling variables, experimenting, researching

What Do Plants Need in Order to Grow?

Materials Needed

- One four-ounce paper cup for each child
- Potting soil
- Lima bean seeds
- Water

Procedure

1. Add potting soil until the paper cup is half full.
2. Plant a bean seed in the potting soil approximately one cm (1/4 in. to 1/2 in.) deep. Be sure to cover the seed.
3. Keep the potting soil moist and warm. Do not over-water.
4. Observe for several days.
5. What happened? What can you say about this?

For Problem Solvers

Plant different types of seeds and keep track of how many days it takes for each seed to germinate (begin to sprout). Figure out a way to test their needs for water, warm temperature, and which type of soil each plant seems to grow best in. Keep that information for use later on—it will always be useful to you, especially when you grow a garden.

Try to find some seeds that have been around for a year or more. Plant several of these seeds, along with several fresh seeds of the same variety. Plant them at the same time, use separate containers, plant the same number of new seeds as old seeds, and mark the containers clearly to be sure you remember which seeds are in each container. Is the germination rate (number of seeds that sprout compared with the total number of seeds) as good for the old seeds as it is for the new seeds?

Do some research and find out how old seeds can be and still germinate. At the time that those seeds were new, what was happening in the world that is remembered in the history books? Here's another chance for some exciting research.

Teacher Information

Seeds kept moist at room temperature should begin to grow within three to five days. In about a week, green sprouts will appear above the potting soil. Until green plants appear, it is not necessary to keep the cups in sunlight.

In place of bean seeds, the children may want to try corn, peas, raw peanuts, wild bird seed, radish, geranium, or other seeds.

Seeds can be dormant for different periods of time and then begin to germinate and grow when conditions are right. Some can be kept only a few weeks, while others may germinate after fifty years or more. Under favorable conditions, scientists have been able to cause lotus seeds that were thought to be thousands of years old to germinate.

Integrating

Math, reading, social studies

Science Process Skills

Observing, inferring, classifying, measuring, communicating, using space-time relationships, formulating hypotheses, identifying and controlling variables, experimenting, researching

How Does Water Travel in a Plant?

(Take home and do with family and friends.)

Materials Needed

- Celery stalk
- Pint jar
- Water
- Red or blue food coloring
- Copies of the "Science Investigation Journaling Notes" for this activity for all students

Procedure

1. As you complete this activity, you will keep record of what you do, just as scientists do. Obtain a copy of the form "Science Investigation Journaling Notes" from your teacher and write the information that is called for, including your name and the date.

2. For this activity, you will find out how water travels in a plant. For item 1, the question is provided for you on the form.

3. Item 2 asks for what you already know about the topic. If you have some ideas about water traveling in a plant, write your ideas.

4. For item 3, write about how you think water travels through a plant, and that will be your hypothesis.

5. Now continue with the following instructions. Complete your Journaling Notes as you go. Steps 6 through 10 below will help you with the information you need to write on the form for items 4 and 5.

6. Fill a pint jar with water.

7. Place a stalk of celery, leaves up, in the jar of water.

8. With the bottom of the celery stalk under water, cut off one centimeter of the stalk.

9. Add four to six drops of food coloring to the water.

10. Observe for several days.

11. What happened? Discuss your observations with the group. (This is item 6 on the form.)

12. For item 7 on the form, think about your hypothesis (item 3) and write what you have learned about how water travels in a plant.

For Problem Solvers

Does colored water flow up the stem and into the flowers of all plants? Design an experiment and find out.

Does the stem have to be cut under the water? Try cutting one and leaving it exposed to the air for a few minutes, another one for an hour, and another for a day, and compare the water flow up the stem. Does it make any difference whether or not the cut stem is exposed to the air? Will you use the same type of plant for all of these experiments? Why?

Split the stem of a carnation and place the two parts of the stem in water of two different colors. Predict what will happen. Draw and color what you think the flower will look like after two days. Compare the flower with your drawing two days later. Discuss the results with your group.

Teacher Information

This activity will work best if the stem is cut under the water and not exposed to the air. In a few days the food coloring will travel up the celery stalk and color the celery leaves.

Note: This can also be done with a white carnation. One color can be used, or the stem can be split carefully and placed in two colors, as shown below.

Integrating

Math, art

Science Process Skills

Observing, inferring, classifying, predicting, communicating, using space-time relationships, formulating hypotheses, identifying and controlling variables, experimenting

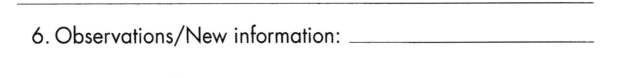

Science Investigation

Journaling Notes for Activity 4.11

1. Question: *How does water travel in a plant?*

2. What we already know: _____

_____

3. Hypothesis: _____

_____

4. Materials needed: _____

_____

5. Procedure: _____

_____

_____

_____

_____

6. Observations/New information: _____

_____

_____

7. Conclusion: _____

_____

How Do Plants Respond to Light?

(Teacher-supervised activity)

Materials Needed

- Utility knife
- Water
- Large shoe box
- Heavy cardboard
- Masking tape
- Small plant such as wandering Jew (genus Zebrina)
- Copies of the "Science Investigation Journaling Notes" for this activity for all students

Procedure

1. As you complete this activity, you will keep a record of what you do, just as scientists do. Obtain a copy of the form "Science Investigation Journaling Notes" from your teacher and write the information that is called for, including your name and the date.

2. For this activity, you will learn about how plants react to light. For item 1, the question is provided for you on the form.

3. Item 2 asks for what you already know about the topic. If you have some ideas about the way plants react to light, write your ideas.

4. For item 3, write a statement about how you expect plants to react to light, based on what you know. This will be your hypothesis.

5. Now continue with the following instructions. Complete your Journaling Notes as you go. Steps 6 through 11 below will help you with the information you need to write on the form for items 4 and 5.

6. Cut a hole in one end of the shoe box 6 cm high (2½ in.) and 2 cm (3/4 in.) wide.

7. Use the end of the box as a pattern to cut four dividers (pieces of cardboard) as tall as the box but 2 cm (3/4 in. to 1 in.) shorter than its width.

Plants and Seeds

179

8. Tape the cardboard dividers upright along the inside of the box, alternating from side to side. Be sure the first divider is attached to the same side as the slot you cut in the box.

9. Put your small plant inside the box, at the end opposite the slot. A box arranged this way is called a maze.

10. Put the lid on the box and turn the opening toward bright sunlight. Every three or four days, remove the lid long enough to water your plant and observe its condition.

11. Observe your plant for several weeks. What is happening? Can you think of reasons why?

12. What happened? Discuss your observations with the group. (This is item 6 on the form.)

13. For item 7 on the form, consider your hypothesis (item 3). Was it accurate? Write what you have learned about how plants react to light.

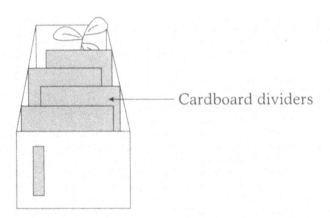
Cardboard dividers

For Problem Solvers

Time the progress of the plant, to determine how long it takes to grow to the opening at the other end of the box. Then do it again with the same type of plant to see whether they are somewhat consistent. Try a different type of plant, and compare your results. How about a third type of plant? Make a graph that will show the time required for each plant to complete the growth through the box. Does the reduced light seem to affect all types of plants the same?

Hands-On Life Science Activities

Compare the physical appearance of the different types of plants. Does the reduced light seem to have affected all types of plants the same?

Learn as much as you can about phototropism. What is it? What does this activity have to do with it?

Where do you think the light-sensing mechanism on a plant is? Can you design an experiment to find out? Try it. Share your ideas with others who are interested in this experiment.

Teacher Information

This activity is designed to help children discover that green plants need sunlight and that some will travel to find it. The plant will grow around the dividers toward the light source. The attraction of plants to light is called phototropism. A sprouting potato may be substituted for the wandering Jew and will not need water.

If you can locate a field of sunflowers near your school, visit it several times on a sunny day. The children should discover that most sunflowers turn their flowers toward the sun and will follow it during the day. (There are usually some that hear Thoreau's "different drummer" and don't conform.)

Integrating

Math, reading

Science Process Skills

Observing, inferring, predicting, communicating, using space-time relationships, formulating hypotheses, identifying and controlling variables, experimenting, researching

Science Investigation

Journaling Notes for Activity 4.12

1. Question: *How do plants respond to light?*

2. What we already know: _____

_____

3. Hypothesis: _____

_____

4. Materials needed: _____

_____

5. Procedure: _____

_____

_____

_____

_____

6. Observations/New information: _____

_____

_____

7. Conclusion: _____

_____

How Do Plants Respond to Gravity?

(Teacher-supervised activity)

Materials Needed

- Clear plastic bottle, half-liter (1 pint) or larger, with large lid (This will be your planter.)
- Water
- Potting soil or peat moss
- Tomato seeds (or seeds from another fairly fast-growing plant)
- Tray or plate (to catch the drain water from the plant)
- Paper towels
- Copies of the "Science Investigation Journaling Notes" for this activity for all students
- Drawing paper
- Crayons

Procedure

1. As you complete this activity, you will keep a record of what you do, just as scientists do. Obtain a copy of the form "Science Investigation Journaling Notes" from your teacher and write the information that is called for, including your name and the date.

2. For this activity, you will learn about how plants react to gravity. For item 1, the question is provided for you on the form.

3. Item 2 asks for what you already know about the topic. If you have some ideas about how plants react to gravity, write your ideas.

4. For item 3, write a statement about how plants react to gravity, according to what you know now. This will be your hypothesis.

5. Now continue with the following instructions. Complete your Journaling Notes as you go. The following steps 6 through 17 will help you with the information you need to write on the form for items 4 and 5.

6. Cut three holes (about the size of a quarter) in the side of the bottle. One of the holes should be centered between the ends of the bottle, with one on each side of the first hole, about halfway to the end of the bottle (see Figure 4.13–1). The center hole is for planting the seeds; the others are access holes for water and fertilizer. The holes will also allow air to circulate through the planter.

7. Along the opposite side of the bottle, cut two smaller holes. These are drain holes, and they will be opposite the access holes. The bottle is now your planter.

8. Fill the planter with potting soil, as shown in Figure 4.13–2.

9. Plant three or four seeds in the large center hole.

10. Place the planter on the tray. Add a small amount of water through the center hole.

11. Make two small wads of wet paper towels and place them on the tray with one on each side of the bottle. Press the wads under the bottle so the bottle will not roll.

Figure 4.13-1. Planter for Geotropism

Hands-On Life Science Activities

Figure 4.13-2. Planter Filled with Soil

12. Now be patient for a few days. After the seeds have germinated and grown an inch or two in height, remove all but one of them, keeping the healthiest one.

13. Make a drawing of your plant, including the planter.

14. When your plant has grown to about 7 or 8 cm (3 inches) in height, first thing in the morning rotate the planter 90 degrees (so the plant extends to the side from the planter), and support the planter with the wads of paper towel.

15. Make a new drawing of the plant, including the planter.

16. Throughout the day, examine the plant every hour or so if you can. Any time you observe changes, make a new drawing and write journal notes describing the changes. Pay close attention to the roots, as well as to the rest of the plant.

17. After two days, turn the planter right-side-up again, and continue your journal entries. Write your prediction of any changes you think might occur in the plant.

18. Write about your observations—what the plant did and why you think it happened. (This is item 6 on the form.)

19. Discuss your observations with your group and with your teacher.

20. For item 7 on the form, think about your hypothesis (item 3) and write your explanation of how the plants reacted to gravity.

For Problem Solvers

Look up the word *geotropism* in the encyclopedia. What is it? What does this activity have to do with it?

Try the same activity with a different type of plant and compare results. How about a third type of plant? Make a graph that will show the time required for each plant to change its course (direction of growth). Do you think all plants would react the same way? Why do you think they do that?

Teacher Information

Caution: For safety reasons, the cutting of the holes in the bottle must be done by the teacher or another adult.

Tropisms are responses to external stimuli. Just as plants typically respond to light (phototropism), they also respond to gravity. This is called *geotropism* or *gravitropism*. The tendency of plant stems to grow against the pull of gravity is called negative geotropism, and the tendency of roots to grow with the pull of gravity is called positive geotropism. In this activity, students will experience the fascinating phenomenon of geotropism. Scientists think the force of gravity is sensed in special cells of a plant.

Integrating

Math, reading

Science Process Skills

Observing, inferring, predicting, communicating, using space-time relationships, formulating hypotheses, identifying and controlling variables, experimenting, researching

Science Investigation

Journaling Notes for Activity 4.13

1. Question: *How do plants respond to gravity?*

2. What we already know: _____

_____

3. Hypothesis: _____

_____

4. Materials needed: _____

_____

5. Procedure: _____

_____

_____

_____

_____

_____

6. Observations/New information: _____

_____

_____

7. Conclusion: _____

_____

Plants and Seeds   **187**

How Can We Make a Visual Record of Plant Growth?

Materials Needed

- A newly started plant
- Chart paper
- Colored construction paper
- Scissors
- Rulers
- Tape or glue

Procedure

1. Write "Days of Measured Growth" at the bottom of the chart paper.

2. Write "Height in Centimeters" (or "Inches" if you prefer) up the left side of the chart paper.

3. Measure the height of your plant, from the soil to the tip of the plant.

4. Cut a narrow strip of colored construction paper the same length as the plant's height.

5. Tape or glue the strip of colored paper to the chart paper, positioned vertically near the lower left (see Figure 4.14–1).

6. Write "1" on the chart paper below the strip of paper, indicating that this strip shows how tall the plant was on the first day it was measured.

7. Measure the height of the plant every other day. For each measure, cut another strip of paper the appropriate length (height of the plant), mount the paper on the chart, and write the number of the day at the bottom, counting days from the day of the first measurement.

8. Does your plant grow faster as it gets older? Does it slow down? Do you notice a change when you forget to water it?

9. Discuss the growth pattern of your plant with your group. Compare the growth pattern with that of other plants included in this study.

188

For Problem Solvers

Set up an experiment to determine the effect of light on plant growth. This is a good time to invite one or more others to work with you, if you want to do that. After you write up your plan, discuss it with your teacher. Be sure you use a control.

Use the technique you learned in this activity to track the growth of each plant. Identify at the top of the chart the experiment (such as "Effect of Light on Plant Growth") and which plant(s) is being recorded on this chart.

Figure 4.14 -1. Plant Growth Chart

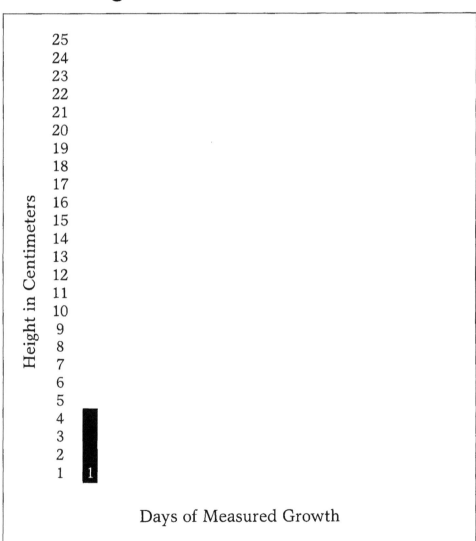

Teacher Information

In this activity, students will use a vertical bar graph to keep a record of the growth of one or more plants. This skill will be useful in future work with plants and in many other applications.

Your problem solvers who wish to extend their study of plants can use this method of charting the growth of plants as they investigate the effect of light on plant growth. You might suggest that they also consider investigating the effect of varying moisture conditions, amounts and types of fertilizer, soil types, age of seed, or any other variable related to plant growth.

Integrating

Math, art

Science Process Skills

Observing, inferring, measuring, predicting, communicating, comparing and contrasting, using space-time relationships, formulating hypotheses, identifying and controlling variables, experimenting

What Are the Parts of Some Common Plants?

Materials Needed

- Large paper (or plastic) bags
- Spoons for digging
- White paper
- Pictures of plants
- Drawing paper
- Crayons

Procedure

1. Take a field trip to a vacant lot near your home or school. Choose several plants and dig them up. Make sure you get most of the root system for each.
2. Put your plants in a bag and bring them back to school. Choose one and spread it out on a piece of white paper.
3. Look at the picture of a plant below and find the same parts on your plant.

4. Make a picture of your own plant and label all the parts.
5. Compare your picture with the one above. Are any parts missing? If so, can you think of why?

Teacher Information

Depending on the season and their stage of maturity, many of the plants may not have all the parts shown.

Remind your students to stay away from poison ivy, poison oak, and so on. ("Leaves of three, let it be.") Also be sure that the students are not picking plants from a restricted area.

Integrating

Math, language arts, art

Science Process Skills

Observing, inferring, communicating

Why Are Leaves Important?

Materials Needed

- Two identical plants, both healthy and growing
- Copies of the "Science Investigation Journaling Notes" for this activity for all students
- Drawing paper
- Crayons
- Ruler

Procedure

1. As you complete this activity, you will keep record of what you do, just as scientists do. Obtain a copy of the form "Science Investigation Journaling Notes" from your teacher and write the information that is called for, including your name and the date.

2. For this activity, you will learn why leaves are important. For item 1, the question is provided for you on the form.

3. Item 2 asks what you already know about the topic. If you have some ideas about why leaves are important, write your ideas.

4. For item 3, you need to think about what you already know about the importance of leaves. Write what you know about the topic, and that will be your hypothesis.

5. Now continue with the following instructions. Complete your Journaling Notes as you go. Steps 6 through 12 below will help you with the information you need to write for items 4 and 5.

6. Observe the two plants very carefully, noting ways they are alike and ways they are different.

7. Draw both plants. Be sure that each of your drawings looks like the plant it is intended to be, and not like the other one.

8. Remove all of the leaves from one of the plants.

9. For several days, treat both plants alike, with the same amount of water (measure the water), the same lighting, and so forth. Whatever you do to one, do the same to the other.

10. Observe your plants each day. Draw them and describe what they look like, especially noting any changes that occur as the days go by. Measure and record the height of the two plants.

Plants and Seeds

193

11. From what you observe, do you think leaves are important to the plant? If so, what difference do they seem to make?

12. Remove both plants from the soil and examine the roots. Compare the roots. Do they look the same? Does one root structure look healthier than the other? Measure and compare the length of the roots.

13. Share your findings with your teacher and with your class. Show them both plants, and discuss your evidence of why plants need leaves. This is item 6 of your Journaling Notes.

14. For item 7, think about your hypothesis (item 3) and write what you have learned about why plants need leaves.

For Problem Solvers

Try the same experiment with another type of plant, and see whether you get the same results. Do some research about leaves and see what you can learn about what they do.

Do this as a science investigation. Obtain a blank copy of the "Science Investigation Journaling Notes" for this activity. Write your name, the date, and your question at the top. Plan your investigation through step 5 (Procedure) and get it approved by your teacher. Complete the Journaling Notes as you perform your investigation. Share your project with your group, and submit your Journaling Notes to your teacher if requested.

Share your information with your group.

Teacher Information

After a few days, the leafless plant will likely appear to be dead. Differences should be evident even in the roots. Students should easily conclude that leaves somehow help the stem and roots to stay alive. Roots supply the plant with water, but even the roots are fed by the leaves. With the leaves removed, even the roots lose their ability to function.

Integrating

Math, language arts

Science Process Skills

Observing, measuring, communicating, comparing and contrasting, researching

Hands-On Life Science Activities

Science Investigation

Journaling Notes for Activity 4.16

1. Question: *Why are leaves important?*

2. What we already know: _____

_____

3. Hypothesis: _____

_____

4. Materials needed: _____

_____

5. Procedure: _____

_____

_____

_____

_____

6. Observations/New information: _____

_____

_____

7. Conclusion: _____

_____

How Are Leaves Alike and How Are They Different?

Materials Needed

- Variety of plants—perhaps some you gather on a nearby field trip
- Pictures of plants similar to your plants
- Paper towels
- Books
- Ruler

Procedure

1. Spread your plants out flat on your desk.
2. Study them carefully and compare their roots, stems, and leaves.
3. In what ways are they alike? In what ways are they different? Can you think of reasons why?
4. Measure the length of the longest leaf and the shortest leaf on each plant. How long is the longest and how short is the shortest? How much difference is there between their lengths? Is the longest leaf also the widest one?
5. Choose some of your most interesting leaves and spread them out on a piece of paper towel. Put another paper towel on top of them, then place a flat, heavy object, such as one or more books, on top. This is called pressing. Wait several days and remove the weight. If you would care to preserve your leaves, ask your teacher for help.
6. Leaves are very important to plants and to many other forms of life on earth. Do you know why? Discuss your ideas with others.

For Problem Solvers

Do some research about leaves. Your encyclopedia will have some very interesting information. Also check the Internet. See what you can find out about the importance of leaves to the plant. Why are they important to animals? Do you ever eat leaves? What are some of the largest and smallest leaves that you can find information about? Why do many leaves

change colors in the autumn? How many different shapes of leaves can you find? Classify your leaves by putting them into groups that seem logical to you. How many different ways can you find that people use leaves?

Share your information with your group.

Teacher Information

The shape, color, and texture of leaves can be an interesting study. Pressing, preserving, and displaying leaves in creative ways may add aesthetic dimensions to the activity. An excellent way to preserve leaves is to laminate them. They may also be preserved by pressing them with a warm iron between sheets of waxed paper. Leaves are important to plants because they manufacture food through their "chlorophyll factories." Plants also "breathe" through their leaves and give off moisture (transpiration). In the daytime (during photosynthesis) they give off oxygen. In darkness their chlorophyll factories shut down. For additional information about leaves, see your encyclopedia.

Integrating

Math, social studies, art

Science Process Skills

Observing, classifying, measuring, communicating, researching

How Can You Preserve the Leaves You Collect?

(Take home and do with family and friends.)

Materials Needed

- Large pieces of poster paper or card stock
- Leaves to preserve
- Wide transparent tape
- Ruler

Procedure

1. Lay a leaf on the card stock.
2. Place a strip of tape over the leaf full length, to completely seal it to the paper.
3. Place more tape over the leaf until the leaf is completely covered.
4. Get together with others who are preserving leaves. Compare your leaves with theirs and see how many different kinds you have altogether.
5. Find the largest and smallest leaves. Measure their lengths and widths, and describe how they compare with each other.
6. How many basic shapes can you find among the leaves? Do they have smooth edges, or are they jagged? Put your leaves into groups according to their shape.

For Problem Solvers

Small flowering plants can also be preserved in this way. Collect several small plants and preserve them by mounting them to card stock with wide transparent tape. Press the plants flat on paper before mounting them, but you don't have to wait until they dry thoroughly.

If you want to be able to remember what type of plant each one in the collection is, find this information before you mount the plants to the card stock and write the names at the bottom of the cards before mounting the plants. A permanent marker would do a nice job for preserving the names.

Teacher Information

This type of mounting will give the plants a fair degree of permanence, without equipment or very much expense. The plants will dry slowly through the back of the card stock, but they will not be crumbly when mounted.

Integrating

Math, reading

Science Process Skills

Observing, inferring, predicting, communicating, using space-time relationships, formulating hypotheses, identifying and controlling variables, experimenting, researching

How Can You Collect Bark Without Damaging the Tree?

Materials Needed

- Plaster of Paris and water
- Clay
- Cardboard
- Straight pins
- Newsprint or plastic table covers
- Vaseline®

Procedure

1. Form a piece of clay into a rectangular shape, at least 10 cm by 10 cm (4 in. by 4 in.) and about 1 cm (1/2 in.) thick.
2. Cover one side of the clay with a thin film of Vaseline.
3. Press the clay onto the bark of a tree (lubricated side next to the bark), forming it to the shape of the bark.
4. Carefully remove the clay from the tree, preserving the shape of the clay the best you can.
5. Cover a table with newsprint or plastic and place the clay on the table.
6. Cut the ends of the clay off straight.
7. Fold the clay to a slight boat-shape and pin a piece of cardboard to each end by pushing straight pins through the card and into the clay (see Figure 4.19–1). The cardboard pieces will serve as end supports.

Figure 4.19-1. Clay Mold with One End Support in Place

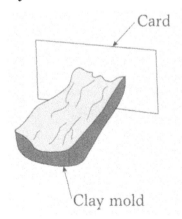

Card

Clay mold

8. The clay, along with its end supports, is now a mold for your plaster of Paris.

9. Mix a small amount of plaster of Paris with water to the consistency of pancake batter and pour it into the mold.

10. Allow the plaster time to cure, and then carefully remove the clay from the plaster.

11. Compare your tree-bark cast with those of others who are doing this activity. Discuss the similarities and differences in their shapes.

12. Paint your bark the color of the tree.

For Problem Solvers

You might want to expand this activity and make a collection of castings of different types of bark. You should be able to use the same clay multiple times.

You can make castings of leaves by simply pouring a shallow layer of plaster of Paris into a container and then laying a leaf on the surface. Press the leaf only slightly to smooth it out and to be sure it will leave its shape in the plaster. Avoid letting plaster get on the top of the leaf.

Make matched sets of bark and leaves.

Teacher Information

Students will enjoy making permanent casts of bark. These can be painted if desired. They make fine paperweights and shelf pieces. Those who choose to continue with the problem solvers' challenge will also enjoy collecting pairs of bark-and-leaf casts.

Integrating

Art

Science Process Skills

Observing, communicating

How Do Roots Grow and Develop?

Materials Needed

- Several young plants that are sprouting in potting soil (same variety)
- Hand lenses
- Copies of the chart for this activity for each student

Procedure

1. Pull up one sprouting plant from the potting soil and examine the roots with a hand lens. Make a drawing of the plant, including its roots, using the chart provided.
2. Pull up a different plant every other day for a week and examine its roots. Make a drawing of the plant, including roots, each time. How tall is the plant? How long are the roots? Measure both the roots and the stem, and record them on the graph.
3. Discuss the progress of the root system of these plants. What changes do you see?

For Problem Solvers

Continue your study of root structures by comparing root systems of other types of plants. Do they all have the same basic parts? Measure their growth on a weekly (or even daily) basis. How do the root structures of the different varieties of plants compare? Which ones grow faster? More slowly? Which ones have the largest and most massive root structures? Which ones do you think are better designed to support a large, heavy plant in a windstorm?

Teacher Information

The plants will likely be more advanced each day, and their root systems will be more highly developed. Small hair-like roots will be growing through the soil. This activity could be continued for several weeks or could lead to a study of other plants and their root systems—especially for your problem solvers who are motivated to continue their study.

Integrating

Math, art

Science Process Skills

Observing, inferring, measuring, communicating, comparing and contrasting, using space-time relationships

Hands-On Life Science Activities

Chart for Activity 4.20

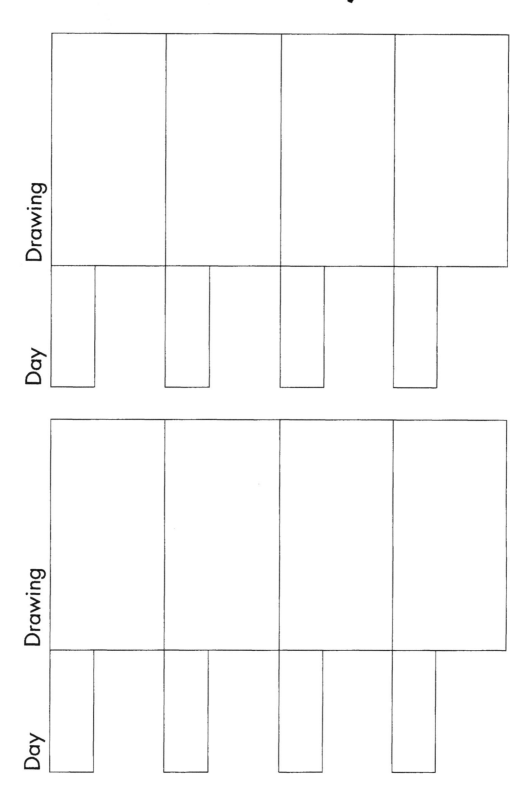

Plants and Seeds

What Are the Parts of a Flower?

Materials Needed

- Large flowers
- Wide transparent tape
- Hand lenses
- White paper
- Roll of plastic wrap

Procedure

1. Put your flower on a sheet of white paper and examine it carefully.
2. Compare your flower with the one in the picture below. Can you find the same parts? You may need a hand lens to help you.
3. Carefully take your flower apart. First find the petals, then the sepals, and then the pistil. Next find the stamens and the anther.
4. Use transparent tape to tape the parts to your sheet of white paper.
5. Label the parts, cover your paper with plastic wrap, and hang it on a wall of your classroom.

Figure 4.21-1.

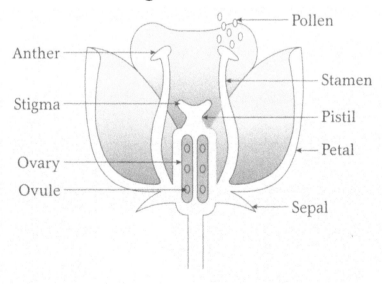

Hands-On Life Science Activities

For Problem Solvers

When you are finished with your flower, try to think of a way to use the parts of it to make a collage or other kind of art project. Perhaps you can share with others, in order to have a greater variety of colors and parts.

Do some research and find out why each part of a flower is important. What is the purpose of the anther, the stamen, the ovary, and each of the other parts? Which parts are responsible for making new flowers? Where do the seeds grow? What has to happen in order for seeds to form? You will find some fascinating information. Share what you learn with your group, and with others.

How many petals does your flower have? Do all flowers have the same number of petals? Do all flowers of this type have the same number?

See how many different ways you can find that people use flowers. Make a list of these and compare your list with the lists of others who do the same activity.

Teacher Information

Typical flowers have four sets of parts: sepals, petals, stamens, and the pistil, which includes the ovary and the stigma. Pollen comes from the top of the stamens, which are supported by thin filaments. When the ovary ripens, the top of the pistil, called the stigma, will become sticky and collect pollen spread in the air or by insects. When a flower has all four parts, it is said to be complete. Flowers lacking any of the four parts are generally classified as incomplete flowers.

This is an excellent individual or small-group activity. Extension and enrichment activities could include collecting flowers and pictures for bulletin boards and studying flower arranging. This activity could motivate children to learn the purpose and function of flowers in nature. Flowers should be appreciated for their beauty. Careful observation and first-hand experience will increase children's awareness of plants and enhance appreciation of their beauty.

Integrating

Math, reading, art

Science Process Skills

Observing, inferring, classifying, measuring, communicating, researching

How Can You Make a "Dandy" Tasting Salad?

(Teacher-supervised activity)

Materials Needed

- Young dandelion leaves, gathered in early spring before they blossom
- Salt water
- Salt
- Pepper
- Chives
- Lettuce and celery leaves
- Salad dressing
- Margarine
- Eating utensils and plates
- Plastic bags
- Heat source
- Saucepan

Procedure

1. Gather a plastic bag full of young dandelion leaves to bring to class.
2. Pull the young plants up, being careful to get as much of the root as possible.
3. Pull the leaves from the root. Rinse the leaves and boil them in salt water for about 10 minutes. Season the cooked leaves with salt and pepper and a pat of margarine. Eat your special vegetable.
4. The crowns (tops) of the roots may also be prepared in the same way to provide another variety of vegetable.
5. Mix young dandelion leaves with lettuce and celery leaves at about the ratio of one dandelion leaf to two lettuce and celery leaves. Add chives and mix thoroughly.
6. Use salad dressing to taste.
7. You now have a new, special, inexpensive salad to try at home.

Hands-On Life Science Activities

For Problem Solvers

Many of the early settlers had to rely on native plants for much of their food. Find out what edible plants grow wild in your area—plants that you don't normally eat. Try eating one or more of these, but be sure it is safe before eating it.

Also try to find out where potatoes, corn, and other common food crops began. How did people first learn about them as a food source? Have these plants been altered over the years to make them more desirable? How does that happen?

Teacher Information

Dandelions must be picked while they are very young to be eaten. Boiling in salt water will help remove the bitter taste. *Caution:* Be sure the leaves are gathered in areas that have not been sprayed. Even young dandelion leaves may be somewhat bitter. In using them in fresh salad, be sure to use plenty of lettuce. This may be an appropriate time to remind children not to eat unknown leaves or other parts of plants, such as berries or flowers. Dandelion leaves are a source of vitamins A and C. Be acquainted with the regulations regarding the serving of food at your school. It may be necessary for you to obtain a food-handlers permit in order to do this activity in your classroom. Check with your school's principal.

Integrating

Social studies

Science Process Skills

Observing, classifying, communicating, using space-time relationships, formulating hypotheses, researching

What Parts of Plants Do You Like to Eat?

(Take home and do with family and friends.)

Materials Needed

- Assorted fresh fruits and vegetables cut in pieces
- Nuts
- Raisins
- Grains
- Soybeans
- All-grain breakfast cereals
- Margarine
- Bread or rolls
- Various juices in small paper cups
- Copy of the Classification Chart for this activity for each student
- Pencils

Procedure

1. Select ten pieces of plant parts and juices from the table and take them back to your desk.
2. Try to organize and classify the foods using the "Fruit and Vegetable Classification Chart."
3. How many do you have in each group?

For Problem Solvers

Make a list of foods that you think are fruits and another list of foods you think are vegetables. Some of the foods that we commonly think of as vegetables are actually fruits. After writing your lists, do some research and find out what the differences really are between fruits and vegetables. Make corrections in your list and put a star beside those that surprised you. Compare your list with the lists of others who did this activity.

Teacher Information

This activity should help children understand the value of plant parts as a food source. This can be an opportunity to help children become acquainted with a wide variety of food plants. (Save as many plants as possible for the next activity.) Children can work individually or in small groups to prepare a basic list and then come together to develop a master list and discuss all plant foods in the room.

There are a number of plants that most people think of as vegetables that are technically fruits. Some examples of these are peas, tomatoes, and beans. If it's formed from a seed, it's a fruit.

Integrating

Math, reading, language arts

Science Process Skills

Observing, inferring, classifying, predicting, communicating, researching

Fruit and Vegetable Classification Chart

Common Name of Plant	Fruit or Vegetable?	Part of the Plant We Eat	Cooked, Raw, or Both?	My Favorite

Can We Make a Whole Meal with Just Plants?

(Teacher-supervised activity)

Materials Needed

- Assorted fresh fruits and vegetables
- Nuts
- Juices
- Salad greens
- Sprouts
- Bread or rolls
- Margarine
- Information and classification lists developed in previous activities
- Paper plates
- Cooking utensils
- Bowls
- Plastic knives, forks, spoons
- Seasoning
- Salt
- Pepper
- Napkins
- Stove or hot plate

Procedure

1. Use the list of plant foods from Activity 4.23 to plan a luncheon meal.
2. Make a menu describing the items you will prepare and serve. Try to use as many adjectives as you can to make everyone want to try all the foods you prepare. Be sure you include in your menu the amount of each plant you are using, not just the item.
3. Have your teacher help cut and cook your meal.
4. Invite special people to have lunch with you. Don't forget the school cook and cafeteria workers.

For Problem Solvers

Learn to bake bread or prepare one or more other specific foods at home. Ask your teacher whether you may bring samples to class for the other students to try. Experiment with one or more of the ingredients to try to improve the dish or at least to find out what effect that particular ingredient has on the texture, taste, and so forth. Before you actually use the altered recipe, write the change you will make and the effect you expect it to have on the finished product.

Teacher Information

This activity, combined with the dandelion salad activity, can be an enjoyable culmination to this study. In addition to preparing and serving food, students may choose to share reports, pictures, songs, and other information acquired during the study. Planning and writing the menu, designing invitations, giving reports, sharing art work, singing songs, decorating the room with plants and flowers they have grown, and learning how to be good hosts and hostesses should be a planned part of this activity.

Note: You will need to plan well in advance to arrange for parents and aides to assist with the preparation and cooking. A prior activity on bread making could be developed (good place for a mother or father to be asked to help). Be acquainted with the regulations regarding the serving of food at your school. It may be necessary for you to obtain a food-handlers permit in order to do this activity in your classroom.

Integrating

Math, reading, language arts, social studies

Science Process Skills

Observing, inferring, measuring, predicting, communicating, formulating hypotheses, identifying and controlling variables, experimenting

How Can We Know What Kind of Tree It Is?

Materials Needed

- Trees
- Internet access
- Field manuals for tree identification
- Encyclopedias
- Digital camera (if available)

Procedure

1. Select a tree on or near your school grounds.
2. Examine its leaves. Leaves of evergreens are often needle-shaped. *Do not remove the leaves from the tree.* Instead, bring your book or portable computer to the tree for comparing characteristics of the leaves with pictures you find. If a digital camera is available, you could take a picture of the leaves with you instead of the leaf itself.
3. Compare the leaves of your tree with photographs of leaves you find in your books or on the Internet. Instead of simply trying to determine the name of your tree, try to find trees that have leaves with similar characteristics, such as size and shape.
4. Of all the trees you find pictured with similar leaf characteristics, which tree do you think is most like your tree?

For Problem Solvers

Following the same policy of respect for nature as we did with tree leaves, compare other parts or characteristics of your tree with similar parts and characteristics found in your information sources. These could include flowers, twigs, bark, or size and shape of the tree. Can you think of still other tree characteristics to compare?

Extend your investigations of tree characteristics to comparing and contrasting the parts of flowers, grasses, shrubs, and other plants. Make a journal of what you do and learn, including pictures that you draw, find, or take with a camera. Make notes of new plants you find that you did not know about before. Make a list of names and descriptions of plants that you have learned to identify and name through your research.

Teacher Information

It is important to teach children to live by the slogan "Take only pictures, leave only footprints" when out in nature. In some locations (for example, national forests and national parks) picking a flower, a leaf, or a twig from any plant is a serious violation of the law. In addition to being law-abiding citizens, we should develop habits of respect for nature and its products and beauties. Flowers are reproductive organs. When we pick a flower, it dies, and it is as though we picked all of the plants from all of the potential future generations of that particular flower. It is better to let the flower remain for others to enjoy. When we remove a leaf, we take away part of the food-producing capacity of the plant.

Today's electronic cameras provide immediate results and make it easy to take the flower, leaf, or twig to the sources of information (book or computer screen) to compare and contrast characteristics of the plant parts, and even to project the picture on a TV or large screen. Encourage students to identify characteristics that match those of similar parts of the plant shown in the book or on the Internet, rather than concentrating only on finding the exact name of the plant being observed.

Integrating

Math, physical education, reading, language arts, social studies, art

Science Process Skills

Observing, inferring, classifying, measuring, communicating, comparing and contrasting, researching

Hands-On Life Science Activities

If We Can't Climb It, How Can We Measure It?

Materials Needed

- Trees
- Partners
- Meter sticks or measuring tape
- Note paper and pencils
- A straight stick, about 50 cm (1.5 ft.) long

Procedure

1. Select a tree on or near your school grounds.
2. Estimate the height of the tree, in meters, and record your estimate.
3. Standing away from the tree, and holding the stick vertically at arm's length, sight across the top of the stick to the top of the tree. Your partner should stand beside the tree.
4. Keeping the upper end of the stick in line with the top of the tree, move your hand up or down the stick until you see the base of the tree in line with your thumb. You should now see the entire tree between your thumb and the end of the stick. (See Figure 4.26–1.)
5. Lay the stick down, adjacent to the ground, keeping your thumb in line with the base of the tree.
6. Your partner should now walk straight out from the tree. Tell your partner to stop when he or she is in line with the end of the stick.

Figure 4.26–1. Capturing a Tree's Height

7. At this point, it is as though you cut the tree down and your partner is now standing where the top of the tree would be if it were lying on the ground. (See Figure 4.26–2.)

8. Measure from the base of the tree to your partner and you should have a good estimate of the height of the tree.

9. Try the entire process at least one more time to be sure you followed the procedure correctly.

10. Compare your original estimate with the number you obtained with this procedure. How close was your estimate?

For Problem Solvers

Try using this technique of measuring height without the use of measurement tools (meter stick or measuring tape). First get with your partner and measure your pace (double steps) or your stride (single steps). You will need a tape or meter stick for this, but then you can set them aside and use your pace or your stride to estimate the height of the tree. Try this technique to measure heights of other tall objects as well, such as flagpoles, light poles, and buildings.

Hands-On Life Science Activities

Figure 4.26-2. "Laying the Tree on the Ground"

With your partner or group, try to devise other ways to measure the height of tall objects.

Teacher Information

Not only is this a fun activity; it can also be used to estimate the height of many tall objects, such as flagpoles, light poles, and buildings. In the process, skills of estimating and measuring are applied and reinforced in a meaningful, active, and fun way. If you involve your students in the problem-solver extension, nonstandard measures are used (pace and/or stride), providing additional learning and application of skills in measuring, estimating, and problem solving.

Integrating

Math, physical education

Science Process Skills

Observing, inferring, measuring, estimating, communicating

Is This a Plant?

Materials Needed

- Bread, jelly, orange, cheese, and other foods
- Hand lenses
- Plastic margarine containers and lids

Procedure

1. Choose four different foods and place each one in a different container. Put the lids on and place each container in a warm, dark place. (If you choose bread, be sure it is moist.)
2. In four or five days, remove the lid of each container and observe the contents.
3. What has happened to the food?

Teacher Information

With the most recently adopted classification system, mold is no longer classified as a plant. This activity will introduce mold in a controlled environment. Most children have seen mold, but only in the context of something that has "spoiled" or been ruined. The following activities will help children learn more about mold and how it is both harmful and helpful in their lives. The containers used in these activities should be clean and thoroughly rinsed. Soap residue may retard the growth of mold.

Most activities are excellent individual or small-group activities. Teacher demonstration and classroom discussion should come only after each child has had first-hand experience with the activities.

Integrating

Math, language arts

Science Process Skills

Observing, inferring, communicating, using space-time relationships, formulating hypotheses

What Is This Strange Growth?

Materials Needed

- Containers and foods used in Activity 4.27
- Hand lenses
- Drawing paper
- Markers

Procedure

1. Examine the contents of each of your containers.
2. Use a hand lens to study the growths on the food in each container.
3. Draw a picture of what you observe. Use as much detail as you can.
4. Touch your strange organism. Wash your hands after you touch it. Sniff it without getting too close. Do you notice an odor?
5. Under your picture, write some words to tell what you saw, felt, and smelled.
6. Be prepared to share your containers and pictures with the rest of the class.
7. Also be prepared with questions to ask your teacher.

Teacher Information

Your media center or school library may have children's books about mold. Children should be encouraged to use the books, but not before they have completed the activities. Elementary and junior high school books are excellent sources for teacher background information and pupil reference for older children. It is recommended that reports be encouraged but not required.

Caution: After children touch the mold, remind them to wash their hands thoroughly before touching anything else, especially their eyes. Children with bronchial problems should be cautioned not to even get close to the mold or sniff it. This might be an opportunity to discuss the dangers of tasting, smelling, or touching unfamiliar materials.

Integrating

Language arts, art

Science Process Skills

Observing, inferring, communicating, formulating hypotheses, researching

Hands-On Life Science Activities

What Does Your Strange Organism Grow On?

Materials Needed

- Miscellaneous living (or once-living) and nonliving things, such as cut-up fruit, melons, potato, cheese, bread, wool, nails, magnets, rocks, and wood
- Plastic margarine containers and lids

Procedure

1. Choose five different items from the table.
2. Put each item in a different plastic container with the top sealed.
3. On which items do you think the strange plants will grow? On which do you think they will not grow? Be prepared to explain your reasons.
4. Place your containers in a warm, dark place.
5. After five or six days, open your containers and observe the results.
6. Compare your observations with the ideas you had about which would and which would not grow. Were your ideas correct? Can you think of reasons why?

For Problem Solvers

Select one material, such as bread, and repeat the activity, changing one variable. For example, place dry bread in a warm, dark place and compare it with moist bread placed for the same length of time in the same place. Do you think dry bread will support the growth of mold as well as moist bread? You might also try a freezer, which provides a cold and dark environment.

What other variables will you try with this experiment? Remember to change only one variable at a time.

Share your findings with your group and compare what you learned with what was learned by others who did this activity.

Plants and Seeds

221

Teacher Information

This activity is designed to help students see relationships, to reason, and to hypothesize. It has been used most successfully with students well into the concrete operational years, grades four through eight. The most obvious conclusion should be that mold grows on living (or once-living) things and not on inorganic material. Molds use the organic materials for food. Given enough time and proper conditions, mold will cause wood to rot, but probably not within the time allowed for this activity.

Integrating

Reading, math

Science Process Skills

Observing, inferring, classifying, measuring, predicting, communicating, using space-time relationships, formulating hypotheses, identifying and controlling variables, experimenting, researching

What Have We Learned About Mold?

(Total-group activity)

Materials Needed

- Containers of mold from previous activities
- Student drawings
- Books and pictures from media center, public library, and homes

Procedure

1. Participate in a class discussion about mold. Share and compare your findings from earlier activities with those of the other students.
2. Ask any questions you may have.
3. Use your pictures and containers to design a display and bulletin board about mold.

For Problem Solvers

Are molds harmful, or are they helpful? Think carefully before you answer that question. Discuss the question with your group. Consider what would be different without molds and other organisms that break down organic material.

Make a list of ways that molds can be helpful and ways they can be harmful.

Teacher Information

After studies about mold, consider preparing an informational audiotape to be used after a class discussion. The tape may help answer questions or reinforce concepts identified during the discussion. Try to help children discover the answers through sharing and studying reference sources. Avoid telling them more than is necessary. The following are concepts you may want to include on the audiotape or in your summary:

1. Most molds look somewhat like cotton. Many are not white, but they have a "cottony" texture.
2. Molds grow best in warm, damp, dark places. Mold is a problem in parts of the United States where the climate is humid and warm.

3. Mold often damages food, leather, clothing, and paper. Some molds cause diseases in people, plants, food crops, and animals.

4. Many molds are helpful. They cause wood, leaves, and other materials to rot, forming humus, which makes the soil rich. People use mold to make drugs, such as penicillin. Molds also produce carbon dioxide, which green plants use to make food. Mold is deliberately allowed to grow on Roquefort and certain other types of cheese to help ripen it.

5. Mold reproduces by releasing spores, which travel through the air or are carried by animals.

Integrating

Reading, language arts, social studies

Science Process Skills

Classifying, communicating

Can You Solve This Plants and Seeds Word Search?

Try to find the following Plants and Seeds terms in the grid below. They could appear in horizontal (left to right), vertical (up or down), or diagonal (upward or downward) position.

stigma	osmosis	transplant
plants	germinate	terrarium
soil	phototropism	leaf
respiration	stem	fruit
roots	stamen	pollen

```
P  L  A  N  T  S  Q  A  Z  R  W  S
Y  H  B  T  R  E  T  D  C  O  X  G
H  U  O  G  S  T  E  M  I  O  K  E
N  M  J  T  A  P  R  O  L  T  O  R
A  S  D  F  O  G  R  H  I  S  S  M
O  P  L  K  L  T  A  U  K  O  M  I
I  R  E  S  P  I  R  A  T  I  O  N
U  Y  A  T  O  F  I  O  G  L  S  A
Y  A  F  I  L  H  U  I  P  Y  I  T
T  W  S  G  L  U  M  O  U  I  S  E
S  T  A  M  E  N  J  K  L  P  S  F
R  T  R  A  N  S  P  L  A  N  T  M
```

Can You Create a New Plants and Seeds Word Search of Your Own?

Write your plants and seeds words in the grid below. Arrange them in the grid so they appear in horizontal (left to right), vertical (up or down), or diagonal (upward or downward) position. Fill in the blank boxes with other letters. Trade your Word Search with someone else who has created one of his or her own, and see whether you can solve the new puzzle.

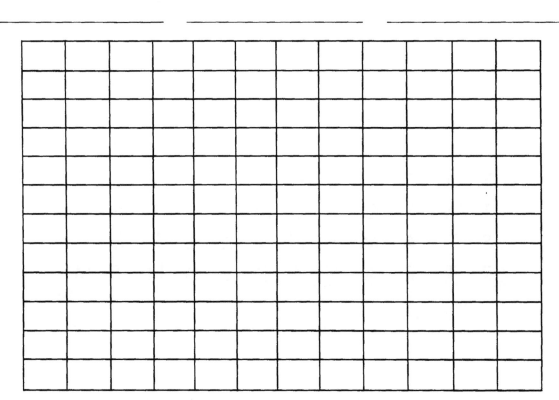

Answer Key for Plants and Seeds Word Search

```
P  L  A  N  T  S  Q  A  Z  R  W  S
Y  H  B  T  R  E  T  D  C  O  X  G
H  U  O  G  S  T  E  M  I  O  K  E
N  M  J  T  A  P  R  O  L  T  O  R
A  S  D  F  O  G  R  H  I  S  S  M
O  P  L  K  L  T  A  U  K  O  M  I
I  R  E  S  P  I  R  A  T  I  O  N
U  Y  A  T  O  F  I  O  G  L  S  A
Y  A  F  I  L  H  U  I  P  Y  I  T
T  W  S  G  L  U  M  O  U  I  S  E
S  T  A  M  E  N  J  K  L  P  S  F
R  T  R  A  N  S  P  L  A  N  T  M
```

Do You Recall?

Section Four: Plants and Seeds

1. If you know the type of plant a seed came from, can you predict what the plant will look like as it matures?

2. When you soak a lima bean seed, then split it open, what do you see inside?

3. Will seeds begin to sprout more quickly in the light than they will in darkness?

4. Name two ways that seeds travel.

5. Name one plant that you can grow without seeds.

6. What can you do with plants that become too large for their containers?

7. Explain why a large terrarium can be used for both plants and animals, but a small terrarium cannot.

Do You Recall? *(Cont'd.)*

8. What happens if you stand a stalk of celery in a glass of colored water and leave it for a few days?

9. What can you do to show that plants need light?

10. How do plants respond to gravity?

11. Name two of the main parts that many plants have.

12. In what ways are leaves alike or different from other leaves?

13. Describe one way to preserve leaves.

14. Name at least two parts of a flower.

Answer Key for Do You Recall?

Section Four: Plants and Seeds

Answer	Related Activities
1. Yes	4.1
2. Plant food and baby plant (embryo)	4.2
3. No. They do not need sunlight until they begin to grow leaves.	4.3
4. Wind, water, animals, etc.	4.4
5. Carrot, potato, sweet potato, onion, beet, philodendron	4.5, 4.6
6. Transplant them into larger containers.	4.7
7. Difficult to balance the supply of oxygen and carbon dioxide	4.9
8. The food coloring will travel up the stalk and color the leaves.	4.11
9. Answers will vary.	4.12
10. The stem grows away from the pull of gravity, and the roots grow toward the pull of gravity.	4.13
11. Stem, leaves, flowers, etc.	4.15
12. Size, shape, etc.	4.16, 4.17
13. Answers will vary.	4.18
14. Petals, sepals, stamens, pistil	4.21

Hands-On Life Science Activities

Body Systems

To the Teacher

This section provides opportunities for students to learn about themselves. Activities involve both the muscular and skeletal systems of the body. Students can discover and learn a great deal about their own body structure by studying the bones and muscles of animals. These parts are usually available from the local meat market. Hair, nails, skin, and lung capacity are also dealt with in the activities of this section.

Invite resource people into the classroom at appropriate times to enrich the experience. Along with the sections "The Five Senses" and "Health and Nutrition," the study of this section provides many excellent opportunities to explore the world of work with respect to the health services occupations and professions.

In a study of the body, the handicapped should be recognized as normal people for whom certain abilities are limited. There is such a broad range of ability among the nonhandicapped, and such a broad range among the handicapped, that it is sometimes difficult to distinguish between the two. It is hoped that in the study of this section physical differences will be recognized and treated as normal. We are all different. Being different is normal. It should be noted and stressed, however, that we are more alike than different.

We suggest that you scan all activities in the section before beginning to use it in the classroom, taking note of materials required. This will aid in making necessary advance preparations.

The following activities are designed as discovery activities that students can usually perform quite independently. Provide students (usually in small groups) with the materials listed and a copy of the activity from the beginning through the "Procedure." The section titled "Teacher Information" is not intended for student use, but rather to assist you with discussion following the hands-on activity, as students share their observations. Discussion of conceptual information prior to completing the hands-on activity can interfere with the discovery process.

Regarding the Early Grades

With verbal instructions and slight modifications, many of these activities can be used with kindergarten, first-grade, and second-grade students. Some of the activities were written specifically with the primary grades in mind. In others, procedural steps that go beyond the level of the child can simply be omitted and yet offer the child experiences that plant conceptual seeds for concepts that will germinate and grow later on.

Teachers of the early grades will probably choose to bypass many of the "For Problem Solvers" sections. That's okay. These sections are provided for those who are especially motivated and want to go beyond the investigation provided by the activity outlined. Use the outlined activities and enjoy worthwhile learning experiences together with your young students. Also consider, however, that many of the "For Problem Solvers" sections can be used appropriately with young children as group activities or as demonstrations. Giving students the advantage of an exposure to the experience can often lay groundwork for connections that will become more meaningful at a later time.

Correlation with National Standards

The following elements of the National Standards are reflected in the activities of this section.

K–4 Content Standard A: Science as Inquiry

As a result of activities in grades K–4, all students should develop

1. Abilities necessary to do scientific inquiry
2. Understanding about scientific inquiry

K–4 Content Standard C: Life Science

As a result of activities in grades K–4, all students should develop understanding of

1. The characteristics of organisms

5–8 Content Standard A: Science as Inquiry

As a result of activities in grades 5–8, all students should develop

1. Abilities necessary to do scientific inquiry
2. Understanding about scientific inquiry

5–8 Content Standard C: Life Science

As a result of activities in grades 5–8, all students should develop understanding of

1. Structures and function in living systems
2. Reproduction and heredity
3. Regulation and behavior

How Do Fingerprints Compare?

(Take home and do with family and friends.)

Materials Needed

- Ink stamp pad
- Paper
- Hand lens

Procedure

1. Have each participant place the tip of his or her right forefinger on the ink pad with a slight right-to-left rolling motion.
2. Immediately after applying ink to the finger, place it on the paper, using the same rolling motion.
3. Examine the fingerprints.
4. How are they alike?
5. How are they different?
6. Do you notice any patterns that are similar in some of the fingerprints?
7. Do you see any two fingerprints that are exactly alike?

For Problem Solvers

Here's another way of making fingerprints. Rub a pencil on a piece of paper, making a heavy smudge of graphite on the paper. Rub the tip of your finger on the graphite. Next, put a piece of clear plastic tape on the graphite-covered finger, then remove the tape and put it on a piece of white paper. The tape will preserve the fingerprint.

Using this method of fingerprinting, study patterns of fingerprints from one person to another and from finger to finger of the same person. Find patterns and draw them. Are they similar from finger to finger for the same person? How many patterns can you find?

Discuss your findings with your group. Why are fingerprints so valuable in police and detective work?

Hands-On Life Science Activities

Teacher Information

Your problem solvers will want to take the prints of all their fingers and study the similarities and differences. They will find that no two fingerprints are exactly alike, not even from two fingers of the same person.

Discuss with the group why fingerprints or footprints are used for identification in some important documents, such as birth records and police records.

Integrating

Math, social studies, art

Science Process Skills

Observing, inferring, classifying, measuring, predicting, communicating, comparing and contrasting, researching

How Big Is the Average Person Your Age?

Materials Needed

- Group of students the same age
- Pencils
- Butcher paper
- Metric measuring tape
- Masking tape

Procedure

1. Have a partner measure and record your height, your arm span, your hand span, and the length of your foot (shoes off).
2. Measure your partner in the same way.
3. Compare your measurements with those of your partner.
4. Compare your arm span with your height.
5. Figure the average height, arm span, hand span, and foot length in your class.
6. Fasten a piece of butcher paper to the wall and mark the average height for your class. Draw on it a hand of average size and a foot of average size.
7. Fasten two more pieces of butcher paper to the wall and record the tallest height and the shortest height, and the longest and shortest of the other measurements. Do not write names on these.
8. Examine and compare the various measurements of the class. Who seems to be closest to average in every measurement? Where do you fit in with each of the measurements taken?

For Problem Solvers

After the average measurements have been computed for the class, draw "Mr. Average" or "Miss Average" on butcher paper.

Try to find out how various forms of measuring were developed: inch, hand, foot, yard, fathom, cord, acre, cubit, meter. Which of these originated from a measure of the human body?

Teacher Information

Students usually enjoy comparing their size with that of others. If you avoid including waist size or weight in the measurements, the risk of offending someone should be very slight. It might be necessary to review the process of computing averages. Students too young to compute averages can still measure each other and compare. They can talk about size ranges and the sizes most students this age seem to be, and you can help them begin to develop a concept of "average." Students should be taught that it is okay to be big or small. Such people are normal. We are all different and we grow at different rates.

Arm span from fingertip to fingertip usually approximates height.

Here are some suggested extensions to this activity:

1. Have a group discussion about the ways people are different—the characteristics we notice in distinguishing one person from another.
2. Assign students in pairs and have each one draw an outline of the other on butcher paper.

Integrating

Math, physical education, art

Science Process Skills

Observing, measuring, communicating, comparing and contrasting

How Can You See Your Pulse?

Materials Needed

- Large thumbtacks
- Used wooden match

Procedure

1. Carefully insert the point of the thumbtack into the end of a wooden match. The match should extend vertically from the thumbtack.
2. Rest your hand, palm up, on a flat surface.
3. Using the thumbtack as a base, place the match in an upright position on your wrist.
4. Move the match to different positions and observe it.
5. What happened? Why?
6. Run in place for one minute.
7. Repeat the activity. Was there a difference?

Teacher Information

Most students have had their pulse taken at some time. Often they don't understand why or what the doctor or nurse is doing.

A wooden match placed on the wrist, especially in an area in approximate line with the index finger, should move back and forth noticeably.

The pulse is difficult to locate in some people. In some cases, medical personnel may use the throat. These differences are normal.

Pulse rate varies from one individual to another, and even for the same person at different times.

Integrating

Physical education

Science Process Skills

Observing, inferring, measuring, communicating, using space-time relationships, identifying and controlling variables

What Is a Blood-Pressure Cuff?

(Teacher demonstration and supervised partners or small groups)

Materials Needed

- Blood-pressure cuff with gauge

Procedure

1. Examine the blood-pressure cuff. Most of you have seen an instrument similar to this. Medical personnel use it to help them monitor (watch) your heart and circulatory system. Identify the cloth cuff, the rubber bulb and tube, and the gauge.

2. Locate the screw knob below the gauge. It regulates the pressure (amount of air) in the cuff. The rubber bulb will pump air into the cloth cuff. By turning the knob, you can control the amount of air in the cuff.

3. Lay the cuff flat on a table. Use the bulb and knob to practice pumping and releasing air from it. Don't pump it too full or you may damage it.

4. Study the gauge. It has a dial with numbers on it and a needle that tells the amount of pressure you have pumped into the cuff. Practice using and reading the gauge.

5. Have your partner wrap the long, wide strip of cloth around your upper arm (above the elbow) and fasten it. Be sure the gauge and bulb are on the outside so you can see and touch them.

6. With a partner, practice pumping and releasing air from the cuff on your arms. Be sure to watch the gauge. As the air is released, notice that you can feel a pumping sensation in your arm. Be careful not to pump the air in the cuff so tight that it hurts. Begin to release the pressure at once. Never leave a tight cuff in place on your arm.

Teacher Information

This activity should begin with a teacher demonstration, and it needs careful supervision throughout. Circulation to the arm should not be cut off for more than a few seconds. If pressure in the cuff is too great, delicate blood vessels could be damaged.

The main objective of this activity is to show how scientists use instruments to help provide information they need. In some ways it is analogous to the gauges and dials in your automobile.

Some of the anxieties many of us have about going to the doctor can be reduced through an understanding of the why and how of many of the instruments used. Many pediatricians today understand this concept and attempt to allay children's fear. School activities such as this should help support the efforts of parents and medical personnel.

After students understand how a stethoscope and blood-pressure cuff work, invite a doctor, nurse, or medical technician to show how to take blood pressure and explain what it means.

Integrating

Physical education

Science Process Skills

Observing, measuring, communicating, using space-time relationships

How Do the Body Systems Work Together?

Materials Needed

- Bicycle

Procedure

1. Examine the bicycle and explain how it works. For each part that moves, tell what makes it move. How do the different parts depend on one another?
2. Look at your body and tell what parts you think depend on other parts.
3. Bend down and pick something off the floor. How did your hand depend on your arm, your arm depend on your shoulders, your shoulders depend on your back, your back depend on your legs, and your legs depend on your feet?
4. Compare the way your body parts depend on one another and work together with the way the bicycle parts depend on one another and work together.

For Problem Solvers

Find a picture of the body's internal organs and study it. From this, can you add to your explanation of parts of the body that depend on one another?

Find a picture that shows the muscular system and the skeletal system. Tell how you think the muscles, bones, and tendons work together.

Teacher Information

Every part of the body depends in some way on many, many other parts of the body. Point out that the control center for all of the body parts is the brain. The "brain" of the bicycle is the person riding it.

Consider making similar comparisons with other machinery in addition to the bicycle, such as a computer, pencil sharpener, door latch, and so forth. If someone in the class knows something about automobiles, this person could be asked to explain some of its interdependent systems. This might be a good time to invite a resource person to the classroom, or for a student to do some research and report findings to the class.

Integrating

Physical education

Science Process Skills

Observing, inferring, communicating, comparing and contrasting

Body Systems   **241**

What Is Your Lung Capacity?

(Take home and do with family and friends.)

Materials Needed

- Gallon bottle
- Sink or large pan
- 1/4-in. flexible tubing
- Soda straw mouthpiece (short piece of soda straw for each student)
- Measuring cup
- Water
- Masking tape

Procedure

1. A bottle with a small opening, such as a cider or vinegar bottle, will work best.
2. Put at least 5 cm (2 in.) of water in the sink.
3. Fill the bottle completely with water.
4. Cover the top of the bottle, turn it over, and stand it upside down in the sink with the opening in the water. When you uncover the opening, no air should enter the jug.
5. Tip the bottle slightly to the side and insert one end of the tube into the opening of the bottle.
6. Have your partner hold the bottle upright while you do steps 7 and 8, as shown in Figure 5.6–1.
7. Insert your piece of soda straw into the other end of the tubing. Take a deep breath, place your soda straw mouthpiece in your mouth, and blow through the tube, emptying the air from your lungs as completely as you can into the bottle.
8. Mark the water level on the bottle with a piece of tape.
9. Empty the bottle, turn it right-side-up, and use the measuring cup to measure the amount of water required to fill it up to your mark. This is the amount of air you blew into the bottle. It is the vital capacity of your lungs.
10. Repeat the activity for your partner and for others if they wish. Compare and compute the average lung capacity of those who participate.

242

Figure 5.6-1. Measuring Lung Capacity

For Problem Solvers

Conduct a survey of the class and find out what types and amounts of physical exercise each person participates in. Study this information, compare it with the information you have about lung capacity, and decide whether you think exercise has an effect on lung capacity. Discuss your information with the class. Do you think singing is an exercise?

Measure the height of class members. Compare height with lung capacity. Do taller people tend to have a greater lung capacity than shorter people?

Teacher Information

The piece of soda straw used for a mouthpiece is very important for sanitary purposes. This is a valuable activity for practice in measuring a volume of air and in getting acquainted with the body. The word "displace" could become a meaningful new vocabulary word as students observe the displacement of water by air. Have some of your problem solvers investigate the amount and types of physical exercise in which each group member participates. Consider that singing is a very good exercise for the lungs. Then search for correlations between lung capacity and exercise. Someone else could measure the height of each person and search for a correlation between height and lung capacity.

The lung capacity measured in this activity is called the "vital lung capacity." It is less than the total lung capacity because some residual air remains in the lungs after exhaling as much as possible.

Integrating

Math, physical education

Science Process Skills

Observing, inferring, classifying, measuring, predicting, communicating, comparing and contrasting, using space-time relationships, formulating hypotheses, identifying and controlling variables, experimenting, researching

Body Systems

How Does an Apple Skin Protect the Apple? (and How Does Our Skin Protect Us?)

Materials Needed

- Four apples
- Straight pin
- Rubbing alcohol
- Four sheets of paper
- Cotton swab or paper towel
- Pencil
- Writing paper
- Copies of the "Science Investigation Journaling Notes" for the activity for each student

Procedure

1. As you complete this activity, you will keep record of what you do, just as scientists do. Use a copy of the "Science Investigation Journaling Notes" at the end of this activity and write the information that is called for, including your name and the date.

2. For this activity you will learn about how the skin of an apple protects the apple. For item 1, the question is provided for you on the form.

3. Item 2 asks for what you already know about the topic. If you have some ideas about how the skin protects the apple, write your ideas.

4. For item 3, write about how the skin protects the apple, based on what you know now. This will be your hypothesis.

5. Now continue with the following instructions. Complete your Journaling Notes as you go. Steps 6 through 14 below will help you with the information you need to write on the form for items 4 and 5.

6. Lay out the four sheets of paper on a table or a shelf. Label the papers A, B, C, and D. Wash your hands carefully before you handle the apples.

7. Wash the four apples and place one apple on each paper. Let the labels on the papers identify the apples. Apple D will remain untouched from this point on.

Hands-On Life Science Activities

8. Use straight pins to puncture four holes in apple B and four holes in apple C. The holes should be within 2 cm (3/4 inch) of each other.

9. Have someone with unwashed hands rub his or her hands around on apples A, B, and C, including the punctured areas of apples B and C.

10. Use the cotton swab or paper towel to apply rubbing alcohol to the punctured areas of apple C.

11. Leave all four apples in place, unhandled, for seven days. Each day, examine (but don't touch) the apples and write a description of any changes you observe.

12. After seven days, compare the four apples. Consider the possible effect of the rubbing with dirty hands, the punctures, and the application of alcohol.

13. Why did we use apple D? (Discuss this question with your group and with your teacher.)

14. Compare the apple skin with your own skin. Write about what you observed with the apples. (This is item 6 of your Journaling Notes.)

15. Discuss your observations with your group. How did the apple skin protect the apple?

16. For item 7, think about your hypothesis (item 3) and write your conclusion. Based on your observations, how did the apple skin seem to protect the apple?

17. Based on that information, how do you think our skin protects us? (Write your answer as an "Inference" for item 8 of your Journaling Notes.)

Teacher Information

Apple D was washed and left untouched to serve as a control. This is an opportunity to stress the importance of the use of controls in many experiments, and the ease of including a control.

The apple skin protects the apple in much the same way as our own skin protects us. This should be evident in comparing apples A and D. When foreign substances do penetrate the skin, such as through an open wound, the importance of using an antiseptic should be evident by comparing apples B and C.

Integrating

Math, language arts

Science Process Skills

Observing, inferring, classifying, predicting, communicating, using space-time relationships, formulating hypotheses, identifying and controlling variables, experimenting

Science Investigation

Journaling Notes for Activity 5.7

1. Question: *How does an apple skin protect the apple?*

2. What we already know: _____

_____

3. Hypothesis: _____

_____

4. Materials needed: _____

_____

5. Procedure: _____

_____

_____

_____

_____

6. Observations/New information: _____

_____

_____

7. Conclusion: _____

_____

8. Inference: _____

_____

How Does the Skin Help Regulate Body Temperature?

Materials Needed

- Water
- Copies of the "Science Investigation Journaling Notes" for the activity for each student

Procedure

1. As you complete this activity, you will keep record of what you do, just as scientists do. Use a copy of the "Science Investigation Journaling Notes" for this activity and write the information that is called for, including your name and the date.

2. For this activity, you will learn about how the skin helps to regulate body temperature. For item 1, the question is provided for you on the form.

3. Item 2 asks for what you already know about the topic. If you have some ideas about how the skin helps to regulate body temperature, write your ideas.

4. For item 3, you need to think about what you already know about how the skin helps to regulate body temperature. Write what you know, and that will be your hypothesis.

5. Now continue with the following instructions. Complete your Journaling Notes as you go. Steps 6 through 9 below will help you with the information you need to write on the form for items 4 and 5.

6. Wet your finger and blow on it. How does it feel?

7. Wet a spot on your arm and blow on it. How does it feel?

8. Think about when you first get out of a shower or a bathtub. How do you feel while you are wet? Do you feel better after you are dry?

9. Think about times you perspire. What do you think the perspiration does for you?

10. Write about your observations—how moisture on the skin affects the temperature of the skin. (This is item 6 of your Journaling Notes.)

11. For item 7, think about your hypothesis (item 3) and write what you have learned about how the skin helps to regulate body temperature.

For Problem Solvers

See what you can learn about evaporative coolers. Check your encyclopedia and talk to people who use evaporative coolers (sometimes called "swamp coolers") on their homes. Think about how the operation of evaporative coolers compares with perspiration and evaporation on the skin. Share your information and ideas with your group.

Teacher Information

Let students discuss their responses to the above questions. Evaporation is a cooling process. When the body perspires, the evaporation of the moisture cools the skin, helping to control body temperature.

If some of the students have been around horses, they will know that when a horse runs it perspires. Some might also know, from experience or from their reading, that pigs are attracted to water holes on hot days. Pigs do not perspire very much, and this seems to be their way of getting the advantage of the cooling effect of evaporation. Many homes in dry climates are cooled by evaporation coolers, which operate on the same principle. Air is blown through water-soaked filters, and the evaporative action cools the air, which in turn cools the home.

The skin helps control body temperature in other ways, too. Have students recall how flushed their faces become when they are hot. This occurs as blood vessels expand, allowing more of the heated blood to flow into the skin to be cooled. Then have them think about the "goose bumps" that form on their skin when they become cold. These occur as blood vessels constrict, closing pores tightly to prevent body heat from escaping.

Integrating

Math, reading, language arts, social studies

Science Process Skills

Observing, inferring, classifying, measuring, predicting, communicating, using space-time relationships, formulating hypotheses, identifying and controlling variables, experimenting, researching

Science Investigation
Journaling Notes for Activity 5.8

1. Question: *How does the skin help regulate body temperature?*

2. What we already know: _____

_____

3. Hypothesis: _____

_____

4. Materials needed: _____

_____

5. Procedure: _____

_____

_____

_____

_____

_____

6. Observations/New information: _____

_____

_____

7. Conclusion: _____

_____

What Do Our Bones Do for Us?

Materials Needed

- Model of a human skeleton

Procedure

1. Examine the skeleton model.
2. Point to where the heart would be located if included in this model.
3. What bones do you see that surround the heart and protect it?
4. What other organs can you think of that are protected by bones? Point to them on your own body and point to where they would be if they were included in this model.
5. Notice how the backbone is constructed. Feel the separate bones in your own back. Why are there so many instead of just one long backbone?
6. Examine the arm and leg bones in the model. Notice how strong they are and where they bend. How do the joints help us?
7. Look at the hands and feet. How many of these bones can you find in your own hands and feet?

Teacher Information

Although some students get an eerie feeling looking at a skeleton, the experience will help them to realize what they really are like beneath the skin. Some of the most obvious functions of the skeletal structure become evident as one examines a model of a human skeleton. Our bones support the flesh and give it shape. Joints are conveniently located to allow the body to bend. Many of the vital organs (heart, lungs, brain) are enclosed in protective coverings of bone.

Integrating

Math

Science Process Skills

Observing, classifying, communicating

Are Human Bones Large or Small?

Materials Needed

- Encyclopedia and other appropriate reference books
- Rulers
- Pencils and paper

Procedure

1. Make a scale drawing of your femur (upper leg bone). Use a scale of 1 to 4 and check the encyclopedia for help with the shape of the bone.

2. Find the size of the same bone of various animals, such as dog, cat, rabbit, mouse, horse, and maybe one of the large dinosaurs. Use the encyclopedia as a source of information. Perhaps you can actually measure this bone for some animals if you have pets or farm animals.

3. Make a chart showing the comparative sizes of the femur—yours and those of the animals you used.

4. Is your bone large or small?

For Problem Solvers

Compare the length of your femur with your height. If others are doing this activity, make a line graph with length of femur along the bottom and height of the person up the left side of the graph. Plot the height and femur length of several people and see whether height seems to be related to femur length. Discuss your results.

Do some research on dinosaurs and see whether scientists seem to think they can estimate the size of dinosaurs by femur length.

Teacher Information

The student will find that size is relative and that human bones could be considered either large or small, depending on the size of the animals with which they are being compared. Students might prefer to make scale drawings of the bodies of various animals, instead of a single bone, and chart these in a way similar to that suggested above.

The lower grades could do this activity by substituting a general comparison of sizes for scale drawings. When students find information in a book about the size of a bone, have them locate something in the classroom or outside that is about the same size, to help them visualize it.

Integrating

Math, reading, language arts, art

Science Process Skills

Observing, inferring, classifying, measuring, predicting, communicating, comparing and contrasting, researching

How Many Bones Can You Count?

Materials Needed

- Paper and pencils
- Encyclopedias, the Internet, and other appropriate references

Procedure

1. Feel the bones in the fingers of one hand with the other hand. Count them.

2. How many bones did you count in your hand? Write that number on your paper.

3. See how many bones you can count from your wrist to your shoulder. Write that number.

4. Now begin with your toes and work up as you count all the bones you can find. As you count the bones in your foot, leg, back, and so on, write down the numbers.

5. Using this procedure, count the bones in your entire body. As you write the numbers, remember to include the number of bones in both hands, both feet, and so forth.

6. Draw a picture of the human skeleton, showing the bones you found.

7. If others in your group do this activity, compare your notes and drawing with theirs. If your numbers are different for some part of the body, each of you count again and try to determine where the differences occurred.

8. When you have counted and drawn all the bones in your body that you can find, go to the encyclopedia and see whether you can find out how many bones there really are in the human skeleton.

9. How close was your count?

10. Which ones did you miss?

For Problem Solvers

Which of your bones are similar to those of a cat or dog? Bird? Other animals? Decide how you can find out, and study the answer to the question for the animals of your choice. Share your information with your group.

Teacher Information

The human body has at least 206 bones. A textbook that has this information could be substituted for the encyclopedia suggested in the materials list. The process of counting and searching the text or encyclopedia will provide a worthwhile and interesting research experience for students.

Lower grades can count, talk about, compare, and draw the bones they think they feel. The use of reference books can be eliminated for students who are not able to use them.

Integrating

Math, reading, art

Science Process Skills

Observing, inferring, classifying, measuring, predicting, communicating, researching

Hands-On Life Science Activities

How Can Doctors Tell Whether a Bone Is Broken and Where?

Materials Needed

- X-rays of broken and unbroken bones

Procedure

1. Hold the X-ray films up to the window, one at a time, and compare them.
2. Can you tell which bone is broken?
3. Do you see any cracked bones?
4. Why do you think the doctor puts a cast on arms and legs when bones are broken?
5. What do you think might happen if an unqualified person moves someone who has been involved in an accident?

For Problem Solvers

Arrange to visit with an X-ray technician who works in a hospital emergency facility. Ask this person to tell you about some of the common types of injuries that come in from accidents in the home. Share these with your group and discuss things you might do to decrease the risk of accidental injury in your home.

Consider asking your friendly X-ray technician to visit your class and answer questions about bicycle safety and safety at home, at school, and when participating in certain recreational activities (swimming, hiking, and four-wheeling, for instance).

Teacher Information

Before beginning, ask whether anyone in the class has ever had a broken bone.

X-rays should be available at a hospital or doctors' clinic if you ask ahead of time and request that some be saved for use in class. Discuss the above questions. Ask students to consider question 5 in terms of a possible broken leg bone, arm bone, or rib bone. You might also wish to discuss it with respect to broken backbones, although this deals with very different and more technical issues.

Integrating

Language arts, social studies

Science Process Skills

Observing, inferring, communicating

Hands-On Life Science Activities

How Is a Splint Applied to a Broken Bone?

Materials Needed

- Newspapers
- Several strips of rags at least 5 cm (2 in.) wide and 60 cm (2 ft.) long

Procedure

1. Pretend your leg bone is in one piece and it is not supposed to bend at the knee. Let the knee represent a break in the bone.

2. Have your partner use newspapers and rag strips to make a splint for your leg. Several sections of newspapers should be wrapped around the leg to make it stiff. A bone must not bend at a break, so be sure it is tied securely. However, it must not be so tight that it stops the flow of blood.

3. Try walking. Can you stand up? Does the leg feel that it would remain stiff so the bone could heal properly?

4. Trade places and make a splint for your partner's leg.

5. Have your partner stand up and test your splint to see whether it feels secure.

Teacher Information

In this activity students practice making splints that will hold a bone securely without shutting off the blood supply. A first-aid manual, such as a Boy Scout First-Aid Merit Badge booklet, would be an excellent resource to have for reference on splint making, but let students try to accomplish the task with minimal assistance.

Integrating

Math, language arts

Science Process Skills

Observing, communicating

Body Systems

How Are Bones Connected at a Joint?

Materials Needed

- Knee joint of an animal
- Encyclopedia
- Pencils

Procedure

1. Examine the joint.
2. Can you see what holds the two bones together?
3. Use your pencil to probe around on the bone near the joint, in the joint, and away from the joint.
4. Is there any difference in the way the material feels with your probe as you move from one part to another? Where is it harder? Where is it softer?
5. Look up "bone" in the encyclopedia and find names for the parts you see, including what holds the two bones together at the joint.
6. Where do you think you have bones similar to those you are looking at?

For Problem Solvers

Your bones might do things for you that you don't even know about. Do some research about bone marrow. Get a piece of a leg bone of a cow or sheep from a butcher. Examine the marrow. Study about bone marrow in the encyclopedia. What does the marrow do that is very important to the body?

Teacher Information

Bones for this activity are usually available at meat markets. A front knee joint of a calf or sheep would work well, but nearly any joint will do. In checking the encyclopedia, students should be able to identify the bone, cartilage, and ligaments. Connecting points of tendons might also be visible.

As they probe with their pencils, students should be able to feel the softer cartilage material that cushions the bones at the joint.

Consider asking the butcher for a second joint, sawed lengthwise through the bone and joint, with which students can see where the cartilage is fused to the bone. Marrow will be in the center of the long part of the bones, providing an excellent research topic when used with the encyclopedia and other available sources.

Integrating
Reading

Science Process Skills
Observing, communicating, researching

What Are Tendons, and How Do They Work?

Materials Needed

- Chicken leg with foot and with tendons exposed

Procedure

1. Pick up the chicken leg and locate the tendons. The tendons are like cords and should be visible at the top of the leg.
2. Pull on the tendons one at a time and observe the foot.
3. What happened?
4. Try it again. What do you think the chicken does to curl its toes? What does it do to straighten them out?
5. How does this compare with the way your own fingers and toes work?
6. Locate some of the tendons that operate your fingers. See whether you can tell where they connect and what makes them work. Wiggle your fingers quickly and watch the action of the tendons.
7. Grasp the large tendon at the back of one ankle with your fingers. Feel it as you move your foot up and down. This is called the Achilles tendon. Which muscles pull on the Achilles tendon?

For Problem Solvers

Do some research on the mythology of the Achilles tendon and report to the class.

Teacher Information

Chicken legs and turkey legs work equally well for this activity. Be sure the tendons have not been removed. If the tendons are not visible at the top of the leg, cut the skin back to expose enough of the tendon for students to grasp. If some students are squeamish about operating the chicken foot, have others demonstrate for them.

Students should be able to easily identify similar structures on their own hands and feet and observe the tendons that attach muscles to bones. With careful observation, they can tell which tendons open each finger and toe and about where they attach to the muscle. Point out that most muscles are attached to bones by tendons.

Integrating
Reading, social studies

Science Process Skills
Observing, communicating, researching

What Is Bone Like Without the Mineral Material?

(Teacher-supervised activity)

Materials Needed

- Chicken leg bones
- Vinegar
- Metal pan
- Gram balance (or other sensitive scale)

Procedure

1. Soak one of the chicken bones in vinegar for four or five days.
2. Remove the bone from the liquid and dry it off.
3. Feel the bone. Bend it. What happened? What does it feel like?
4. What do you think is now missing from the bone?
5. How do you think the materials these bones are made of compare with your own?

For Problem Solvers

Do some research and find out what was removed from the bone by the vinegar. Discuss what problems might occur if our bodies don't get enough of these materials.

Teacher Information

With the minerals removed, this bone will be soft and flexible enough to tie in a knot.

Integrating

Reading

Science Process Skills

Observing, inferring, communicating, comparing and contrasting, researching

Hands-On Life Science Activities

How Many Muscles Can You Identify?

Materials Needed

- Paper
- Pencils

Procedure

1. Raise your arm slowly. As it moves, try to identify the muscles that make it move.

2. Write down the movement and describe where you think the muscles causing the movement are located. For instance:

Movement	Muscle Location
Raise the arm	From shoulder to top of upper arm

3. Lower the arm onto a table. Then push against the table top in an effort to lower the arm further. Find the muscles that seem to pull the arm down.

4. Write down the movement and describe where you think the muscles causing the movement are located.

5. Continue this for all the different arm movements you can think of. Do the same with the hand, then the legs and feet, then other body parts.

6. Compare your list of body movements and muscle locations with those of others. See how many more you can identify together.

For Problem Solvers

Using the references you have available, find a chart that shows the human muscular system. Find out how many muscles there are in the human body. Does the chart show all of the muscles that you found in the above activity? What other muscles can you find on your body, with the help of the chart, that you did not find earlier? Add these muscles to your list.

Teacher Information

Essentially every movement of the body is produced by muscular action. Since muscles pull (contract) but do not push, a different set of muscles is used for opening the fingers than for closing them. The same can be said for many other body movements, such as moving the leg forward and backward, raising and lowering the arm, and so on. (Gravity should be taken into account.) Where ball joints are involved, muscular arrangements also allow a twisting motion.

The human body has over 650 different muscles. Students will be able to locate many of these as they examine their own body movements. There is some advantage in putting students in groups of two or three for this activity so that they can analyze their movements together, discuss their observations, and learn from one another.

Integrating

Math, physical education

Science Process Skills

Observing, inferring, classifying, communicating, researching

How Do Voluntary and Involuntary Muscles Differ?

Materials Needed

- Mirrors

Procedure

1. Do the following:

   a. Close one hand and open it.

   b. Lift one foot and put it down.

2. Did your muscles move because you decided to move them? Do they ever move other than when you decide to move them?

3. Do the following:

   a. Look in the mirror and watch your eyes. Notice the size of the pupils (black spot in the middle). Shade one eye with your hand as you observe the pupil.

   b. Put your hand over your heart and feel it beat.

4. Did the size of the pupil change? Did you decide to change it? Can you change the size of the pupil without changing the light? Can you make your heart beat just when you want it to, or make it beat faster or slower?

5. How does your control over the muscles you used in step 1 compare with your control over the muscles in step 3?

6. Now do the following:

   a. Look at your eyes in the mirror for 30 seconds. Did they blink? Do they blink even if you don't decide to make them blink? Can you make them blink faster or more slowly?

   b. Notice how fast you are breathing. Does this happen even if you don't think about it? Can you breathe faster or more slowly if you want to?

7. Compare what you did in steps 1, 3, and 6. How do they compare in the amount of control you have?

For Problem Solvers

Make a list of voluntary actions and involuntary actions. Make a third list that includes actions that are sometimes voluntary and sometimes involuntary. Compare and discuss your list with others who are doing this activity.

Teacher Information

Students will discover that some body movements are controlled by voluntary muscles (step 1) and some by involuntary muscles (step 3). Still other muscles are both voluntary and involuntary (step 6). For instance, we can speed up our breathing or the blinking of the eyes, but if we don't think about it, automatic mechanisms take over. Breathing and blinking go on without conscious effort on our part. We can also delay these actions temporarily, but if we interfere too long, the involuntary actions will override our efforts.

Many involuntary muscles are constantly at work inside our bodies. The stomach and intestines contract and relax to aid digestion and to move food material along the digestive track. Arteries contract and relax to help move the blood to various parts of the body. These processes take place, regardless of any conscious effort on our part.

Not all people have equal control of voluntary muscles. Differences are evident when considering handicaps, such as palsy, which have a wide range of effects on muscular control. It should also be pointed out that, even among those not considered handicapped, there are great differences in the ability to control the muscles. This is, in part, responsible for varying abilities in art, athletics, and many other skills.

Integrating

Social studies, physical education

Science Process Skills

Observing, inferring, classifying, communicating, comparing and contrasting, using space-time relationships, formulating hypotheses

Hands-On Life Science Activities

What Is Muscle Sense?

Materials Needed

- Blindfolds

Procedure

1. Blindfold your partner.
2. Place your partner's left arm in a raised position and ask him or her to hold it there. Then instruct your partner to put his or her right arm in the same position as the left.
3. Was your partner able to match the position of the left arm with that of the right arm?
4. Move your partner's left arm to a different position and again ask him or her to put the right arm in the same position.
5. Repeat this process several times, sometimes positioning the right arm and asking your partner to match its position with the left arm.
6. Is your partner able to match the position of one arm with the other each time without looking? Why do you think this is so?
7. Trade places. You wear the blindfold and have your partner test your ability to match the position of one arm with the other.

Teacher Information

Certain nerves leading from the muscles to the brain tell the position of the muscles. This is called muscle sense. As a result of muscle sense, people have automatic knowledge of the position of the muscles.

Integrating

Physical education

Science Process Skills

Observing, communicating

How Fast Are Your Reactions?

(Take home and do with family and friends.)

Materials Needed

- Meter sticks

Procedure

1. During this activity, you will test your reaction time. Reaction time is one indicator of health condition.

2. Have your partner hold the meter stick vertically. Your partner should hold it at the top, and the lower end should be between your thumb and index finger.

3. Ask your partner to drop the meter stick without warning. When the stick drops, grasp it as quickly as you can with your thumb and index finger. Note how far it fell by reading the centimeter scale where you grasped the meter stick.

4. Try it three or four times and see whether you can improve your reaction time.

5. Trade places with your partner. This time you drop the meter stick.

6. Practice and see whether you can both improve your reaction time.

7. Have you ever had a physical examination by a doctor? If so, did the doctor check the reflexes of your knees?

For Problem Solvers

Place a dime on the back of your hand, then tip it off and try to catch it before it hits the floor. Try with your left hand, right hand, and both at the same time. Share this activity with another, and each of you try to improve your skill.

Find other reaction-challenging activities to try together. Check your resource books. Ask others if they know of one or more of these types of activities.

Teacher Information

Students will enjoy comparing reaction times and trying to improve their own with this and other reaction-testing activities you might care to use. A competitive reaction-time activity is the hand slapper. The first person holds a hand palm up and the second places his or her hand on that of the first, palm down. Person 1 tries to slap the back of the hand of person 2 before person 2 can move out of the way. Again, try each hand separately and both together. Caution students not to slap hard enough to hurt the other person.

Integrating

Math, physical education

Science Process Skills

Measuring, communicating, comparing and contrasting

How Fast Do Your Nails Grow?

Materials Needed

- Nail polish
- Rulers
- Paper and pencils
- "Science Investigation Journaling Notes" for each student

Procedure

1. As you complete this activity, you will keep a record of what you do, just as scientists do. Obtain a copy of the Journaling Notes for this activity from your teacher and write the information that is called for, including your name and the date.

2. For this activity you will learn about how fast your nails grow. For item 1, the question is provided for you on the form.

3. Item 2 asks for what you already know about the topic. If you have some ideas about how fast your nails grow, write your ideas.

4. For item 3, you need to think about what you already know about how fast your nails grow. Write what you know about the question, and that will be your hypothesis.

5. Now continue with the following instructions. Complete your Journaling Notes as you go. Steps 6 through 10 below will help you with the information you need to write on the form for items 4 and 5.

6. Put a tiny spot of nail polish next to the cuticles of one fingernail and one toenail. Let it dry. Plan to leave it there for several weeks.

7. Check the nail polish each day. If it begins to wear away, put another spot of polish on, but be sure to put the new spot exactly on top of the old.

8. Each week, measure the distance from the cuticle to the spot of polish and record it. Do this until the spot of polish grows out to the point that you cut it off when you clip your nails.

9. What was the average weekly growth of your fingernail? Your toenail?

10. Did either your fingernail or toenail grow faster than the other? If so, which one, and how much faster?

11. Write about your observations. How fast did your nails grow? (This is item 6 of your Journaling Notes.)

12. For item 7, think about your hypothesis (item 3) and write what you have learned about how fast your nails grow.

270

Hands-On Life Science Activities

For Problem Solvers

Prepare a graph on which all class members can plot their fingernail growth and toenail growth. Then determine what the average fingernail growth is for the class. Compute the average toenail growth also. Do fingernails and toenails grow at the same rate? Is there a difference in nail growth rate between males and females?

Do you think fingernails and toenails grow at the same rate for all ages of people? How could you find out?

Do you think the rate of nail growth could be hereditary? Can you find out?

Select one of these questions (or write a new one of your own) and get a blank copy of the Journaling Notes from your teacher. Write your name, the date, and your question at the top. Plan your investigation through step 5 (Procedure) and get it approved by your teacher. Complete the Journaling Notes as you perform your investigation. Share your project with your group and submit your Journaling Notes to your teacher if requested.

Teacher Information

A line could be scratched into the nail with a nail file and the polish applied on the scratch. This will increase the life of the polish on the nail and help to assure accurate replacement if it does wear off.

If several students are involved in this activity, some of your problem solvers will enjoy compiling the results and making a graph. If one person or group makes the graph, each student could plot his or her own results. From the group results, with or without the graph, average fingernail and toenail growth rates could be computed for the class. Perhaps some could carry the research a bit further and include other members of their families, thus finding out whether age seems to be a factor in nail growth rate. Comparing results between families will provide indicators of heredity as a factor.

Fingernails normally grow about three times as fast as toenails.

Integrating

Math, social studies

Science Process Skills

Observing, inferring, classifying, measuring, predicting, communicating, comparing and contrasting, using space-time relationships, formulating hypotheses, identifying and controlling variables, experimenting, researching

Science Investigation

Journaling Notes for Activity 5.21

1. Question: *How fast do your nails grow?*

2. What we already know: _____

_____

3. Hypothesis: _____

_____

4. Materials needed: _____

_____

5. Procedure: _____

_____

_____

_____

_____

6. Observations/New information: _____

_____

_____

7. Conclusion: _____

_____

What Does Hair Look Like Under a Microscope?

(Teacher-supervised activity or teacher demonstration)

Materials Needed

- Microscope
- Razor blade

Procedure

1. Remove a hair from your head.
2. Put the hair under the microscope and examine it.
3. Describe the hair. What do you notice about the hair by looking through the microscope that you cannot see without the microscope?
4. Ask your teacher to slice through the hair diagonally with the razor blade.
5. Now examine the hair under the microscope again. Notice particularly the diagonally cut end. Do you see layers? How many? Where does the color seem to be darkest?
6. Trade hairs with someone else and compare the structure and coloring with yours. What similarities do you see? What differences?

For Problem Solvers

Remove an eyelash and a hair from your eyebrow and examine these under the microscope. How do they compare with the hair from your head?

Compare coarse and fine hair. Also see whether you can find any visible differences between curly hair and straight hair.

Can you think of any other characteristics to examine and compare?

Teacher Information

Caution: The razor blade must be operated only by the teacher, for obvious safety reasons.

Students should be able to see three layers in the diagonally cut hair. The middle layer is the one that contains the pigment, providing color. This, of course, will be more evident with hairs of darker color. As people grow older, the pigment sometimes disappears and the hair turns white.

Integrating

Language arts

Science Process Skills

Observing, inferring, classifying, communicating, comparing and contrasting, formulating hypotheses, identifying and controlling variables, researching

Name _____   Date _____

Can You Solve This Body Systems Word Search?

Try to find the following Body Systems terms in the grid below. They could appear in horizontal (left to right), vertical (up or down), or diagonal (upward or downward) position.

pulse	blood	protect
fingerprint	pressure	skin
system	temperature	lung
muscles	reaction	joint
voluntary	tendon	involuntary
bones		

```
M Y F P R O T E C T A S
U I I V C E P U L S E Y
S Q N W B E A R T Y R N
C P G V L T Z C A A S U
L S E V O C E X T S E I
E Y R B O L I N R I N O
S S P N D U U P D D O P
L T R J Y L O N F O B N
U E I J O I N T T K N L
N M N V B S K I N A H G
G R T X P R E S S U R E
T E M P E R A T U R E Y
```

Body Systems

275

Can You Create a New Body Systems Word Search of Your Own?

Write your Body Systems words in the grid below. Arrange them in the grid so they appear in horizontal (left to right), vertical (up or down), or diagonal (upward or downward) position. Trade your Word Search with someone else who has created one of his or her own, and see whether you can solve the new puzzle.

_____   _____   _____

_____   _____   _____

_____   _____   _____

Answer Key for Body Systems Word Search

```
M   Y     F     P   R   O   T   E   C   T   A   S
U   I     I   V   C   E   P   U   L   S   E   Y
S   Q   N   W   B   E   A   R   T   Y   R   N
C   P   G   V   L   T   Z   C   A   A   S   U
L   S   E   V   O   C   E   X   T   S   E   I
E   Y   R   B   O   L   I   N   R   I   N   O
S   S   P   N   D   U   U   P   D   D   O   P
L   T   R   J   Y   L   O   N   F   O   B   N
U   E   I   J   O   I   N   T   T   K   N   L
N   M   N   V   B   S   K   I   N   A   H   G
G   R   T   X   P   R   E   S   S   U   R   E
T   E   M   P   E   R   A   T   U   R   E   Y
```

Name _____   Date _____

Do You Recall?

Section Five: Body Systems

1. Why are fingerprints so useful in identifying persons?

2. What is meant by "checking your pulse"?

3. When a doctor or nurse checks your blood pressure, does it hurt?

4. How can the body be compared to a bicycle?

5. How does your skin protect you?

6. What can you do to help your skin to protect your body?

7. How does your skin help your body cool off on a hot day?

8. How do joints help you to move?

Do You Recall? *(Cont'd.)*

9. What are some of the larger bones of your body?

10. You should never try to move someone who has been involved in an accident. Why?

11. What does the cartilage in a joint do?

12. What do tendons do?

13. Do muscles pull, push, or do they do both?

14. What is the difference between voluntary muscles and involuntary muscles?

15. Name one voluntary muscle and one involuntary muscle. Explain how they work.

Body Systems

Answer Key for Do You Recall?

Section Five: Body Systems

Answer	Related Activities
1. Each one is unique.	5.1
2. Finding out how fast your heart is beating	5.3
3. No	5.4
4. The different parts work together as the body functions.	5.5
5. It helps to keep harmful substances out of your body.	5.7
6. Wash your hands often.	5.7
7. Perspiration evaporates from the skin.	5.8
8. They allow the legs, arms, and back to bend.	5.9
9. Leg bones, arm bones, pelvis	5.10
10. You might cause more serious injuries.	5.12
11. The cartilage provides a cushion.	5.14
12. Tendons attach muscles to bones.	5.15
13. Muscles only pull.	5.17
14. We consciously control voluntary muscles.	5.18
15. Answers will vary.	5.18

280

The Five Senses

To the Teacher

The human body is a topic of interest, curiosity, and importance to all ages. Formal study of it should begin in the elementary grades. Many things can be done at this early age to increase awareness of the capacities and needs of this marvelous system. As awareness increases, so do appreciation and the ability to care for our bodies properly.

Everything we do involves one or more of the five senses. All that we learn is learned through the senses. Getting acquainted with their bodies is a logical topic for young learners. Scores of activities can be undertaken that involve concrete, first-hand experiences. Many concepts have been encountered before, but new insights and awarenesses should be acquired as those concepts are spotlighted and discussed.

A study of the five senses should include recognition of the handicapped. Those who have lost part, or all, of one or more senses deserve to be recognized and respected as normal human beings. Children should develop an attitude of appreciation for their capabilities without perceiving the handicapped as something less. Indeed, people with full capability of the senses can learn a great deal from those with some degree of loss of hearing, sight, or other capabilities. Frequently, other senses have compensated by becoming sharper and stronger through use, resulting in enhanced awareness.

The following activities are designed as discovery activities that students can usually perform quite independently. You are encouraged to provide students (usually in small groups) with the materials listed and a copy of the activity from the beginning through the "Procedure." The section titled "Teacher Information" is not intended for student use, but rather to assist you with discussion following the hands-on activity, as students share their observations. Discussion of conceptual information prior to completing the hands-on activity can interfere with the discovery process.

Regarding the Early Grades

With verbal instructions and slight modifications, many of these activities can be used with kindergarten, first-grade, and second-grade students. Some of the activities were written specifically with the primary grades in mind. In others, procedural steps that go beyond the level of the child can simply be omitted and yet offer the child experiences that plant conceptual seeds for concepts that will germinate and grow later on.

Teachers of the early grades will probably choose to bypass many of the "For Problem Solvers" sections. That's okay. These sections are provided for those who are especially motivated and want to go beyond the investigation provided by the activity outlined. Use the outlined activities and enjoy worthwhile learning experiences together with your young students. Also consider, however, that many of the "For Problem Solvers" sections can be used appropriately with young children as group activities or as demonstrations. Giving students the advantage of an exposure to the experience can often lay groundwork for connections that will become more meaningful at a later time.

Correlation with National Standards

The following elements of the National Standards are reflected in the activities of this section.

K–4   Content Standard A: Science as Inquiry

As a result of activities in grades K–4, all students should develop

1. Abilities necessary to do scientific inquiry
2. Understanding about scientific inquiry

K–4   Content Standard C: Life Science

As a result of activities in grades K–4, all students should develop understanding of

1. The characteristics of organisms

5–8   Content Standard A: Science as Inquiry

As a result of activities in grades 5–8, all students should develop

1. Abilities necessary to do scientific inquiry
2. Understanding about scientific inquiry

5–8   Content Standard C: Life Science

As a result of activities in grades 5–8, all students should develop understanding of

1. Structures and function in living systems

In What Ways Do We Depend on Our Eyes?

Materials Needed

- Pencils
- Two sheets of paper for each student
- Blindfolds

Procedure

1. On one of the pieces of paper, draw a simple picture and write your name at the bottom of the paper.
2. Have someone blindfold you. Then, using the other piece of paper, draw the same picture again and write your name on it in the same place as you did on the first.
3. Compare your pictures. How well were you able to draw the picture when you couldn't see?
4. Name some other ways in which we depend on our eyes.

Teacher Information

As students compare their pictures and consider the difficulty in placing elements of the picture in the right places and connecting the lines, their dependence on their eyesight should be emphasized. They will probably think of many ways and times we depend heavily on our eyes.

Integrating

Social studies

Science Process Skills

Observing, communicating, comparing and contrasting, using space-time relationships, identifying and controlling variables

How Well Can You Judge Depth with One Eye?

(Take home and do with family and friends.)

Materials Needed

- Ping-Pong ball
- Soda bottle
- Table (lower than waist high)

Procedure

1. Stand the soda bottle on the table, about 15 cm (6 in.) from the edge.
2. Place the Ping-Pong ball on the top of the bottle.
3. Walk away at least 3 meters (10 ft.).
4. Face the bottle, cover one eye with your left hand, and walk toward the bottle.
5. As you pass the bottle, try to flip the ball with your finger. Flip only one time and do not pause to flip.
6. What happened?
7. Try it again, covering the other eye.
8. Were the results any different?
9. Try it a third time, leaving both eyes uncovered.
10. What happened this time? Compare the three attempts and explain as best you can.
11. Have someone else try flipping the ball, using the same procedures. Compare the results with your own.

For Problem Solvers

How do you think the use of two eyes makes our judgment of depth and distance more accurate than using only one eye? Write your hypothesis, then research the question and find out whether your hypothesis was right.

Learn about triangulation and how distances can be determined by this technique. You might want to talk to someone who knows something about surveying. Share your information with the class.

Teacher Information

In this activity, students will learn that having two eyes serves more of a purpose than simply providing a spare. Accurate depth and distance perception requires two eyes, each of which see objects from a slightly different angle. It is usually difficult to flip the Ping-Pong ball with one eye covered. Students might enjoy practicing to see whether they can increase their skill. You might also have them chart the results of several attempts and find out whether their accuracy is any greater with one eye than with the other.

Integrating

Reading, language arts, math

Science Process Skills

Observing, inferring, measuring, communicating, comparing and contrasting, using space-time relationships, formulating hypotheses, identifying and controlling variables, experimenting, researching

Hands-On Life Science Activities

Which Is Your Dominant Eye?

(Take home and do with family and friends.)

Materials Needed

- None

Procedure

1. Look at an object that is at least 3 meters (10 ft.) away from you.
2. With both eyes open, point at the object.
3. Without moving your pointing finger, close your left eye. Does your finger still appear to be pointing at the object?
4. Now open your left eye and close your right eye. Does your finger appear to be pointing at the object?
5. Select another object and repeat steps 2 through 4.
6. What happened? Try to explain why.

Teacher Information

The two eyes, being a short distance apart, see objects from a slightly different angle. This has certain advantages, including helping us to perceive depth and distance with much greater accuracy than would otherwise be possible (see Activity 6.2). When we point at an object, our finger is in the line of vision of only one eye. This is called the dominant eye, as it is nearly always the same eye. People with two good eyes usually have one that is dominant.

Integrating

Language arts

Science Process Skills

Observing, inferring

How Well Do You Remember What You See?

(Take home and do with family and friends.)

Materials Needed
- Tray
- Variety of small objects

Procedure

1. Put a variety of small objects on the tray, such as a pencil, eraser, marble, paper clip, toy car, bracelet, or wad of paper.
2. Ask one or more participants to examine the items on the tray for thirty seconds.
3. Remove the tray from sight. Remove one of the items.
4. Return the tray and ask participant(s) to look over the contents and try to determine which item was removed. Ask them not to say it aloud until all participants have decided what they think it was.
5. Did everyone get it right? Did no one get it right?
6. If time allows, do the same activity again with the same group but a different set of objects. See whether they can, with practice, improve their visual memory skills.

For Problem Solvers

Repeat this activity many times with different people, changing the items and the number of items. Find out how many items most people can remember well. How many would you predict?

When you know how many items most people can remember with a thirty-second examination of the tray, reduce the viewing time to twenty seconds and find out whether the number of items most people can remember is the same. What difference do you predict it will make, if any?

Hands-On Life Science Activities

Teacher Information

This activity is effective in evaluating visual memory skills. With repeated use, it also provides practice in developing visual memory skills. As skills improve, try increasing the number of objects or rearranging them.

Integrating

Language arts

Science Process Skills

Observing, predicting, communicating, comparing and contrasting, using space-time relationships, formulating hypotheses, identifying and controlling variables, experimenting

Why Do We Need Five Senses?

Materials Needed

- Five blindfolds
- Five sheets of paper
- Five pencils
- Chart paper and markers
- Five baby food jars, each containing one of the following: salt, sand, granulated sugar, powdered sugar, and cornstarch

Procedure

1. Choose five volunteers. Be sure they have not seen the jars containing the five substances.
2. Seat the volunteers at a table and blindfold them.
3. Place one of the jars in front of each volunteer. Also give each one a piece of paper and a pencil.
4. Ask each person to feel the contents of the jar in front of him or her and write on the paper what he or she thinks the substance is. The volunteers are not to taste anything, and they are not to say aloud what they think it is.
5. Record the written responses on a chart.
6. Rotate the jars one position to the right.
7. Again have the volunteers feel the contents of their jars and write down what they think the substance is. Record the results on the chart.
8. Continue until each of the volunteers has identified all five substances using only the sense of touch.
9. Be sure the chart is where it will not be seen by the volunteers and remove the blindfolds.
10. Place the jars in front of the volunteers in a different order from that of step 3.
11. Ask each volunteer to look at the substance in the jar in front of him or her and write what he or she thinks it is. The volunteers are not to taste or feel the substances. They are not to give their answers aloud, and they must not look at one another's responses.

12. Again rotate the jars, recording the responses of each participant.

13. When all five substances have been identified by all five participants by both touch and sight, let them use other ways to identify the substances. If they suggest tasting, assure them that none of these substances is harmful to taste.

14. Discuss the results. How accurate were the responses from the sense of touch alone? From the sense of sight alone? From a combination of these, and possibly with help from the sense of taste?

15. How do the senses depend on one another? How do all five senses help us to know what is happening around us?

Teacher Information

This activity should emphasize that the senses are interdependent. Discuss the fact that everything we learn is learned through the use of the five senses—frequently a combination of two or more of them. Also discuss how we rely on what we have already learned—information stored in the brain. We acquire certain information about these substances, for instance, by looking, touching, and tasting, but it is only from previous experience that we can decide whether something is sugar, salt, or sand.

Integrating

Language arts

Science Process Skills

Observing, inferring, classifying, predicting, communicating, comparing and contrasting

How Do Our Eyes Help Us "Hear"?

Materials Needed

- Storybook with pictures

Procedure

1. Get a group of your fellow students to help you with this activity. They will be your listeners.

2. The storybook you choose should have interesting pictures and illustrations. It should be one the listeners have not heard or read before.

3. Have half of the listeners close their eyes and keep their heads down while the story is read to the group.

4. Read the story to the group, showing the pictures to those who have their eyes open. Don't talk about the pictures.

5. Discuss the story. Let those who had their eyes closed tell about it first; then see whether those who had their eyes open can add any information or details the others were not aware of.

6. If those who had their eyes open could add information the others did not know, discuss the reason. If not, discuss the author's ability to help listeners form pictures in their minds.

For Problem Solvers

Draw a picture. Then, without letting your group see your picture, write a description of it. Read your description to your group and ask them to draw the same picture, from the description alone. Do not add information to the description you wrote. Compare all pictures to the one you drew. Talk to your group about what was helpful in your description and what information was missing.

Do this again, and see whether you can improve your written description. Discuss the results each time. In what ways was your description strong or weak? In what ways did the readers not read carefully enough?

Teacher Information

The story in this activity could be read to the class or to a small group of students by the teacher or by one of the students.

Discuss ways our ears are often assisted by our eyes, not only as we read and listen to stories but also at the many other times our eyes and ears help each other.

Students might wish to find a second story and change roles, having the other half of the group close their eyes.

Your problem solvers will improve their ability to describe verbally and to interpret verbal descriptions as they practice these skills together.

Integrating

Reading, language arts, art

Science Process Skills

Observing, communicating, identifying and controlling variables

How Does a Picture Stimulate Your Senses?

Materials Needed

- Pictures from books and magazines (food, outdoor scene, wintery day, and others)

Procedure

1. Find a picture in a book or a magazine.
2. Tell some ways that what you see involves the senses of touch, hearing, smell, and/or taste.
3. Share your ideas with others and make a list.

Teacher Information

You might wish to use this as an introductory activity or as a culminating activity for a study of the senses. A winter scene plays on the sense of touch as one infers from it cold temperatures and scratchy branches on the trees. A picture of delectable food stimulates the senses of taste and smell. When we look at a scene of a busy street corner or a football game, we can almost hear the honking horns or the roar of the crowd as a touchdown is made. Artists and photographers are able to enhance perceptions and enjoyment by involving more than the sense of sight on the part of the observer.

Students might also enjoy drawing their own pictures to see how many of the senses they can involve.

Discussion accompanying this activity should include not only the inference of other senses from the sense of sight, but the intertwining of all the senses and their ability to stimulate each other. For instance, when we hear something sizzling on a stove before breakfast, we might visualize bacon and eggs frying.

Publishers have added the sense of smell to pictures in a very real way with "scratch and smell" pictures. Consider adding some of these to the discussion of this activity.

Integrating

Language arts, art

Science Process Skills

Observing, inferring, classifying, communicating

Hands-On Life Science Activities

What Happens to the Iris as Light Changes?

Materials Needed

- Hand mirrors

Procedure

1. Hold the mirror close enough to your face so that you can easily see the iris (colored part) of your eyes.
2. Look at the iris of one eye carefully and see whether you can detect any movement.
3. Hold one hand up to the side of your eye to shade the light. As you do, watch the iris carefully.
4. Move your hand, allowing more light to reach the eye again, still watching the iris.
5. Close one eye or put your hand over it to shut out the light. When you open it, observe the iris immediately.
6. What happens to the iris as you change the amount of light around it? Why do you think this happens?

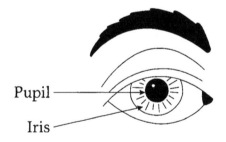

Pupil

Iris

Teacher Information

The iris opens and closes to adjust the amount of light entering the eye through the pupil. The diaphragm of a camera operates much the same way (see Activity 6.9).

You might pair students up and have them observe the iris in each other's eyes as light conditions change. Caution them not to shine bright light in their eyes or look directly at bright lights. The movement of the iris is easily observed in room light by closing the eyes or by temporarily shading with the hand.

Integrating

Language arts

Science Process Skills

Observing, communicating, identifying and controlling variables

How Is the Eye Like a Camera Diaphragm?

(Teacher-supervised activity)

Materials Needed

- Camera (35-mm SLR with no film in it) with an adjustable lens

Procedure

1. The camera must not have film in it and must have an adjustable lens.

2. Ask your teacher to be close by for this activity, to assure that no damage will be done to the camera and to help you locate the parts you need to work with.

3. Open the back of the camera.

4. Set the shutter speed on "time" (B) so it will remain open while the shutter release button is depressed.

5. Look through the lens from the back of the camera. Press the shutter release button and hold it down. You should be able to see a dot of light.

6. Move the f-stop setting as you look through the lens.

7. What happened? How does it compare with the movement of the iris of your eye from your observations in Activity 6.8?

For Problem Solvers

The amount of light that reaches the film in a camera is adjusted in two ways, one of which is the f-stop that you experienced in this activity. Find out where this setting is and how it works, and share your information with the class.

Another adjustable setting on the camera is the focus. This also must be set correctly to get a good picture. Your eye focuses automatically when you look at things that are different distances away from you. Do some research (read about it and/or ask someone) and find out how the focus is adjusted on the camera and what your eye does to focus on things you look at. Share your information with your group.

Why do some people wear glasses, and what do glasses do for the wearer? Write your hypothesis; then find the answer to this question while you are researching the focus of the eye and the camera.

Teacher Information

This activity should be carefully supervised. You will need a single-lens reflex (SLR) camera with an adjustable lens. If you have to borrow a camera and are not acquainted with the operation of it, it will take only a few minutes for someone to brief you on it for this activity. This is also an excellent time for inviting a resource person into your classroom if you have a camera buff available. That person could talk about the light and focusing adjustments of the camera and compare these to the adjustments made by the eye. Many cameras use light-sensitive cells to adjust the diaphragm automatically.

Integrating

Math, reading

Science Process Skills

Observing, inferring, communicating, comparing and contrasting, using space-time relationships, formulating hypotheses, identifying and controlling variables, experimenting, researching

Hands-On Life Science Activities

How Can You See Through a Solid Object?

(Take home and do with family and friends.)

Materials Needed

- Cardboard tubes, such as toilet-tissue tubes or paper-towel tubes
- Books

Procedure

1. Look through the cardboard tube at an object across the room. Keep your other eye open, too.
2. While staring at the object with both eyes, bring your open hand (or a book) against the side of the tube near the far end so that your eye that is not looking through the tube is blocked from seeing the object (remember to keep both eyes open).
3. What happened? Discuss this with your teacher.

Teacher Information

Your hand or the book, when brought against the side of the tube, will appear to have a hole in it. You will see the object farther away through the hole. Those of us who are fortunate enough to have two eyes have two receptors sending images to the brain simultaneously. The brain combines the two images, and the distant object seems to be seen through a hole in your hand.

Integrating

Language arts

Science Process Skills

Observing, communicating

What Is a Blind Spot?

(Take home and do with family and friends.)

Materials Needed

- Prepared 5 by 7-inch index card as shown below

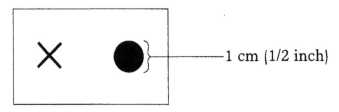

1 cm (1/2 inch)

Use black felt-
tipped pen

Procedure

1. Close and cover your left eye.
2. Hold the index card at arm's length.
3. Stare at the X on the card.
4. Slowly bring the card closer to your right eye.
5. What happened to the dot? Repeat this activity several times.
6. Discuss this with your teacher and the class.

For Problem Solvers

Find a diagram of the eye. Locate the lens and the optic nerve. Study about how the lens focuses an image on the back of the eye and what happens at the spot where the optic nerve is attached. What does this have to do with the disappearing dot on the card?

Experiment with this, varying the size of the X and the dot and varying the distance between them.

Hands-On Life Science Activities

Teacher Information

As the student slowly brings the card near while staring at the X, at some point the dot will momentarily disappear. This is because each eye has a blind spot where the optic nerve exits the eye. At this point there are no rods or cones to detect an image. The blind spot occurs only at a specific distance. We usually see beyond or within this distance, and we use two eyes, so we usually don't notice the blind spot.

Integrating

Reading

Science Process Skills

Observing, inferring, communicating, researching

How Effective Is Your Side Vision?

(Take home and do with family and friends.)

Materials Needed

- Pencils or rulers

Procedure

1. Do this activity with a partner.
2. Have your partner sit down and look straight ahead.
3. Hold the pencil vertically about one meter (or one yard) away from your partner's ear.
4. Move the pencil forward slowly and ask your partner to tell you when he or she can see it (eyes still straight ahead).
5. Move the pencil slowly forward and back as necessary to find the point at which your partner can first see it.
6. Test your partner's side vision of the other eye in the same way.
7. Trade places and have your partner help you test your side vision.
8. Compare results. Are they the same? Discuss situations where good side vision might be important.
9. Have you ever had an eye specialist perform this examination?

For Problem Solvers

Side vision is called peripheral vision. Test the peripheral vision of many people and see how they compare. Is it the same for everyone? Does it become stronger or weaker with age? Is it about the same for people who wear glasses as for people who do not? What about for people who wear contact lenses? Before you begin testing the peripheral vision of these people, write your prediction of how the different groups will compare.

Interview a professional driver (truck driver, taxi driver, or delivery driver) or a pilot and find out how important side vision is for them.

Do it as a Science Investigation. Get a blank copy of the "Science Investigation Journaling Notes." Write your name, the date, and your question at the top. Plan your investigation through step 5 (Procedure)

and have it approved by your teacher. Complete the Journaling Notes as you perform your investigation. Share your project with your group and submit your Journaling Notes to your teacher if requested.

Teacher Information

Peripheral vision (side vision) is the ability to see at the side while focusing straight ahead. It is used frequently by everyone, but for some it is narrower than for others. In some situations, good peripheral vision is critical, such as when driving an automobile or walking across a busy street. Students should easily recognize the importance of side vision to a football player or basketball player. Many other examples can be discussed.

Integrating

Language arts, social studies

Science Process Skills

Observing, classifying, measuring, predicting, communicating, comparing and contrasting, formulating hypotheses, identifying and controlling variables

Can You Save the Fish?

(Take home and do with family and friends.)

Materials Needed

- Prepared index cards, mounted on pencils

Procedure

1. Hold the pencil between the open palms of your hands.
2. Move your palms back and forth rapidly so the pencil spins around.
3. Observe the fish on the card. What happened?
4. What can you say about this?

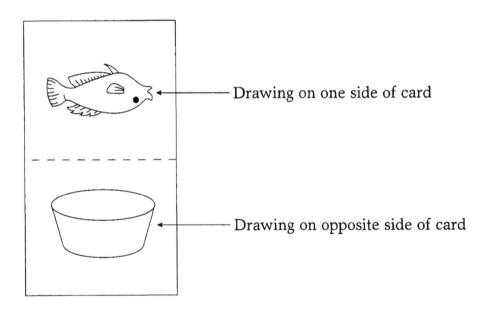

Drawing on one side of card

Drawing on opposite side of card

For Problem Solvers

Prepare other two-part pictures that you can use in the same way and share them with others. You might consider a bird in a cage, a basketball in a basket, or a baby in a crib. Think of others.

Do some research about movies and find out how the film and projector use a series of still pictures to fool your eyes into seeing movement. And what about television? Share your information with others.

Hands-On Life Science Activities

Teacher Information

Fold and cut an index card so that you have a two-inch square on two sides. Draw a fish on one side of the card and a bowl on the other. Glue the card together with the pin in the middle. Stick the pin in the eraser of a pencil. When the pencil is rotated in the palms of the hands, the fish will appear to be in the bowl. This demonstrates the idea of persistence of vision. When we see an image, it persists for about 1/16 of a second. If another image appears within that time, we will see both. Thus the fish appears to be in the bowl. Other related objects such as a lion and a cage or a basketball and a basket can be substituted.

Because of this phenomenon, if approximately twenty-four pictures move in front of the eye each second, they can change slightly and blend together into a "moving picture."

Integrating

Reading, language arts

Science Process Skills

Observing, communicating, using space-time relationships, identifying and controlling variables, researching

How Can Our Eyes Make Colors Seem to Change?

(Take home and do with family and friends.)

Materials Needed

- Prepared 5 by 7-inch index cards

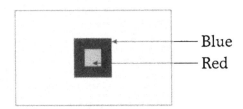

Use blue and red
felt-tipped pens

Procedure

1. Stare at the blue and red squares for thirty seconds.
2. Now stare at the flat, white surface.
3. What happened? What can you say about this?

For Problem Solvers

Make another card, using the same pattern but with different colors, and try the activity again. Make different patterns and use different colors. Each time you use a new color or a new pattern, predict what colors will show up on the blank wall.

Can you make a picture of the U.S. flag that shows up in its true colors when you look at the blank wall?

Learn about complementary colors and find out how they relate to this activity. Do it as a Science Investigation. Get a blank copy of the "Science Investigation Journaling Notes." Write your name, the date, and your question at the top. Plan your investigation through step 5 (Procedure) and have it approved by your teacher. Complete the Journaling Notes as you perform your investigation. Share your project with your group and submit your Journaling Notes to your teacher if requested.

Teacher Information

A simple explanation for elementary children might be: "When we stare at bright colors for a length of time, the cones in our eyes that see the bright colors get tired. When we look at a white surface, the tired cones rest and the other cones near the same place in the eye take over. We will still see the image we have been staring at, but it will be in different colors." (This may be a place to explore the idea of complementary colors in art.)

A related idea is the after-image effect. Darken the room and stare at a vivid object for several seconds (try a large black X on a white sheet of paper). After the object is removed, you will still be able to see it faintly; however, the colors will be reversed (white X on a black square) just as in a negative of a black-and-white photograph.

Integrating

Art

Science Process Skills

Observing, measuring, predicting, communicating, comparing and contrasting, using space-time relationships, formulating hypotheses, identifying and controlling variables, experimenting

How Well Can You See in the Dark?

Materials Needed

- At least twelve pairs of clean socks (variety of colors) per student

Procedure

1. Put all of the individual socks (not in pairs) in a pile and mix them up.
2. Turn the room lights off and immediately sort the socks into pairs. Do it as quickly as you can.
3. Turn the lights on and count the number of pairs of socks that are matched correctly and the number of pairs that are not matched correctly. Write these numbers on paper or on the board.
4. Mix the socks up again into a single pile.
5. Turn the lights off, close your eyes, and have someone time you for two minutes.
6. After two minutes, open your eyes and sort the socks.
7. Record the number of correctly matched socks and the number of incorrectly matched socks and compare these numbers with the numbers from the first try.
8. Did you do better the second time? Discuss the results of all who tried the activity. What made the difference?

For Problem Solvers

Find a flashlight; some red, green, and blue cellophane; and a rubber band to fasten the cellophane over the flashlight. Discuss how well you think you can match the socks in the different colored lights. What differences do you think there will be in your accuracy?

Put red cellophane over the flashlight and repeat the activity with the filtered light shining on the socks.

After you have checked and recorded the number of correctly matched pairs and the number of mismatched pairs, repeat with blue cellophane, then with green.

How well did you do? Did you mismatch different colors when you used the different filters? What do you think makes the difference?

Teacher Information

To make this activity the challenge it is intended to be, the socks should be as much alike as possible except for color. Use a room that is fairly dark when the lights are turned off, but not totally dark. The intent is to show that when the eyes have a few minutes to adjust to the dark, the pupils open up, allowing more light to enter the eye, and the person can see better. Thus, the child is expected to be able to sort the socks more accurately on the second try.

The problem solvers will work with a different variable, finding that we can see only the colors that are reflected to our eyes. The colors of the socks will not appear the same with a red filter as with a green filter or a blue filter. Ask students to notice the color of cars in a parking lot at night. Compare this experience with that of sorting socks under different colors of filtered light.

Colored paper can be substituted for the socks.

Integrating

Math, language arts

Science Process Skills

Observing, inferring, communicating, comparing and contrasting, formulating hypotheses, identifying and controlling variables, experimenting

How Fast Can You Judge What You See and Take Appropriate Action?

Materials Needed

- Two meter sticks per group
- Two spacers; for example, crayons or short pencils
- Masking tape
- Several marbles (same size but different color patterns) per group
- One ruler per group
- Stack of books or containers
- Groups of four students

Procedure

1. You are police officers being trained to make quick decisions. In your work, your split-second decisions will sometimes be a matter of life and death for you or for someone else. Your decisions must be quick and accurate.

2. Place the two meter sticks side by side. Put one crayon (or another spacer) between them at each end, then tape the two meter sticks together. This is your ramp. (See Figure 6.16–1.)

3. Mark three points on the ramp with tape. One will be at 5 cm (write A on this tape), one at 20 cm (write B on this tape), and one at 90 cm (write C on this tape).

4. Prop one end of the ramp on a short stack of books or containers.

5. Roll a marble down the ramp, releasing it at point A. Time the marble between points B and C several times, adjusting the slope of the ramp until the marble gets from B to C in approximately one second.

6. Identify one of the marbles as the Armed Criminal. All members of the group need to know which marble this is.

Figure 6.16-1. Meter-Stick Ramp

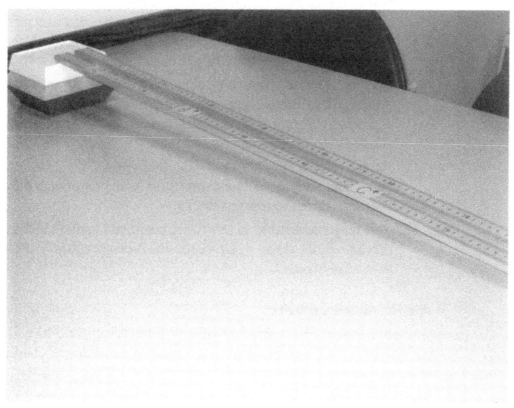

7. You will rotate in four roles. One person will begin as the Gate Keeper and another person as the Officer. A third person will be the Judge and a fourth person will be the Recorder. The Gate Keeper will release a marble on the ramp at point A and the Officer will determine whether the marble being rolled is the Armed Criminal.

8. Place a stack of books (or another object) near the upper end of the ramp, to block the Officer's view of the ramp above point B, and another stack of books (or another object) to block the Officer's view of the ramp below point C. The Officer should be able to see the ramp only between points B and C.

9. With this setup, as the Gate Keeper releases a marble, it will already be rolling when it comes into view for the Officer, and the Officer will see it for only about one second, as the marble rolls from point B to point C. During this brief moment, the Officer will determine whether the marble is the Armed Criminal. If it is the

Criminal, the Officer will take action (tap the table with the ruler) before the marble disappears from view. If it is any other marble, the Officer will not tap the table. The Judge will determine whether the Officer made the correct judgment and took the appropriate action before the marble disappeared from view.

10. Let the Officer have five turns. The Recorder will keep track of points. The Officer gets one point for a correct decision, but if the Criminal appeared, the point is given only if the ruler was tapped while the marble was still in view.

11. Rotate roles from Officer to Gate Keeper to Judge to Recorder, until each group member has been in all four positions, rolling the marbles five times for each Officer.

12. You might want to let the first round of turns be for practice and do the whole thing again. See whether you can do better the second time around.

For Problem Solvers

Do some research on the life of a police officer and the situations in which the police have to make quick decisions. Check the Internet and other resources available to you. Try to find an opportunity to interview a police officer. Write a report on what you learn and ask your teacher whether you may report it to the class. Perhaps the police officer would be able to come to your school and speak to your class. He or she would have some valuable information for you about keeping yourself safe and avoiding foolish behaviors.

Teacher Information

The setup for this activity gives students about one second to make a decision and take action. In the day-to-day work of police officers, life-and-death decisions and actions must often be made in less than one second. They might need to determine whether the person who suddenly appears is dangerous, whether the object being pointed at them is a real gun, a toy gun, or some other object, whether to shoot or not to shoot, and, if the decision is to shoot, get the shot off—all in less than a second. Making the wrong decision somewhere in that series of questions can result in the officer being killed, killing a criminal who was not armed, or killing an innocent person.

Caution: This activity could be sensitive with some people, or even offensive. You will need to make the judgment call on that. Consider such situations as a possible shooting within the family or neighborhood or general sensitivity about the use of firearms. If you use the activity, it is hoped that it will result in greater respect and appreciation for those who put their lives on the line for our safety. A visit to the classroom by an officer of the law could have a very positive effect on student perceptions of these men and women as our friends.

For those who find the references to guns, police officers, and criminals objectionable, but otherwise would like to use the activity, the solution is easy. Change the role labels with no reference to these, and use the activity simply as an exercise in quickness of perception and action.

Integrating

Math, language arts, social studies, art

Science Process Skills

Observing, inferring, measuring, communicating, comparing and contrasting, using space-time relationships, identifying and controlling variables, experimenting, researching

How Fast Do Odors Travel?

(Teacher-directed activity)

Materials Needed

- Bowls or saucers
- Perfume or after-shave lotion
- Timers or clocks with second hands

Procedure

1. Have the students on one side of the room put their heads down and close their eyes.
2. At the front of the room, put a few drops of the perfume in the bowl and ask the students with their heads down to raise their hands when they smell the perfume. They are not to open their eyes until told to do so.
3. Record the number of seconds it takes for the aroma to reach the first row, second row, third row, and so on.
4. When you are finished, have the students open their eyes.
5. Discuss with the class the results of the investigation.

Teacher Information

This activity will show not only the speed with which aromas move through the air, but the differences in sensitivity of the sense of smell from one person to another. Students might wish to test and compare different perfume brands and fragrances. If so, the bowl will need to be rinsed and the room aired out between trials.

Use the other half of the class to repeat the activity, adding plain water as a "secret" brand of perfume. Find out how many students "smell" perfume just because they think it's there.

Integrating

Math

Science Process Skills

Observing, inferring, using space-time relationships, formulating hypotheses

How Long Can You Retain a Smell?

Materials Needed

- Slices of orange
- Blindfolds

Procedure

1. Find a partner to do this activity with you.
2. Hold the slice of orange under your partner's nose.
3. Tell your partner to close his or her eyes and to tell you when you move the orange slice away.
4. Leave the orange slice under your partner's nose for two minutes, or until he or she reports that it has been removed.
5. What happened? Try to explain why.
6. Try the same activity with other people and with substances other than the orange slice.

For Problem Solvers

Prepare a graph that shows the duration of smell in seconds. Plot on your graph the results from several people, and perhaps with several foods. Compare and discuss the results.

Do this activity as a Science Investigation. Obtain a blank copy of the "Science Investigation Journaling Notes" from your teacher. Write your name, the date, and your question at the top. Plan your investigation through step 5 (Procedure) and have it approved by your teacher. Complete the Journaling Notes as you perform your investigation. Share your project with your group, and submit your Journaling Notes to your teacher if requested.

Teacher Information

Other items can be substituted for the orange slice, but each one should have a distinct odor and the odor should not be too strong. The odor-sensitive nerves seem to become accustomed to a given smell in a short

The Five Senses   **315**

time and cease to recognize that odor. The person smelling the orange slice or other substance will usually report in a short time that the item has been removed, even though it is still there.

This is a good time to develop or practice graphing skills. Have students make a graph showing smell duration of several people, using the same substance. Other graphs could be made using a variety of substances with the same person.

Integrating

Math, language arts

Science Process Skills

Observing, inferring, classifying, measuring, communicating, comparing and contrasting, using space-time relationships, identifying and controlling variables, experimenting

What Foods Can Your Nose Identify?

Materials Needed

- Variety of food samples
- Paper cup for each sample
- Toothpicks
- Blindfolds
- Markers
- Chart paper

Procedure

1. Choose a partner to help you with this activity.
2. Blindfold your partner.
3. Select one of the food samples and use a toothpick to hold it under your partner's nose for a few seconds. Ask him or her to identify the food.
4. Record your partner's response and indicate whether the food sample was identified accurately.
5. Follow the same procedure for the remaining food samples. For any food sample your partner did not identify correctly, use a toothpick and place a small amount on your partner's tongue. Then see whether he or she can tell what the food is.
6. Trade places and ask your partner to give you the same food identification test.
7. Examine the charted results and compare your chart with your partner's chart. Which foods did his or her nose identify correctly without help? Which did yours? Were there any differences? If so, what ideas do you have about the reasons?

The Five Senses   **317**

For Problem Solvers

With your partner blindfolded, hold a piece of apple under his or her nose while you place a piece of potato in his or her mouth. With the apple still under his or her nose, ask your partner to identify the food being eaten.

Can you find other foods of similar texture? If so, try them, too.

Teacher Information

This activity will be more revealing if food samples with varying strength of odors are selected. Students will find that some people can smell certain odors better than others, and that the nose relies, at times, on assistance from the tongue. The nose returns the favor, however, and the sense of taste is often assisted or enhanced by the sense of smell.

Integrating

Math, language arts

Science Process Skills

Observing, inferring, classifying, predicting, communicating, comparing and contrasting, formulating hypotheses, identifying and controlling variables, experimenting

How Is Taste Affected by Smell?

Materials Needed

- Variety of food samples
- Paper cups (one for each type of food)
- Box of toothpicks
- Blindfolds
- Markers

Procedure

1. Find a partner to do this activity with you.
2. Blindfold your partner.
3. Have your partner hold his or her nose so the foods being tasted cannot be smelled.
4. Using a toothpick, place a small amount of one type of food in the center of your partner's tongue.
5. Have your partner close his or her mouth and move his or her tongue around for a thorough taste of the sample, then describe the food as sweet, sour, salty, or bitter. Record the results on a chart something like this:

   Name of taster:_____

Food	**Taste**
a. _____	Sweet Sour Salty Bitter
b. _____	Sweet Sour Salty Bitter

6. Follow the same procedure for each of the food samples, using a new toothpick for each food. The person tasting should rinse his or her mouth with water between food samples. Place the food in the center of the tongue each time.

7. After your partner has tasted all the food samples, trade places and have your partner put the food samples on your tongue. Put the food in the center of the tongue each time and use a new toothpick for each type of food. Your partner should record your judgment of each food type as sweet, sour, salty, or bitter.

8. When finished, compare each person's taste judgments with those of the same person in Activity 6.18. Are there any differences? If so, what do you think made the difference?

Teacher Information

People are sometimes heard to say that food just doesn't taste the same when they have a cold. Taste is affected by smell, sometimes enough to alter the judgment of the type of taste if the salty, sweet, sour, or bitter tastes are not very strong. Have students share their findings and discuss them.

Integrating

Language arts

Science Process Skills

Observing, inferring, classifying, communicating, comparing and contrasting, identifying and controlling variables

How Can You Tell Whether Taste Is Affected by Smell?

Materials Needed

- Small slices of potato, apple, and onion
- Three blindfolds
- Chart paper
- Markers

Procedure

1. Find three volunteers to help you do this activity.
2. Blindfold all three volunteers. Seat them about two meters (six feet) apart.
3. Hold a slice of one of the three foods under the nose of one volunteer as you put another of the foods in the same person's mouth. Ask him or her to identify the food in his or her mouth.
4. Use various combinations of the food slices with the same volunteer, placing a slice of apple in the mouth as you hold a slice of onion under the nose. Place a slice of potato in the mouth as you hold a slice of apple under the nose, and so forth.
5. Record the foods used and what the volunteer identifies them to be.
6. Follow steps 3 to 5 with the other two volunteers.
7. Analyze and discuss the results. Did the volunteers identify the foods accurately in all cases? Were the results consistent from one volunteer to the next? If identifications were inaccurate in some cases, which smells seem to fool the tongue?

For Problem Solvers

Do this activity with several more people. Keep accurate records and compare people's ability to identify food types when distracting smells are introduced. Discuss the results with your group.

Do it as a Science Investigation. Get a blank copy of the "Science Investigation Journaling Notes." Write your name, the date, and your question at the top. Plan your investigation through step 5 (procedure)

and have it approved by your teacher. Complete the Journaling Notes as you perform your investigation. Share your project with your group and submit your Journaling Notes to your teacher if requested.

Teacher Information

The senses of taste and smell work together in helping us to identify what we are eating and to enjoy it. Either of these senses can be affected by strong signals from the other. Students might enjoy trying this same activity with other combinations of foods.

Integrating

Math, language arts

Science Process Skills

Observing, inferring, classifying, communicating, comparing and contrasting, identifying and controlling variables, experimenting

Hands-On Life Science Activities

How Can You Match Things Without Seeing Them?

Materials Needed

- Bean seeds (at least ten)
- Small erasers (at least six)
- Paper clips (at least ten)
- Thumbtacks (at least ten)
- Buttons (at least ten)
- Ten film canisters or other small opaque cans with lids
- Masking tape
- Marker

Procedure

1. Number the canisters with masking tape.
2. Mix them up.
3. Randomly select two numbered canisters.
4. Place half of the bean seeds in each of these two cans, put the lids on, and record which two numbers have beans in them.
5. Do the same with the erasers, paper clips, thumbtacks, and buttons.
6. Be sure all lids are on tight. You should now have two containers with bean seeds in them, two with erasers, two with paper clips, two with buttons, and two with thumbtacks.
7. Mix the cans up.
8. Shake the cans one at a time and try to match them in pairs, according to what they have inside. Do not look inside the lid to match contents. Use only your ears to pair them up.
9. Have someone who doesn't already know what is inside try matching the shaker cans.

Teacher Information

By using the numbering and random selection as suggested, the accuracy of matching can be checked without the participant getting clues from the number sequence.

We frequently classify things according to visual characteristics. This activity requires the use of the sense of hearing alone in matching pairs of cans containing identical items. Other small items can be substituted for those listed above, and the canisters can be replaced by other suitable containers.

As an interesting variation, use an odd number of cans and have students identify the can that does not have a mate. You might also try having only one matching pair in the entire set, with the objective being to identify the matching pair. The activity can be further extended by having students try to guess what is in each container. If students already know what the items inside the containers are, replace one or more of them with something else.

If you are using containers with transparent or translucent lids, glue or tape a piece of paper inside the lid so the contents cannot be seen. Also consider decorating the outside of the containers. This could be done as an art activity before the items are put inside.

Integrating

Language arts

Science Process Skills

Comparing and contrasting

What Sounds Do Your Ears Recognize?

Materials Needed

- Paper
- Pencils

Procedure

1. Close your eyes and listen for about three minutes.
2. Write a list of all the sounds you heard and their sources.
3. Discuss this experience with others. Did you hear the same things everyone else heard? Did you notice sounds that you don't usually notice? If so, why did you and others hear some sounds this time when they sometimes go unnoticed?

For Problem Solvers

Use a tape recorder to capture a variety of sounds, such as a blender running, the shutting of a refrigerator door, ice cubes being broken from their tray, a busy street corner, or other common sounds. Play the tape to the class and see how many of the sound sources they can identify. Be sure to include a flushing toilet!

Teacher Information

This should be a group activity, as the sharing of sounds heard and ideas about them is an important part of the experience. Students will note that when they listen deliberately for all sounds, they will be aware of sounds that frequently go unnoticed.

The problem solvers will enjoy preparing a hearing test for the group to see how many recorded common sounds they can identify.

Integrating

Language arts

Science Process Skills

Observing, inferring

What Sounds Do You Hear in Paper?

Materials Needed

- Sheets of paper

Procedure

1. Have all your students put their heads down and close their eyes.
2. Make sounds with the paper and have the group try to guess what you are doing with the paper to make each sound. For instance, fold it, cut it, tear it, crumple it up, shake it, drop it on the floor, smooth out the crumpled paper, blow on it.

Teacher Information

This activity lets students use their sense of hearing and their experience with the sounds that can be made with paper. Students might want to take turns making one sound at a time to see whether the others can determine what is happening to the paper using the sense of hearing alone. Have them try different kinds of paper, such as kraft paper and construction paper. See whether the group can tell what kind of paper is being used as well as what is being done with it.

Integrating

Language arts

Science Process Skills

Observing, inferring

How Well Do You Know Your Classmates' Voices?

Materials Needed

- Blindfolds
- Chairs

Procedure

1. Do this activity with a group of classmates.
2. Place a chair at the front of the room.
3. Select a volunteer to sit on the chair. This is person 1.
4. Blindfold person 1.
5. Choose a person (person 2) to come up and stand behind person 1.
6. Person 2 knocks on the back of the chair person 1 is sitting in.
7. Person 1 asks, "Who is knocking?"
8. Person 2 answers, "It is I," with a disguised voice.
9. Person 1 has three chances to guess who answered "It is I."
10. If the guesses are all wrong, another person is selected to be person 2. If the guess is right, person 2 becomes person 1, sits on the chair, and is blindfolded. Another person is selected to come up and knock on the chair.

Teacher Information

This is an exercise in using the sense of hearing, coupled with familiarity with the voices of classmates. The student in the role of person 2 needs to come up to the front of the room very quietly so person 1 doesn't know what part of the room he or she came from. The challenge is in trying to determine whose voice is being disguised.

Integrating

Language arts

Science Process Skills

Observing, inferring, comparing and contrasting

How Well Can Your Ears Alone Tell You What's Happening?

Materials Needed

- Paper and pencils
- Carrots and graters
- Chalkboard and chalk
- Other optional props

Procedure

1. Do this activity with several partners.
2. Ask the other participants to close their eyes and put their heads down.
3. Instruct them that they are to listen and try to decide what you are doing by using only their ears. They may raise their hands when they think they know.
4. Walk across the floor and see who guesses first what you are doing.
5. Write on the chalkboard.
6. Grate a carrot.
7. Open a drawer.
8. Do a variety of other things and see whether the others can tell what you are doing.
9. Make a list of the things the others could identify by using only their ears and a list of things you did that they could not identify.
10. Examine your two lists and discuss reasons you think some of your actions were easier or more difficult for other people to identify by listening.

Teacher Information

Because of our familiarity with some sounds, certain ones are easily recognized. Some are less obvious to us because we don't hear them very much or because they are similar to other sounds we know. This activity should emphasize to students that, although we often need the help of our eyes and other senses, our ears alone frequently provide us with rather accurate information.

You might want to discuss with the class how certain senses become more keen through added use when others are lost or weakened. People who are blind, for instance, learn to rely more on their ears, and they might notice sounds that the rest of us sometimes do not.

Integrating

Language arts

Science Process Skills

Observing, inferring, communicating, comparing and contrasting

How Much Can You "See" with Your Ears?

Materials Needed

- Curtain or other opaque barrier
- A "sound" skit
- Props (optional)

Procedure

1. Find two or three partners to do this activity with you.
2. Create a short skit, such as a trip to the grocery store, going swimming, or mountain climbing. Your skit is to be heard only, not seen, so write the speaking parts and include any sound effects that might help.
3. Behind the curtain, perform your skit for your class.
4. Tell the class that after your skit is finished, you'd like them to describe the events of the play. The class members are to use only their sense of hearing, as all actions are hidden from view.
5. Perhaps other groups in the class would like to try producing a "sound skit."

Teacher Information

Usually, skits are both seen and heard, so we use two senses in getting the meaning of the play. In this activity, students are to use only their sense of hearing. Encourage them to close their eyes as they "observe" with their ears and try to visualize the scenes being acted out in sound.

Integrating

Language arts

Science Process Skills

Observing, inferring, communicating

What Is a Stethoscope?

(Teacher-supervised partners or small groups)

Materials Needed

- Stethoscopes (one for each two or three participants)
- Soft facial tissue or toilet paper

Procedure

1. Stethoscopes are delicate instruments specially designed to help us listen to functions inside the body. Examine your stethoscope. Notice that it resembles the letter Y.

2. Can you find the two small, rounded ends, held together with a spring? These fit into your ears.

3. Use a soft tissue to clean the rounded ends and carefully put one in each ear. The spring should keep the ends in place. Be sure to clean the ends before each use.

4. Notice that the two hollow tubes coming from the ends in your ears join together to make a single tube.

5. The single tube is attached to a large, flat disc. Carefully examine the flat disc. It has a sensitive vibrator or diaphragm that magnifies sound.

6. Put the disc against the part of your body where you think your heart is.

7. Use the stethoscope to listen to other parts inside your body: stomach, throat (try swallowing), lungs (breathe deeply and listen both front and back). Try other places.

8. A stethoscope helps our hearing in the same way hand lenses help our vision. Can you explain how?

For Problem Solvers

Did you know that mechanics sometimes use stethoscopes? What do you suppose the mechanic would use it for? Does a car have a heartbeat? Visit a mechanic and ask to see his or her stethoscope, and ask the person to explain how and why he or she uses it. Make a drawing of it and compare it with the medical stethoscope. Share your information with your group, and discuss your ideas about it. Can you think of any other purpose a stethoscope might be useful for?

Teacher Information

With younger children, demonstrate first. Stethoscopes are available from medical personnel—doctors, nurses, dentists, and medical technicians. Some students may have them in their homes. The diaphragms are delicate and should be handled with care.

Some students are familiar with stethoscopes, but many are not. Students can hear many of the normal functions in their own bodies and may be surprised at the normal sounds (such as those in the intestinal tract) that go on regularly inside them. Listening to throats, hearts, and breathing may require partners or teams. Modesty should be observed.

Stethoscopes can also be used to hear the small sounds around us (for example, small insect noises). If possible, have one available at all times for students to use.

Integrating

Physical education

Science Process Skills

Observing, inferring, classifying, measuring, communicating, researching

Hands-On Life Science Activities

What Differences in Taste Do People Have?

Materials Needed

- Variety of food samples in small pieces
- Paper cups (one for each type of food)
- Box of toothpicks
- Blindfolds
- Markers
- Chart paper

Procedure

1. Find a partner to help you with this activity.
2. Blindfold your partner.
3. Using a toothpick, place a small amount of one type of food in the center of your partner's tongue.
4. Have your partner close his or her mouth and move the tongue around for a thorough taste of the sample. Then describe the food as sweet, sour, salty, or bitter. Record the results on a chart something like this:

   Name of taster:_____

   Food   **Taste**

   a. _____   **Sweet Sour Salty Bitter**

   b. _____   **Sweet Sour Salty Bitter**

5. Follow the same procedure for each of the food samples, using a new toothpick for each food. The person tasting should rinse his or her mouth with water between food samples. Place the food in the center of the tongue each time.
6. After your partner has tasted all the food samples, trade places and have your partner put the food samples on your tongue. Put the food in the center of the tongue each time and use a new toothpick for each type of food. Your partner should record your judgment of each food type as sweet, sour, salty, or bitter.

Teacher Information

Tastes are usually described as sweet, sour, salty, or bitter. These tastes are strong in some foods and weak in others. Some foods even have combinations of tastes. The purpose of this activity is to compare taste judgments of different people. The different taste-sensitive areas of the tongue are compared in Activity 6.30, and should not become a factor in the above activity; for consistency it is important that each food sample be placed at the center of the tongue.

Integrating

Language arts

Science Process Skills

Observing, inferring, classifying, communicating, comparing and contrasting, identifying and controlling variables

Which Part of the Tongue Is Most Sensitive to Taste?

Materials Needed

- A copy of Figure 6.30–1 for each student
- Variety of food samples
- Paper cups (one for each type of food)
- Box of toothpicks
- Blindfolds
- Water
- Chart paper
- Markers

Procedure

1. Find a partner to do this activity with you.
2. Blindfold your partner.
3. Using a toothpick, place a small amount of one type of food on the region of the tongue identified as "1" in the illustration. Your partner is to judge the taste with his or her mouth still open so the food sample is not spread to other regions of the tongue. The taste judgment this time is to indicate strength as well as type of taste: strong sweet, weak sweet, strong salty, weak salty, strong sour, weak sour, strong bitter, or weak bitter.
4. Record your partner's judgment of taste, have him or her rinse the mouth with water, then place the same type of food on region 2, then 3, then 4, then 5. Record the taste judgment each time. Be sure the mouth is rinsed with water between tastes.
5. When you have placed the first food type on all five regions of the tongue and recorded your partner's judgment of taste, do the same with the next food type.
6. After recording your partner's taste judgment of each type of food, trade places and have your partner give you the same taste tests.
7. Analyze the information you have collected in this activity and see whether some regions of the tongue seem to be more sensitive to certain tastes than other regions. Make a chart showing your findings.

The Five Senses

Teacher Information

While doing this activity, students should have a copy of Figure 6.30–1, but *not* Figure 6.30–2. When finished with the activity, the results can be compared with Figure 6.30–2.

Certain regions of the tongue are known to be more sensitive to certain tastes. These are shown in Figure 6.30–2. Results of the above investigations should approximate this information. Have students share and compare their findings. Where differences are found, encourage students to try to identify reasons for the differences. Possible factors include not placing the food sample in the exact same locations, closing the mouth, or spreading the food sample to other parts of the tongue. Also consider differences in taste sensitivities from one person to another (refer to Activity 6.29), or simply the subjectivity of the judgment.

Integrating

Language arts

Science Process Skills

Observing, inferring, classifying, communicating, comparing and contrasting, identifying and controlling variables

Figure 6.30-1. Taste Regions of the Tongue

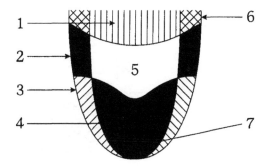

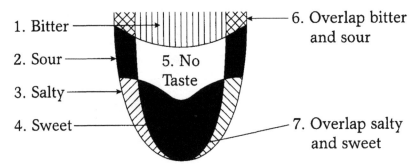

Figure 6.30–2. Taste Regions of the Tongue Labeled

1. Bitter

2. Sour

3. Salty

4. Sweet

5. No Taste

6. Overlap bitter and sour

7. Overlap salty and sweet

How Can We Classify Foods by Taste?

Materials Needed

- Chart paper
- Markers

Procedure

1. For a period of one day, keep a list of all the food items you eat.
2. As you eat something, think about ways you could describe its taste.
3. As you write each item in your list, write a description of its taste. A word or two is usually sufficient.
4. When you have finished your list, look it over and find foods that in some way have a similar taste. Group these together. How many of each group did you find?
5. Compare your list with those of others. Does someone else have some of the same foods? Did he or she describe the taste the same way you did? Talk together about it.

Teacher Information

If students cannot think of ways to describe taste in order to classify the foods they eat, suggest or discuss the terms normally used to describe taste: sweet, sour, salty, and bitter.

A fun way to do the above activity is to have a party to which each member of the group contributes one food item. Then, before anything is eaten, have students list all food items involved and classify each one as sweet, sour, salty, or bitter. They could work individually, in small groups, or as a whole class.

Integrating

Math, language arts

Science Process Skills

Observing, inferring, classifying, predicting, communicating, researching

How Does a Sudden Change in Temperature Affect Us?

Materials Needed

- Large pan or bowl filled with hot water (not hot enough to burn the skin)
- Large pan or bowl filled with warm water
- Large pan or bowl filled with cold water

Procedure

1. Observe the three pans. One has hot water in it, one has warm water in it, and one has cold water in it.
2. Carefully put one hand in the hot water and one in the cold. Leave them there for thirty seconds.
3. Now put both hands in the warm water.
4. What happened? What can you say about this?

Teacher Information

When placed in the warm water, the hand that was in the hot water will feel cool while the hand from the cold water will feel warm. A simple explanation for elementary children is that our body has a control system to help us adjust to hot and cold. After one hand has adjusted to hot water and the other has adjusted to cold water, the warm water will feel quite cool to the one and quite warm to the other. This happens because of contrast with that to which they have become accustomed. This is the reason a room feels hot when we first come in from the cold outdoors or vice versa.

Integrating

Language arts

Science Process Skills

Observing, inferring, measuring, communicating, comparing and contrasting, identifying and controlling variables

How Well Can You "Observe" with Your Sense of Touch?

Materials Needed

- Paper
- Pencils
- Blindfolds
- Variety of objects, such as sandpaper, cotton balls, oranges, baseballs, seashells, rocks, feathers, books, erasers, pencils, or other objects from around the classroom or home

Procedure

1. Find a partner to do this activity with you.
2. Blindfold your partner.
3. Hand one of the objects to your blindfolded friend and ask for a description of the object. The other person is not to name the object, but only to describe how it feels.
4. Write the name of the object and some of the descriptive words used by the blindfolded person on a piece of paper.
5. Do the same with several other objects.
6. Have someone else try some of the same objects blindfolded and compare descriptions.

For Problem Solvers

Repeat the same activity, but using bare feet to feel with in describing the objects. Compare the sense of touch of the feet with that of the hands.

Do this activity as a Science Investigation. Obtain a blank copy of the "Science Investigation Journaling Notes" from your teacher. Write your name, the date, and your question at the top. Plan your investigation through step 5 (Procedure) and have it approved by your teacher. Complete the Journaling Notes as you perform your investigation. Share your project with your group, and submit your Journaling Notes to your teacher if requested.

Teacher Information

Descriptions given in this activity are to be limited to those characteristics of the objects that can be felt, such as smoothness, sharpness, roughness, size, shape, and so forth. If this is used as a whole-class activity, any items selected ahead of time should be put out of sight so that each person, in turn, is experiencing some element of surprise. An alternative would be to select items for each person after the blindfold is in place.

Another option is to use a "feely box." Prepare a box that is closed except for an opening large enough for inserting the hand. A variety of small items are placed inside, and students reach in, take one object (keeping the object inside the box and out of sight), and describe what the object feels like. With this version of the activity, the blindfold is not necessary.

Integrating

Language arts

Science Process Skills

Observing, classifying, predicting, comparing and contrasting

How Much Can You "See" with Your Hands?

Materials Needed

- Paper
- Pencils
- Assortment of buttons (many shapes, sizes, and colors)
- Blindfolds

Procedure

1. Find a partner to do this activity with you.

2. Put the blindfold on your partner.

3. Pour the buttons out on the table and ask your blindfolded friend to separate them into groups according to whatever characteristic he or she chooses (such as size). Do not answer any questions about the appearance of the buttons. These characteristics must be determined by the sense of feel.

4. When your partner is finished sorting the buttons, ask him or her to try to think of another way to sort them (such as according to shape).

5. If your partner can think of still another way to sort the buttons, have him or her do it.

6. Write a list of the characteristics your partner uses for sorting the buttons.

7. Remove the blindfold and ask your partner to try to sort the buttons in still more ways. Add these to your list of characteristics. These might include color and texture.

8. After the blindfold was removed, what characteristics were used that were not used before? Could any of these characteristics have been felt, even though they weren't thought of until they were also seen? (How about texture, for instance?)

9. Can you think of other times when our sense of touch is aided by our sense of sight?

The Five Senses

For Problem Solvers

Do you think your sense of touch is as good with your feet as it is with your hands? Try the same activity again, but this time do it with the feet (bare feet) instead of the hands. No fair looking. Can you sort the buttons now? In how many ways? Which characteristics were you able to detect with your hands but not with your feet? Did you find any new ways to sort them when you used your feet?

What makes the difference? Study it out, and share your information with your group.

Teacher Information

As a supplement to this activity, you might bring some things to class that feel similar but are not the same and do not look the same. Have blindfolded students try to decide what these things are. For example, try small jelly beans and candy-coated peanuts.

Integrating

Reading, math

Science Process Skills

Observing, inferring, classifying, predicting, communicating, comparing and contrasting, formulating hypotheses, identifying and controlling variables, experimenting, researching

Where Is Your Sense of Touch Most Sensitive?

Materials Needed

- None

Procedure

1. Do this activity with a partner.
2. Ask your partner to close his or her eyes.
3. Place the tips of three of your fingers about 3 cm (1 in.) apart on your partner's back. Ask your partner to tell you how many fingers are touching.
4. Touch the palm of your partner's hand with one finger, then two. See whether your partner can tell without looking how many fingers you are using.
5. Do the same on the shoulder, the forearm, the neck, the forehead, and the back.
6. In what areas is your partner able to tell with the most accuracy how many fingers are touching?
7. Trade places and have your partner test your sense of touch in the same manner.
8. Compare the results. Is your sense of touch the most sensitive in the same areas as that of your partner?

For Problem Solvers

Draw an outline of the human body and identify areas of greater or lesser sensitivity. Use a 1, 2, 3 rating. First, mark the outline with your predicted ratings, based on the above activity, then test the areas of the body and mark the areas again, showing your findings with a different color of ink. Compare your information with that of others who are doing the activity.

Do this activity as a Science Investigation. Obtain a blank copy of the "Science Investigation Journaling Notes" from your teacher. Write your name, the date, and your question at the top. Plan your investigation

through step 5 (Procedure) and have it approved by your teacher. Complete the Journaling Notes as you perform your investigation. Share your project with your group, and submit your Journaling Notes to your teacher if requested.

Teacher Information

Sometimes it is surprising to find out how little sensitivity we have on some parts of the body. Students usually find that on their hands, fingers, and face they can tell quite accurately how many fingers are touching. On the back and arms, the sense of touch is noticeably less sensitive. They might like to discuss times when they have noticed that injuries are much more painful in some places than in others.

Students who do the "For Problem Solvers" extension might need to be reminded of rules of modesty.

Integrating

Physical education

Science Process Skills

Observing, inferring, classifying, predicting, communicating, comparing and contrasting, formulating hypotheses, identifying and controlling variables

What Parts of Your Body Can Feel Things Best?

Materials Needed

- Blindfold
- Variety of objects, such as a ball, a pencil, a book, an eraser, a piece of crumpled paper

Procedure

1. Find a partner to help you with this activity.
2. Blindfold your partner.
3. Select one of the objects and place it on the table in front of your partner.
4. Tell your partner that he or she is to identify the object on the table by feeling it, but the hands are not to be used. The arms, face, feet, or anything but the hands may be used.
5. Have someone else try the same thing, but with a different object to identify.
6. Discuss the experience. Was it easy? What part of the body did you want to use? What parts of the body have the greatest sense of touch?

Teacher Information

The children should note that the sense of touch is the only one of the five senses that is not confined to the head area. The organ of the body that is usually associated with the sense of touch is the skin, although areas inside the body have varying amounts of touch sensitivity as well.

Not all areas of the skin have the same degree of sensitivity to touch. One of the areas of greatest sensitivity is the fingertips. Because of this and the dexterity of the fingers, we usually use our fingers to feel something. This activity should help participants realize why we use our fingers to do this and how little sensitivity some of the other parts of the body have.

If you have been using a "feely box" for activities with the sense of touch, items from it would be excellent to use in the above activity. These are items the children have already experienced with the fingers, and they will be able to compare the task of identifying them with other parts of the body.

Integrating

Language arts

Science Process Skills

Observing, communicating, comparing and contrasting, identifying and controlling variables

What Is Warm and What Is Cold?

Materials Needed

- Three pans or bowls
- Hot, lukewarm, and cold water
- Blindfolds

Procedure

1. Find another student to do this activity with you.
2. Fill one pan with cold water, one with lukewarm water, and one with hot water. The hot water must not be hot enough to burn or hurt.
3. Blindfold your partner.
4. Have your partner put his or her left hand in the hot water and then put the right hand in the lukewarm water.
5. Ask your partner to describe the temperature of the water in the two bowls.
6. Have your partner remove both hands from the water.
7. Shift the bowls around; then have your partner put his or her left hand in the cold water and the right hand in the lukewarm water.
8. Ask your partner to again describe the temperature of the water in the two bowls.
9. Think about the result. Did your partner describe the lukewarm water as lukewarm both times? Did his or her judgment of the lukewarm water seem to be affected by the temperature of the water the other hand was in? How was it affected? What can you say about this?
10. Try the same activity with another person and see whether you get the same results.

The Five Senses   **349**

Teacher Information

When we say something is hot or cold, we are usually thinking in terms of its comparison to something else. Boiling water isn't very hot compared with molten steel, for instance. We sometimes get a glass of water from the cold-water tap and complain about the water being warm, but if we were to take a shower in water of the same temperature, we would probably consider it very cold. This activity is designed to point out that our reactions to temperatures are relative. We frequently judge something to be hot or cold relative to the temperature of the skin. The lukewarm water used in this activity should be such that it feels neither hot nor cold to the skin. When the blindfolded person puts one hand into it after the other hand is already in hot water, however, the lukewarm water will probably be described as cold or cool because of the contrast with the hot water. To the hand that has been in cold water, the lukewarm water will feel warm.

Integrating

Language arts

Science Process Skills

Observing, inferring, communicating, comparing and contrasting, identifying and controlling variables

How Many Touch Words Can You Find?

Materials Needed

- Paper
- Pencils
- Bowl or small box

Procedure

1. Do this activity with a group of your classmates.
2. Write a touch word (such as hard, soft, smooth, rough) on each of several small pieces of paper. The words used should describe objects that are in the room or otherwise accessible.
3. Fold the papers and put them in the bowl.
4. Divide into two teams.
5. Draw a paper from the bowl and read the word aloud.
6. Each team should find something that will match the word that is read. The first team to find an item to match the touch word gets a point.
7. Draw another piece of paper. Repeat the process until the time is up or a predetermined number of points is reached.

Teacher Information

This activity gives students an opportunity to use many descriptive words that are associated with the sense of touch and to match those words with objects they describe. Here is a beginning list of touch words you or your students can choose from in making the papers to go in the bowl:

Hard	Heavy	Smooth	Soft	Solid	Wet
Dry	Spongy	Hairy	Dusty	Stiff	Scratchy
Rough	Hot	Cold	Lukewarm	Slippery	Silky
Sticky	Bumpy	Lumpy	Bristly	Coarse	Woolly
Furry	Oily	Prickly	Limp	Gooey	Greasy
Gritty	Flabby	Fluffy	Fuzzy	Slimy	Squishy
Thorny	Stretchable	Springy	Slick	Cuddly	

The Five Senses

As a follow-up activity, consider having the children think of some touch experiences that are sometimes associated with emotions or feelings. Have them describe touch experiences that make them feel warm, cold, itchy, tingly, frightened, excited, safe, happy, eerie, and so forth.

Integrating

Language arts

Science Process Skills

Observing, inferring, classifying, communicating

Hands-On Life Science Activities

Name _____   Date _____

Can You Solve This Five Senses Word Search?

Try to find the following Five Senses terms in the grid below. They could appear in horizontal (left to right), vertical (up or down), or diagonal (upward or downward) position.

eyes	taste	senses
ears	tongue	nose
hearing	vision	observe
sight	color	touch
smell	reaction	voice
odor	feel	observation

```
O  Z  A  Q  T  A  S  T  E  X  C  E
S  B  W  E  D  O  E  G  C  V  O  C
N  O  S  E  F  R  N  T  G  S  L  I
B  N  H  E  Y  I  S  G  U  R  O  O
S  U  J  M  R  K  E  I  U  A  R  V
I  M  K  A  L  V  S  O  P  E  M  T
E  Y  E  S  N  B  A  V  C  X  H  O
X  H  S  L  Q  W  S  T  D  G  C  U
R  F  E  E  L  F  R  T  I  G  V  C
O  B  S  E  R  V  E  S  B  O  N  H
D  H  Y  T  G  V  I  S  I  O  N  J
O  M  G  R  R  E  A  C  T  I  O  N
```

The Five Senses   **353**

Can You Create a
New Five Senses Word Search
of Your Own?

Write your Five Senses words in the grid below. Arrange them in the grid so they appear in horizontal (left to right), vertical (up or down), or diagonal (upward or downward) position. Then fill in the blank boxes with other letters. Trade your Word Search with someone else who has created one of his or her own, and see whether you can solve the new puzzle.

_____   _____   _____

_____   _____   _____

_____   _____   _____

_____   _____   _____

Answer Key for Five Senses Word Search

```
O  Z  A  Q  T  A  S  T  E  X  C  E
S  B  W  E  D  O  E  G  C  V  O  C
N  O  S  E  F  R  N  T  G  S  L  I
B  N  H  E  Y  I  S  G  U  R  O  O
S  U  J  M  R  K  E  I  U  A  R  V
I  M  K  A  L  V  S  O  P  E  M  T
E  Y  E  S  N  B  A  V  C  X  H  O
X  H  S  L  Q  W  S  T  D  G  C  U
R  F  E  E  L  F  R  T  I  G  V  C
O  B  S  E  R  V  E  S  B  O  N  H
D  H  Y  T  G  V  I  S  I  O  N  J
O  M  G  R  R  E  A  C  T  I  O  N
```

Do You Recall?

Section Six: The Five Senses

1. Why do we need five senses?

2. What does the iris do when lights get brighter and dimmer?

3. Why is side vision important to someone while driving a car?

4. How do the senses of taste and smell work together?

5. How do the senses of hearing and sight work together?

6. What does a stethoscope do?

7. Are all areas of the tongue equally sensitive to the tastes of sweet, sour, salty, and bitter?

8. Are all areas of the body equally sensitive to touch?

Answer Key for Do You Recall?

Section Six: The Five Senses

Answer	Related Activities
1. They support each other in giving us more complete information.	6.5, 6.6
2. The iris constricts and enlarges, controlling the amount of light that enters the eye.	6.8, 6.9
3. The driver needs to be able to see cars and other objects while focusing straight ahead.	6.12
4. Answers will vary.	6.19–6.21
5. Answers will vary.	6.22–6.27
6. It magnifies sound, just as a hand lens magnifies light.	6.28
7. No, each of these tastes is stronger on certain parts of the tongue.	6.29, 6.30
8. No, some areas of the body are more sensitive than others.	6.33–6.36

Section Seven

Health and Nutrition

To the Teacher

Every person needs to develop wise eating habits and understand some basic concepts and principles for proper care of the body. Some children have access to little food and need to be especially careful that what they do eat is nutritious. Many have excessive amounts of junk food available to them and considerable social pressure or desire to consume unhealthful amounts of it. The activities of this section will help to increase awareness of good eating habits, proper hygiene, and care of the teeth.

Someone said commitment comes partly through ownership of an idea. This is a good time to involve students in researching, writing, and sharing reports on topics related to the activities herein, and in teaching one another. The process of teaching someone else good health habits will increase the level of commitment on the part of the presenters to develop those habits themselves.

The following activities are designed as discovery activities that students can usually perform quite independently.

359

You are encouraged to provide students (usually in small groups) with the materials listed and a copy of the activity from the beginning through the "Procedure." The section titled "Teacher Information" is not intended for student use, but rather to assist with discussion following the hands-on activity, as students share their observations. Discussion of conceptual information prior to completing the hands-on activity can interfere with the discovery process.

Regarding the Early Grades

With verbal instructions and slight modifications, many of these activities can be used with kindergarten, first-grade, and second-grade students. Some of the activities were written specifically with the primary grades in mind. In others, procedural steps that go beyond the level of the child can simply be omitted and yet offer the child experiences that plant conceptual seeds for concepts that will germinate and grow later on.

Teachers of the early grades will probably choose to bypass many of the "For Problem Solvers" sections. That's okay. These sections are provided for those who are especially motivated and want to go beyond the investigation provided by the activity outlined. Use the outlined activities and enjoy worthwhile learning experiences together with your young students. Also consider, however, that many of the "For Problem Solvers" sections can be used appropriately with young children as group activities or as demonstrations. Giving students the advantage of an exposure to the experience can often lay groundwork for connections that will become more meaningful at a later time.

Correlation with National Standards

The following elements of the National Standards are reflected in the activities of this section.

K-4   Content Standard A: Science as Inquiry

As a result of activities in grades K-4, all students should develop

1. Abilities necessary to do scientific inquiry
2. Understanding about scientific inquiry

K-4   Content Standard C: Life Science

As a result of activities in grades K-4, all students should develop understanding of

1. The characteristics of organisms

K-4   Content Standard F: Science in Personal and Social Perspectives

As a result of activities in grades K-4, all students should develop understanding of

1. Personal health

5-8   Content Standard A: Science as Inquiry

As a result of activities in grades 5-8, all students should develop

1. Abilities necessary to do scientific inquiry
2. Understanding about scientific inquiry

5-8   Content Standard C: Life Science

As a result of activities in grades 5-8, all students should develop understanding of

1. Structures and function in living systems

5-8   Content Standard F: Science in Personal and Social Perspectives

As a result of activities in grades 5-8, all students should develop understanding of

1. Personal health

What Are We Made Of?

(Teacher demonstration in a sink, large bucket, or dishpan)

Materials Needed

- Opaque garbage bag, 20- to 40-liter (5- to 10-gallon)
- Water
- Food products in small quantities such as hard-boiled eggs; milk; green, leafy vegetables; yellow vegetables (squash); piece of whole-wheat bread; soy or any dry beans; potatoes with skin left on; small pieces of fruit, such as oranges, apples, or pears; nuts
- Slice of pizza (avoid fresh meat and fish)
- Flashlight batteries
- Tablespoon of salt
- Pinch of dirt

Procedure

1. Add water to the bag until it is about three-fourths full.
2. As you add small quantities of the other materials on the list, discuss the importance (to human health and nutrition) of each item.
3. Continue to add items (especially leafy vegetables and fruit) until the bag is full.
4. Seal the top of the bag. Carefully shake the contents.
5. Although the amounts are not in proportion, this bag is the way a chemist might see us. In order to grow, we must continue to add water and nutritional foods to our bag.

Teacher Information

You can keep costs down by using small quantities and perhaps asking your produce department at the local grocery store for scraps.

This simple idea may help introduce the following concepts:

a. Our body is mostly water.

b. Various foods contain different amounts of elements our body must have.

c. A balanced diet means giving our bodies the right kinds and quantities of many foods.

d. One important purpose of our skin is to prevent harmful things from entering the body. In our model, the garbage bag represents the skin, which is the largest organ of the body.

The salt and dirt represent bacteria and compounds that are natural and essential to body functions. You may want to discuss health problems that require limitations in salt and other substances and the difference between harmful and helpful bacteria in the human body.

The flashlight battery is optional and probably should be used only with older students, although younger ones may relate to the concept of energy in the body. It represents the chemical reactions that produce electrical energy from which our brain and nervous system operate.

Life processes such as digestion, respiration, and elimination are not included in this simple model. However, the model could trigger many creative and challenging questions, such as: "Now that we have all the necessary chemical contents in this bag, why isn't it alive?" or "What does your body do that this bag cannot?"

Integrating

Language arts

Science Process Skills

Observing, inferring, classifying, measuring, communicating, using space-time relationships, identifying and controlling variables

Why Do We Wash Our Hands Before Handling Food?

Materials Needed

- Two small potatoes (washed)
- Potato peeler
- Two sterilized jars (with lids that will seal)
- Masking tape or two gummed labels
- Marker

Procedure

1. Without washing your hands, peel a potato and put it into one of the jars.
2. Wash the potato peeler and scrub your hands well, using soap, then peel the other potato and put it in the second jar.
3. Seal both jars with their lids.
4. Using gummed labels or masking tape, label the first jar "Hands unwashed" and the second "Hands washed."
5. Place the two jars in a warm place where they can be observed but untouched for several days.
6. Leaving the lids on the jars, examine the two potatoes daily. Compare them. Do you see any changes? If so, write a description of the changes you see.
7. Continue your daily observations and note-taking.

For Problem Solvers

Put pieces of peeled and washed potato into sterilized jars, one piece per jar. Seal one of the pieces of potato in its jar. Just before putting the other pieces of potato into the jars, touch each of them with someone's finger, lips, or other body part, and some of them with a pencil, paper clip, and other things that people often put into their mouths. Seal the jars with lids and predict what will happen to the potato pieces. Label each jar according to what the item inside is and what it was touched by.

364

Observe the potatoes for several days. Share your results.

How does the untouched potato piece compare with the others? This one is called a control. Ask your teacher to help you decide what a control is.

Do this as a Science Investigation. Obtain a blank copy of the "Science Investigation Journaling Notes" from your teacher. Write your name, the date, and your question at the top. Plan your investigation through step 5 (Procedure) and have it approved by your teacher. Complete the Journaling Notes as you perform your investigation. Share your project with your group, and submit your Journaling Notes to your teacher if requested.

Teacher Information

The potato peeling should be done by someone whose hands appear to be clean but that have not been washed for several hours. Be sure students notice that the hands appear to be clean. After a few days, mold is likely to form on the potato peeled with unwashed hands, as mold spores that were transferred from the hands to the potato multiply. Little or no growth will likely be noted on the potato that was peeled after the hands were scrubbed.

Daily observation, particularly after the mold begins rapid growth, should help students realize the importance of washing their hands before handling food. Remind students that the hands looked clean before the first potato was peeled.

Your problem solvers will grow other cultures that will remind them of good reasons to keep themselves clean and to not put pencils and other such things in their mouths.

Integrating
Language arts

Science Process Skills
Observing, inferring, classifying, predicting, communicating, comparing and contrasting, using space-time relationships, formulating hypotheses, identifying and controlling variables, experimenting

Why Are the Basic Food Groups Important?

Materials Needed

- Paper and pencils
- Encyclopedia
- Health books
- Other books about food
- Small groups of students

Procedure

1. With your class or group, select one of the following basic food groups to study:

   a. Vegetables and fruits

   b. Meat

   c. Bread and cereals

   d. Milk and milk products

2. Search the reference books you have for answers to the following questions regarding your food group:

   a. What do these foods have in common?

   b. What do these foods do for our bodies?

   c. What vitamins and minerals do these foods provide?

   d. How many calories are usually in a normal serving?

   e. Are these foods expensive?

3. Report your findings to the class.

For Problem Solvers

Arrange to interview a nurse or other nutrition expert. Prepare your questions in advance. Use a tape recorder or camcorder to record the interview. (Be sure to ask for the person's permission to record the interview.) Include the recording of this interview as a part of your report.

Search the Internet for information about a group of people who do not receive adequate nutrition. Study and prepare a report on this information.

Hands-On Life Science Activities

Teacher Information

A balanced diet is necessary for our bodies to have energy to keep warm, to do our work, and to play. Our bodies must also have materials for repair and growth and to keep the organs functioning properly.

This exercise works well as a class activity, with each group of students assigned a different food group to explore. When they have gathered their information, have each group share its findings with the rest of the class. Preparation for these reports provides an excellent opportunity for students to practice their skills at illustrating with pictures and compiling information into charts. With all information in, have students plan a balanced diet, using the information learned in this activity. This could be done either by individuals or in groups, according to the interest and ability of the students.

Note: The food activities in this section use four basic food groups: vegetables and fruits; meat; bread and cereals; and milk and milk products. However, the U.S. Department of Agriculture revised the food groups in 2000 and developed the Food Guide Pyramid consisting of six food groups: Bread/Cereal/Rice/Pasta; Fruit; Vegetables; Milk/Yogurt/Cheese; Meat/Poultry/Fish/Beans/Eggs/Nuts; and Fats/Oils/Sweets.

Integrating

Math, reading, language arts, social studies

Science Process Skills

Communicating, formulating hypotheses, identifying and controlling variables, experimenting, researching

What Are the Most Common and the Most Popular Foods?

Materials Needed

- Copies of the "Food I Like and Food I Eat" worksheet
- Chart paper
- Pencils
- Marker

Procedure

1. Make several copies of the "Food I Like and Food I Eat" worksheet and write "Breakfast" at the top of each for the meal.

2. Give copies of this sheet to each of several people and ask them to write the *food items they most commonly eat* for breakfast (at least once each week) in the left column and the *foods they prefer* for breakfast in the right column.

3. Collect the worksheets.

4. Write all the food items people included in the left column on a "Common and Popular Foods" chart like the one shown on the next sheet.

5. For each item on the list, count the number of people who eat that item regularly and write the number in the "How Many Eat" column on the chart.

6. For each item on the list, count the number of people who prefer that item and write that number in the "How Many Prefer" column on the chart.

7. Display the chart on the wall.

Common and Popular Foods

Food Item	How Many Eat	How Many Prefer

For Problem Solvers

Repeat this activity for lunch foods and for dinner foods. Share your information, along with the information on breakfast foods.

Teacher Information

This activity could be done by an individual or by a committee. A class discussion of the popular and common foods and the reasons we eat what we do could be a valuable follow-up. The discussion should include the relative nutritional value of various foods.

While this activity is being conducted, other individuals or groups could be gathering similar information for lunch and dinner foods. Or this could be done by your problem solvers who are motivated to do more after doing their research on breakfast foods.

You might want to have students begin by writing a list of the foods they predict are the most common and popular foods.

Integrating

Math, reading

Science Process Skills

Communicating, researching

Food I Like and Food I Eat

Meal: _____

Food I eat most: Food I like most:

How Well Balanced Is Your Diet?

Materials Needed

- Paper
- Pencils
- Encyclopedia or health texts

Procedure

1. Write a "Three-Meal Menu" of everything you eat for breakfast, lunch, and dinner today. Do this for three days.
2. Find the Food Guide Pyramid of the food groups in an encyclopedia or health book.
3. Examine your menus of food you consumed for three days. Beside each food item, write which food group that item belongs to.
4. At the bottom of each "Three-Meal Menu," write the names of the food groups and the number of items you consumed that day from each group.
5. Do you show a balanced diet (at least one serving from each of the food groups) for each day? If not, write down which food group(s) you need to include in your diet more frequently.

For Problem Solvers

Collect the results from all students in the class, without names attached, and prepare a chart that shows the frequency of consumption of the food groups by the class. Discuss the results with your class, and emphasize the weak spots you find in the chart, that is, the food groups that are most frequently lacking in the diets of the class members.

Teacher Information

If school lunch is served at your school, be sure to include it as one of the daily meals used for this activity.

Students should easily be able to find, in their health book or encyclopedia, reference to the food groups. If students have already completed Activity 7.4 and still have their record of food eaten, they could use that information instead of rewriting the food items for nine meals as indicated above.

Hands-On Life Science Activities

After students have completed this activity, discuss their findings. They should be cautioned to include frequent servings of each of the food groups in their diet (at least one from each group every day), and to avoid excessive amounts of sugar and of foods that contain a lot of fat, such as ice cream and fatty meat. You might even make a class chart (without names) showing the frequency of consumption of the food groups. This will spotlight the extent to which the class is getting a balanced diet and which, if any, food groups are being short-changed. This is a good extension for your problem solvers.

Integrating

Language arts

Science Process Skills

Classifying, communicating, using space-time relationships, researching

How Can We Test Foods for Protein?

(Teacher-supervised activity)

Materials Needed

- Lime powder
- Copper sulfate
- Water
- Two stirring sticks
- Two eyedroppers
- Small measuring cup
- Small amounts of common foods, such as meat, flour, butter, eggs, cheese, bread, salt, and sugar
- Paper towels
- Two cup-size containers

Procedure

1. Measure about two tablespoons of water into each of two containers.
2. Mix lime powder in one of the containers and copper sulfate in the other. Put in as much as you can get to dissolve.
3. Keep the two solutions separate. Put a clean dropper in each.
4. Put a small piece of meat on a paper towel.
5. Put two or three drops of lime water on one spot on the meat. Then put an equal amount of the copper sulfate solution on the same spot.
6. What happened?
7. Try putting equal amounts of the two solutions on some sugar.
8. Do the same with a piece of bread.
9. The different reactions you see are an indication of the amount of protein present. Which of these substances has the most protein? Which does not have any?

10. Test the other foods you have and make a list, beginning with the foods having highest protein content and ending with those that have none. Before you begin, write your prediction of the outcome, based on the information you have from the above procedure. This is your hypothesis.

11. Now continue with this as a Science Investigation. Obtain a blank copy of the "Science Investigation Journaling Notes" from your teacher. Write your name, the date, and your question at the top. Plan your investigation through step 5 (Procedure) and have it approved by your teacher. Complete the Journaling Notes as you perform your investigation. Share your project with your group, and submit your Journaling Notes to your teacher if requested.

Teacher Information

Proteins help to make up the protoplast, or living portion, of body cells. Our bodies cannot manufacture their own protein, so we depend on the plants and animals we eat for our protein supply. Proteins are a vital food element, so it is important that we know which foods are the best sources of protein.

If a food containing protein is mixed with lime and copper sulfate, the mixture will turn a violet color. The higher the protein content of the food, the darker the violet color will be.

Your high school or junior high school chemistry teacher can help you obtain lime powder and copper sulfate.

Integrating

Math

Science Process Skills

Observing, inferring, classifying, comparing and contrasting, formulating hypotheses, identifying and controlling variables, experimenting

Which Foods Contain Sugar?

Materials Needed

- Empty food containers with labels intact
- Pencils
- Paper
- Chart paper
- Markers

Procedure

1. Write a list of the foods your food containers represent. Put a check mark beside each food on your list that you think contains sugar.
2. Select one of the food containers. Write the name of the food on a chart.
3. Look at the list of contents on the container. Does the list include sugar? If so, write the type(s) of sugar used. Here are some types of sugar that might be included:

Corn syrup	Dextrose
Maltose	Glucose
Sucrose	Lactose
Fructose	Molasses
Corn sweetener	

4. The food contents are listed in order of quantity used. If one or more types of sugar are in the list, indicate on the chart whether they are listed first, second, third, and so forth.
5. Continue steps 2 to 4 for the food containers you have.
6. Now go back to the list you made in step 1 and put an X beside those foods you found that do contain sugar. Compare these with your predictions (check marks from step 1).
7. Are you surprised?

For Problem Solvers

Find several more food containers and repeat the activity. This time, however, write your hypothesis of the outcome, based on the background you have from the above activity and considering the new set of foods represented by the containers.

Do this as a Science Investigation. Obtain a blank copy of the "Science Investigation Journaling Notes" from your teacher. Write your name, the date, and your question at the top. Plan your investigation through step 5 (Procedure) and have it approved by your teacher. Complete the Journaling Notes as you perform your investigation. Share your project with your group, and submit your Journaling Notes to your teacher.

Teacher Information

The object of this activity is to make students aware that most foods we eat contain sugar and that sugar comes in many different forms. It is important that students complete step 1, including their predictions. Their findings will be more meaningful as they compare them with their own predictions if they complete step 1.

Integrating

Math, reading

Science Process Skills

Predicting, communicating, formulating hypotheses, researching

Which Foods Contain Starch?

Materials Needed

- Tincture of iodine
- Stirring sticks
- Eyedroppers
- Paper cups
- Cornstarch
- Raw potatoes
- Bread
- Other foods, such as cooked egg white, cooked macaroni, meat, sugar, salt, crackers, and boiled rice
- Paper and pencils

Procedure

1. Fill a paper cup about half full of water and add a small amount of cornstarch.

2. Using an eyedropper, add a drop or two of iodine to the cornstarch solution and stir. The blue-black color indicates the presence of starch.

3. Using the eyedropper, place a drop of tincture of iodine on a slice of raw potato.

4. What happened? Does potato contain starch?

5. Use the iodine test on a variety of other foods. With each one, make your prediction before you do the iodine test.

6. Do this as a Science Investigation. Your prediction will become your hypothesis. Obtain a blank copy of the "Science Investigation Journaling Notes" from your teacher. Write your name, the date, and your question at the top. Plan your investigation through step 5 (Procedure) and have it approved by your teacher. Complete the Journaling Notes as you perform your investigation. Share your project with your group, and submit your Journaling Notes to your teacher if requested.

Teacher Information

Have one or more students look up "starch" in the encyclopedia or other reference books and prepare a short report on the nutritional value of starchy foods. They will learn that carbohydrates, including sugar and starch, provide heat and energy and are a necessary part of the diet. Excessive amounts, however, can be harmful.

Integrating

Math, language arts

Science Process Skills

Observing, inferring, classifying, predicting, communicating, comparing and contrasting, formulating hypotheses, experimenting, researching

Which Foods Contain Fat?

Materials Needed

- Water
- Eyedroppers
- Paper
- Pencils
- Brown paper bags
- Butter (melted)
- Variety of foods, such as salad dressing, boiled egg, leafy vegetable, meat, bread, nuts

Procedure

1. Tear up a brown paper bag into small pieces, about 5 cm (2 in.) in diameter.
2. Put a small amount of butter on one of the small pieces of paper. If the butter is not melted, hold the paper in the sun for a few minutes.
3. Put a few drops of water on a second piece of paper.
4. Hold both pieces of paper up to the sunlight. Notice that they are both translucent, letting some light through.
5. Leave both pieces of paper in the sun until the water dries.
6. Hold both pieces of paper up to the sunlight again. Are they both still translucent?
7. Fatty foods, such as the butter, leave a permanent stain on the paper. Use the brown paper test on several other foods. With each one, predict whether they contain fat before you test them.
8. Do this as a Science Investigation. Your prediction will become your hypothesis. Obtain a blank copy of the "Science Investigation Journaling Notes" from your teacher. Write your name, the date, and your question at the top. Plan your investigation through step 5 (Procedure) and have it approved by your teacher. Complete the Journaling Notes as you perform your investigation. Share your project with your group, and submit your Journaling Notes to your teacher if requested.
9. Make a list of foods you found to contain fat and those in which you did not detect fat.

Hands-On Life Science Activities

For Problem Solvers

Do some research about fats in foods and find out whether fats are always bad for you. Do we need any fat in our food at all? If so, why? If not, how can we avoid it? Is it healthful for us to be fanatical about avoiding fats in foods? Discuss your findings with your group.

Teacher Information

Have one or more students look up "fatty foods" in their health books, on the Internet, or in the encyclopedia and report to the class. They will learn that fats provide energy. If excessive amounts of carbohydrates are consumed, these are changed to fat and stored in the body. Fats have a much higher caloric content than do carbohydrates.

Integrating

Math, reading, language arts

Science Process Skills

Observing, inferring, classifying, predicting, communicating, formulating hypotheses, comparing and contrasting, experimenting, researching

How Do People Count Calories?

Materials Needed

- Encyclopedia, cookbooks, the Internet
- Calorie chart for each student

Procedure

1. For one full day, record on a "Calories for a Day" chart everything you eat. Be sure to include the number of servings of each item.

2. Find a calorie chart in one of your resources.

3. Determine as closely as you can the number of calories in each of the food items you consumed. Record these numbers with the foods on your list.

4. Compare the number of calories you consumed with the average indicated for your age and height.

5. Make a realistic judgment as to whether the number of calories you consumed is appropriate. Don't be concerned about your total calories being a little above or below average. You might want to ask your teacher or your parent for his or her opinion.

6. If you determine that you should change your caloric intake, make adjustments in your diet and keep track of what you eat for an additional day or more.

7. Compare the results from step 6 with those from the first day. How did you do?

Teacher Information

Caution students that to some people the number of calories eaten is considered personal information, so they shouldn't ask others for information from their lists. Before, during, or after this activity is an excellent time to invite a school nurse (or other available nurse, doctor, or nutrition expert) to talk to the group about nutrition and normal caloric intake.

Integrating

Math, reading

Science Process Skills

Observing, inferring, classifying, measuring, communicating, formulating hypotheses, identifying and controlling variables, experimenting

Hands-On Life Science Activities

How Many Calories Do You Use?

Materials Needed

- Three copies of "My Daily Exercise Chart" for each student
- Calorie table
- Pencils

Procedure

1. Keep a record of the types of exercise you do for one full day and the number of minutes you spend with each one. Use your "My Daily Exercise Chart."

2. From information in the calorie table, write on your chart the number of calories used per minute for each exercise you listed.

3. Compute the total number of calories you used in each exercise and record it on your chart.

4. Determine the total number of calories you used in exercising during the entire day.

5. Keep a record of your exercising for an additional two or three days and compare with the first day. What kinds of exercises are you doing most? How many calories do you seem to be using with exercise on an average day?

For Problem Solvers

Ask your teacher to gather all of the individual calorie charts, remove the names, and assign a number to each one. Prepare a chart of the information without names, so that each member of the class can compare his or her calorie information with that of the class.

Try to get a nurse or other nutrition expert to visit the class and discuss the implications of the information on the chart. Ask everyone to respect the privacy of the information on the chart and to not try to guess which numbers belong to specific individuals.

Teacher Information

A calorie table can be found in a health book or encyclopedia. In addition to keeping track of their own calories used in exercising, students might enjoy comparing their charts with those of others. Make a class chart, without names, showing the types of exercises that seem to be the most popular and the number of calories used by each. Your problem solvers can do this. Total numbers of calories used daily in exercising can also be charted without names so that each student can compare his or her results with those of the group. Students should understand that these figures represent only part of the total calories used. The body uses calories constantly, whether it is walking, running, resting, or even sleeping.

Integrating

Math, reading

Science Process Skills

Observing, inferring, classifying, communicating, comparing and contrasting, formulating hypotheses, identifying and controlling variables

Hands-On Life Science Activities

Name _____   Date _____

🪑 My Daily Exercise Chart

Type of Exercise	No. of Minutes Spent Doing It	No. of Calories Used per Minute	Total No. of Calories Used During This Exercise

Total No. of Calories
Used Exercising Today

Health and Nutrition

How Are Teeth Shaped for Their Task?

Materials Needed

- Model of a full set of teeth
- Encyclopedia and health books
- Pencils and paper
- Mirrors

Procedure

1. Examine the model set of teeth and notice the different shapes.
2. Which teeth are sharpest? Which are most pointed? Which are flattest?
3. Use a mirror to look at your own teeth. Are yours shaped about the same as those in the model?
4. How are the front teeth shaped? What do you think they do best: cut, tear, or crush? How many of these are there? Write your answers on a sheet of paper.
5. How many teeth come to a single point? What do you think they do best? Write your answers on the piece of paper.
6. Answer the same questions for teeth with two points and for those that are broad and flat.
7. When you are through, look up "teeth" in the encyclopedia and find the names of the four types of teeth on your piece of paper. Read about them and see whether the information you wrote agrees with that in the encyclopedia.

For Problem Solvers

Now that you have examined human teeth and considered the specialized jobs they perform, compare these with the teeth of various animals. Study about them in the encyclopedia and other references you have available. What differences are there in the teeth of carnivores and herbivores? Compare the numbers and types of teeth of the various animals you find. Also compare the numbers and types of teeth with the numbers and types of human teeth.

Teacher Information

A full set of adult teeth includes the following types and numbers in the upper jaw (the same types and numbers are found in the lower jaw):

Four incisors, located in the center and front of the mouth. These are sharp and are used for cutting food.

Two cuspids, located at the corners of the mouth. These are pointed and are used to tear food.

Four bicuspids, located just behind the cuspids. These are used to tear and crush food.

Six molars, located at the back of the mouth. These are broad and flat and are used for grinding food.

In addition to examining human teeth and considering the specialized jobs they perform, your problem solvers might enjoy comparing these with the teeth of various animals. Note the differences in the teeth of carnivorous and herbivorous animals.

This is an excellent time to invite a dental technician into your classroom to talk about teeth and their proper care.

Integrating
Math, reading, language arts

Science Process Skills
Observing, inferring, classifying, predicting, communicating, comparing and contrasting, researching

What Does Tooth Decay Look Like?

Materials Needed

- A healthy human tooth (or model)
- A decayed human tooth (or model)
- X-ray showing tooth decay
- Mirrors
- Paper
- Pencils or crayons

Procedure

1. Examine the samples of healthy and decayed teeth. What differences can you see?
2. Use a mirror to look in your own mouth. Which of your teeth are most like the samples?
3. While you are examining your own teeth, look for places that are discolored or for possible signs of tooth decay.
4. Examine the X-ray. Can you tell where there is tooth decay? If not, ask your teacher to help you.
5. Draw a picture of a healthy tooth and a decayed tooth. Then draw a picture of what you think each of them would look like in an X-ray. You might need to look at the sample X-ray again and notice where the light and dark colorings are.

For Problem Solvers

Survey the class and find out how many have had teeth filled because of tooth decay. Find out how many go for a dental checkup at least once each year (every six months is better). Also find out how many brush their teeth regularly and floss regularly.

Prepare a chart with your information, with numbers only (no names), and discuss this information with the class. Decide what might be done by the class members to take better care of their teeth and avoid tooth decay.

Teacher Information

If sample teeth or models cannot be obtained at your dentist's office, ask your school nurse to help you locate some samples. If they are not available, use pictures, but the real thing will leave a more lasting impression on students. You should be able to obtain one or more X-rays from your dentist. When you get the sample X-ray, have the dentist, a technician, the school nurse, or other qualified person brief you on reading the X-ray.

During discussions related to this activity, point out that the outer layer of the tooth is a hard enamel covering. When decay extends through this protective shell, the decay progresses more rapidly and becomes painful. This is one reason why it is important for such problems to be detected and corrected early.

Integrating

Math, language arts

Science Process Skills

Communicating, comparing and contrasting, using space-time relationships, formulating hypotheses, identifying and controlling variables, researching

Why Are Healthy Teeth Important to You?

(Teacher-directed small-group activity)

Materials Needed

- Pictures of smiling people of all ages and different nationalities with healthy teeth
- Dentist or dental hygienist as resource person
- Pictures of primitive people (eating if possible)
- Newsprint
- Pencils

Procedure

1. As you listen to the dentist or hygienist, use your pencil and paper to list as many reasons as you can that healthy teeth are important and some things you can do to keep your teeth healthy.

2. Look at the pictures of different people with healthy teeth. Some work very hard to keep their teeth healthy and clean. Others do very little. Can you think of reasons why? Before you do step 3, write down any reasons you can think of for the differences.

3. Look at the pictures of the cave men and primitive people. Scientists have found evidence that these cave men and primitive people ate their food almost as they found it. They gnawed bones, chewed skins, and ate vegetables and fruit without boiling, softening, or tenderizing them. Because their teeth worked hard and were scraped, scratched, and brushed by tough foods, tooth and gum problems were rare. Broken teeth, however, were common. Was this one of the reasons you listed on your paper?

4. Some highly developed and civilized people such as American Indians and Eskimos have very healthy teeth when they follow the customs and eating habits of their culture. Before white people came, most American Indians and Eskimos had very healthy teeth. Now many do not. Can you think of reasons why?

390

Hands-On Life Science Activities

5. Good dental hygiene (brushing and flossing) is very important for everyone, but even if we try very hard, some people will have better teeth than others. This is also true of eyesight, hearing, and many other things. People adapt to different problems in different ways. Following is a list of some reasons for poor teeth and gums. Some you can change and some you cannot. Make a list of the things you can change and tell how.

   a. Tooth decay from eating and drinking foods with sugar

   b. Tooth decay from improper care, such as not brushing and flossing

   c. Tooth decay due to lack of fluoride in your drinking water

   d. Crooked teeth

   e. Overbite

   f. Sore gums

   g. Color of teeth

   h. Tooth problems of parents and grandparents

   i. Eating foods that are hard to chew

6. Discuss the list in step 5 with your teacher and your group.

Teacher Information

Although teeth have not changed significantly in the history of modern people, lifestyle and eating habits have. Good dental care, hygiene, and nutrition (sugar control) are ways of adapting teeth to constant change.

Different cultures and varying lifestyles influence the amount and type of care human teeth require. Heredity must also be considered when evaluating tooth development and care.

Integrating

Language arts

Science Process Skills

Observing, inferring, classifying, measuring, predicting, communicating, comparing and contrasting, using space-time relationships, formulating hypotheses, identifying and controlling variables, experimenting, researching

How Can You Clean Your Teeth Best?

Materials Needed

- Plaque-indicator pills (one for each student)
- Toothbrushes (one for each student)
- Toothpaste
- Toothpicks
- Dental floss
- Model set of teeth
- Sink and water
- Paper cups

Procedure

1. Chew the pill you were given.
2. Rinse your mouth with water and notice how much of the red coloring is left on your teeth.
3. Brush your teeth using a back-and-forth motion. Rinse your mouth and notice how much of the red coloring is left in your mouth.
4. Brush your teeth again, this time using an upward motion on your lower teeth and a downward motion on the upper teeth. Rinse your mouth and notice how much of the red coloring is left in your mouth.
5. Use dental floss between your teeth. Rinse your mouth and check for red coloring again.
6. Use a toothpick to clean places where the toothbrush and dental floss did not clean. Rinse your mouth and check for red coloring again.
7. Did each of these methods clean out some of the red coloring that was missed by the others? What can you say about that?

Teacher Information

If possible, have the students bring their toothbrushes from home wrapped in plastic or foil. Each of the techniques used for cleaning teeth in this activity should clean out some of the red coloring that was missed by the other methods. Relative effectiveness in cleaning food out of the teeth is similar. Food that is between the teeth and missed by the toothbrush continues to provide feeding ground for bacteria. The waste product of the bacteria is called plaque. Plaque contains acid, which decays the teeth.

Integrating

Language arts

Science Process Skills

Observing, inferring, communicating, formulating hypotheses, identifying and controlling variables

🪑 Can You Solve This Health and Nutrition Word Search?

Try to find the following Health and Nutrition terms in the grid below. They could appear in horizontal (left to right), vertical (up or down), or diagonal (upward or downward) position.

wash	vegetables	hygiene	floss
fruits	vitamins	nutrition	fat
bread	nutrients	meat	eat
calories	healthy	teeth	diet
protein	sugar	dentist	soap

```
M  K  O  P  H  E  A  L  T  H  Y  E
J  I  N  L  Y  Y  T  G  A  F  M  V
N  B  U  H  G  U  V  S  F  V  E  R
N  U  T  R  I  T  I  O  N  E  A  H
B  P  R  F  E  A  T  A  X  G  T  C
D  R  I  T  N  R  A  P  U  E  D  S
E  O  E  G  E  D  M  S  E  T  C  W
N  T  N  A  U  H  I  T  K  A  V  F
T  E  T  Y  D  Y  N  E  M  B  B  L
I  I  S  T  W  A  S  H  T  L  N  O
S  N  U  C  A  L  O  R  I  E  S  S
T  E  T  K  F  R  U  I  T  S  M  S
```

🪑 Can You Create a New Health and Nutrition Word Search of Your Own?

Write your Health and Nutrition words in the grid below. Arrange them in the grid so they appear in horizontal (left to right), vertical (up or down), or diagonal (upward or downward) position. Now fill in the blank boxes with other letters. Trade your Word Search with someone else who has created one of their own, and see if you can solve the new puzzle.

_____   _____   _____

_____   _____   _____

_____   _____   _____

_____   _____   _____

Health and Nutrition

Answer Key for Health and Nutrition Word Search

```
M  K  O  P  H  E  A  L  T  H  Y  E
J  I  N  L  Y  Y  T  G  A  F  M  V
N  B  U  H  G  U  V  S  F  V  E  R
N  U  T  R  I  T  I  O  N  E  A  H
B  P  R  F  E  A  T  A  X  G  T  C
D  R  I  T  N  R  A  P  U  E  D  S
E  O  E  G  E  D  M  S  E  T  C  W
N  T  N  A  U  H  I  T  K  A  V  F
T  E  T  Y  D  Y  N  E  M  B  B  L
I  I  S  T  W  A  S  H  T  L  N  O
S  N  U  C  A  L  O  R  I  E  S  S
T  E  T  K  F  R  U  I  T  S  M  S
```

Hands-On Earth Science Activities For Grades K–6, Second Edition

Marvin N. Tolman, Ed.D.

Paper/300 pages   ISBN: 0-7879-7866-3

www.josseybass.com

The perfect complement to any elementary school science program, these activity books foster discovery and enhance the development of valuable learning skills through direct experience. The updated editions include an expanded "Teacher Information" section for many of the activities, enhanced user friendliness, inquiry-based models, and cooperative learning projects for the classroom. Projects use materials easily found around the classroom or home, link activities to national science standards, and include other new material. Many of the activities could become, or give rise to, science fair projects.

The study of earth science at the elementary school level is best conducted through an exploration of the following topical areas: air, water, weather, the earth (mapping, topography, rocks, minerals, and earthquakes), ecology, gravity and flight, and celestial bodies. This book consists of more than 160 easy-to-use, hands-on activities in the following areas of sciences:

- Air
- Water
- Weather
- The Earth
- Ecology
- Above the Earth
- Beyond the Earth

Current trends encourage teachers to use an activity-based program, supplemented by the use of textbooks and many other reference materials. Activities, such as those in this series, that foster hands-on discovery and enhance the development of valuable learning skills through direct experience are key to the exploration of new subject matter and to the goal of attaining mastery.

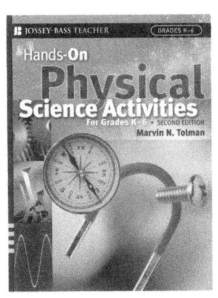

Hands-On Physical Science Activities For Grades K–6, Second Edition

Marvin N. Tolman, Ed.D.

Paper/300 pages   ISBN: 0-7879-7867-1

www.josseybass.com

The perfect complement to any elementary school science program, these activity books foster discovery and enhance the development of valuable learning skills through direct experience. The updated editions include an expanded "Teacher Information" section for many of the activities, enhanced user friendliness, inquiry-based models, and cooperative learning projects for the classroom. Projects use materials easily found around the classroom or home, link activities to national science standards, and include other new material. Many of the activities could become, or give rise to, science fair projects.

The study of physical science at the elementary school level is best conducted through an exploration of the following topical areas: the nature of matter, energy, light, sound, simple machines, magnetism, static electricity, and electromagnetism. This book consists of more than 175 easy-to-use, hands-on activities in the following areas of sciences:

- Nature of Matter
- Energy
- Light
- Sound
- Simple Machines
- Magnetism
- Static Electricity
- Current Electricity

Current trends encourage teachers to use an activity-based program, supplemented by the use of textbooks and many other reference materials. Activities, such as those in this series, that foster hands-on discovery and enhance the development of valuable learning skills through direct experience are key to the exploration of new subject matter and to the goal of attaining mastery.

Dr. Art's Guide to Science: Connecting Atoms, Galaxies, and Everything in Between

Art Sussman, Ph.D.

Cloth/250 pages   ISBN: 0-7879-8326-8

www.josseybass.com

Dr. Art's Guide to Science teaches major science ideas that are relevant to people's lives in ways that are very enjoyable. It expands the approach successfully used in his popular and award-winning previous book, *Dr. Art's Guide to Planet Earth*. As in that book, *Dr. Art's Guide to Science* uses a "systems thinking" framework to connect major ideas in the physical, life, and earth sciences. This book also helps the reader recognize, develop, and apply skills in using literacy strategies to enjoy and learn by reading science nonfiction.

Here's What's Inside:

- Why Science
- Two Plus Two Equals Hip-Hop
- What's The Matter?
- Energy And Dr. Art's 50th Anniversary Ball
- Forces Be With Us
- Putting The You In Universe
- Home Sweet Home
- Energy On Earth
- Life On Earth
- How Life Works
- The Famous E Word
- The Day The Dinosaurs Died
- Where Are We Going?

Art Sussman, Ph.D., is a science educator, and the author of the award-winning book, *Dr. Art's Guide to Planet Earth*. He presents "Dr. Art's Planet Earth Show" at education conferences and science centers nationally.

Science Essentials, Elementary Level: Lessons and Activities for Test Preparation

Mark J. Handwerker, Ph.D.

Paper/320 pages   ISBN: 0-7879-7576-1

www.josseybass.com

Science Essentials, Elementary Level gives classroom teachers and science specialists a dynamic and progressive way to meet curriculum standards and competencies. Science Essentials are also available from Jossey-Bass publishers at the middle school and high school levels.

You'll find the lessons and activities at each level actively engage students in learning about the natural and technological world in which we live by encouraging them to use their senses and intuitive abilities on the road to discovery. They were developed and tested by professional science teachers who sought to give students enjoyable learning experiences while preparing them for district and statewide proficiency exams.

For easy use, the lessons and activities at the elementary school level are printed on a big 8 1/2" x 11" lay-flat format that folds flat for photocopying of over 150 student activity sheets, and are organized into four sections:

I. Methods and Measurement Lessons & Activities

II. Physical Science Lessons & Activities

III. Life Science Lessons & Activities

IV. Earth Science Lessons & Activities

Mark J. Handwerker, Ph.D., has taught science in the Los Angeles and Temecula Valley Unified School Districts. As a mentor and instructional support teacher, he has also trained scores of new teachers in the "art" of teaching science. Dr. Handwerker is the author/editor of articles in several scientific fields and the coauthor of an earth science textbook currently in use.

Science Puzzlers!
150 Ready-to-Use Activities to Make Learning Fun, Grades 4-8

Robert G. Hoehn

Paper/255 pages   ISBN: 0-7879-6660-6
www.josseybass.com

For the upper elementary and middle school teacher, this unique resource offers 150 science puzzle activities ranging from word scrambles, word searches and categorizing, to variations on crosswords and mini-problem solvers to help you add challenge and humor to instruction while keeping lessons moving at a steady pace.

With puzzles like these, you can present science in a light-hearted manner, give a break from the daily routine, and provide an intrinsic motivator. Students feel good when they solve a puzzle.

Life Science

- The Cell • Genetics • Evolution • Plants • Invertebrates • Vertebrates
- Human Skeleton • Human Body Systems • Health and Human Diseases

Physical Science

- Energy • Sound • Light • Electricity/Magnetism • Matter • Atomic Structure
- Chemistry • Heat • Force and Motion • Potpourri

Earth Science

- Minerals • Rocks • Weathering and Erosion • Earth Features • Fossils • Meteorology
- Oceanography • Nonrenewable Energy Sources • Renewable Energy Sources

Robert G. Hoehn (B.A., San Jose State University) has taught earth science, physical science, and biology in the Roseville Joint Union High School District of California high schools since 1963 and uses wit and humor daily as an educational tool. Author of numerous publications, including *What's Up in Science* (Jossey-Bass, 2004), he counts seven National Summer Science grants from the National Science Foundation among his many accomplishments.

Lightning Source UK Ltd.
Milton Keynes UK
UKHW052156180320
360576UK00003B/3